THE PATTERN OF TRAGI-COMEDY IN BEAUMONT AND FLETCHER

By Eugene M. Waith

An attempt to define the nature of the drama created by Beaumont and Fletcher, based on the view that an awareness of rhetoric current in Augustan Rome and still operative in Jacobean England makes their tragicomedy understandable.

S0-AYT-112

109708

PR
2434
W2.85
1969

THE PATTERN

OF TRAGICOMEDY IN

BEAUMONT AND FLETCHER

BY EUGENE M. WAITH

87
BIP
BCL

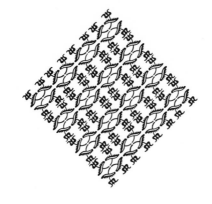

ARCHON BOOKS
1969

GOSHEN COLLEGE LIBRARY
GOSHEN, INDIANA 46526

Copyright, 1952, by Yale University Press
Reprinted 1969 with permission of Yale University Press
in an unaltered and unabridged edition

{*Yale Studies in English, Vol. 120*}

SBN: 208 00777 6
Library of Congress Catalog Card Number: 69-15694
Printed in the United States of America

TO EDITH MERSEREAU WAITH

PREFACE

THE GENESIS of this study was the conviction that the nature of the drama created by Beaumont and Fletcher had never been satisfactorily defined—that in spite of many perceptive comments by the best of literary critics the essence of a distinct dramatic genre had eluded analysis. The problem of understanding this genre presented itself to me as an investigation of a special variety of tragicomedy, for I agreed with Una M. Ellis-Fermor—*The Jacobean Drama* (London, Methuen, 1936), p. 205—that the creation of a "middle mood" was the outstanding contribution of Beaumont and Fletcher. O. J. Campbell's analysis of the plays of Marston and Jonson in *Comicall Satyre and Shakespeare's Troilus and Cressida* (San Marino, Calif., Huntington Library, 1938) suggested to me a significant relationship between dramatic satire and the new tragicomedy. As I looked further into the literary traditions with which Beaumont and Fletcher had an affinity I came finally to the ancient practice of declamation and to a theory of rhetoric current in Augustan Rome and still operative in Jacobean England. It is my belief that an awareness of this special branch of classical rhetoric makes the tragicomedy of Beaumont and Fletcher understandable. In presenting my findings I begin with a detailed analysis of the pattern of tragicomedy in these plays, after which I interpret the distinctive features of the pattern in the light of certain contemporary literary forms and, ultimately, of the rhetorical tradition.

Some of the research for this study was done at the Huntington Library, to whose staff I am indebted for its courtesy and hospitality. To the Yale University Library, where most of my work was done, I am indebted for constant assistance and particularly for the facilities put at my disposal during the year which was wholly devoted to this project. My thanks are due to the Cambridge University Press for permission to quote from *The ¡Works of Francis Beaumont and John Fletcher,* ed. Arnold Glover and A. R. Waller (Cambridge, 1905–12), and to the editors of *Modern Language Quarterly, PMLA,* and *The Review of English Studies* for permission to use material which has appeared in these periodicals in slightly different form. A number of my colleagues have read my manuscript and have given me criticism for which I am most grateful. John C. Pope took time from pressing academic obligations to read the entire rough draft and to make invaluable suggestions. At a later period Cleanth Brooks, E. Talbot Donaldson, Maynard Mack, and Stanley T. Williams all gave me similar assistance. To

Edmund T. Silk I am indebted for his guidance in the field of classical studies into which my research led me. Benjamin C. Nangle, editor of the Yale Studies in English, helped me in more ways than I can enumerate. My greatest debt of all, however, is to my wife whose detailed criticism, based on the reading and rereading of the manuscript at every stage of its development, aided as nothing else could have in sharpening my perceptions and clarifying my presentation.

Bibliographical Note

In quoting from sixteenth- and seventeenth-century works I have sought to use the most reliable texts currently accessible. In most cases these texts preserve the old spelling, to which I adhere except in play titles, which I have modernized throughout, since the inconsistency of the older practice provides no standard. I have departed from the typography of the original texts in the following ways: by changing the straight *s,* by using the modern *j* and *v,* and, where long passages are printed in italics with occasional words in roman, by reversing this procedure.

Since the First Folio (1647) of Beaumont and Fletcher contains only plays previously unpublished, the Second Folio (1679) is the earliest collected edition with any claim to completeness. The editors entitled it *Fifty Comedies and Tragedies. Written by Francis Beaumont and John Fletcher, Gentlemen.* It contains, in addition to Beaumont's *Masque* and the playlets called *Four Plays in One,* fifty-one plays, including *The Coronation,* which is now recognized as the work of James Shirley and will not be considered in this study. The corpus of Beaumont and Fletcher plays also includes three plays not published in the Second Folio, *Henry VIII, Barnavelt,* and *A Very Woman,* in all of which Fletcher's participation is virtually certain. Other plays such as *The Widow, The Faithful Friends,* or *The Double Falsehood* are of much less certain authorship and will be excluded from my discussion.

The Second Folio is the basis of the best modern text, that of the Cambridge edition, described below under "Cam." All quotations from plays printed in the Second Folio are taken from this edition: since the lines are unnumbered and the scene division erratic, I supplement each reference by indicating volume and page in the Cambridge edition. The editions used in quoting from all other plays are referred to in the notes.

The following cue titles and abbreviations are used:

Cam.   *The Works of Francis Beaumont and John Fletcher.* Arnold Glover and A. R. Waller, eds. Cambridge, University Press, 1905–12.

Dryden, *Essays*	*Essays of John Dryden.* W. P. Ker, ed. Oxford, Clarendon Press, 1926.
E.E.T.S.	The Early English Text Society.
ELH	*ELH, A Journal of English Literary History.*
Harbage, *Annals*	Alfred Harbage. *Annals of the English Drama, 975–1700.* Philadelphia, University of Pennsylvania Press, 1940.
MLQ	*Modern Language Quarterly.*
MLR	*The Modern Language Review.*
MP	*Modern Philology.*
PMLA	*Publications of the Modern Language Association of America.*
RES	*The Review of English Studies.*
G. G. Smith	*Elizabethan Critical Essays.* G. Gregory Smith, ed. Oxford, Clarendon Press, 1904.
Spingarn	*Critical Essays of the Seventeenth Century.* J. E. Spingarn, ed. Oxford, Clarendon Press, 1908.

CONTENTS

THE PATTERN OF TRAGICOMEDY IN BEAUMONT AND FLETCHER

I

The Emergence of the Pattern

THE PLAYS OF Beaumont and Fletcher are almost never performed today, in spite of a reawakened interest in the drama of the seventeenth century. The few readers who eventually turn to Beaumont and Fletcher out of curiosity, because they have enjoyed Jonson, Webster, Tourneur, or Ford, are inclined to dismiss the plays as trivial and decadent—a debauchery of what is best in Jacobean drama. This prevalent attitude poses a major critical problem, for we are confronted with the contempt or, far more devastating, the neglect of playwrights once rated the equals if not the superiors of Shakespeare and Jonson. Nor can the shift of opinion be attributed entirely to the lightheadedness of the fickle playgoer. Beaumont and Fletcher were extravagantly praised by Dryden, who was not only a sensitive critic but a practicing playwright, and they have been damned by T. S. Eliot, another sensitive critic, who happens to be an admirer of Dryden. The reputations of Shakespeare and Jonson, in spite of some notable changes, have been stable by comparison. One is forced to conclude that the drama of Beaumont and Fletcher is in some way a special case which merits critical investigation.

Neither dramatist was successful in his first efforts. Theater audiences had no bouquets for Beaumont's *The Woman-Hater* or for *The Knight of the Burning Pestle,* and Fletcher's *The Faithful Shepherdess* did not even keep the spectators in the theater. *Philaster,* on which the two men collaborated, was the first play to succeed.[1] It was then that they were whirled to the high point of their popularity, and while they were alive it seemed as if the wheel of fortune had stopped. Only post-

NOTE ON HEADPIECE. The ornamental headpieces occurring here and at the beginning of each chapter are reproduced from a copy of the Beaumont and Fletcher First Folio (1647) in the Elizabethan Club of Yale University.

1. Dryden's statement to this effect in "An Essay of Dramatic Poesy" has been generally accepted. See Dryden, *Essays, 1, 81.*

humously, many years later, were they humbled.[2] As often happens when reputations fluctuate so drastically, one extreme has been in part responsible for the other: the critics, in their zeal to demonstrate that Beaumont and Fletcher were by no means the equals of Shakespeare and Jonson, have relegated them to an oblivion which they do not deserve.

One part of this critical process has been the comparison of the Beaumont and Fletcher plays with the comedies and tragedies of their contemporaries, and it is not difficult to show that Jonson realizes more fully the potentialities of comedy, that Shakespeare, Webster, and Tourneur make the tragic view of life far more compelling. But here injustice is done to Beaumont and Fletcher, for their most characteristic work is in another form, tragicomedy, which cannot be properly judged by the standards of tragedy and comedy. Furthermore, just as the concept of tragedy in Shakespeare differs greatly from that in Webster or Tourneur, so the concept of tragicomedy in Beaumont and Fletcher is unlike any other. A sober revaluation of the Beaumont and Fletcher plays must begin with a description of what they are—with an analysis of the distinct version of tragicomedy which takes shape in them. The limitations of these plays will then be no less plain, but it will be possible to appreciate the brilliance of a unique dramatic experiment.

The large corpus of so-called "Beaumont and Fletcher" plays[3] is remarkably homogeneous, although we now know that Massinger, Middleton, Field, and probably others took part in the composition of certain ones. Approximately a third of them, though published under the general title of "Comedies and Tragedies," are separately designated as tragicomedies, and all but a few, regardless of designation, conform to one pattern of dramatic entertainment, which I shall refer to as the pattern of Fletcherian[4] tragicomedy.

A critical examination of this pattern is the object of the present study. Since the Beaumont and Fletcher plays resemble each other strongly and other plays only imperfectly, it is especially valuable to compare them with each other and study them as a group. The quali-

2. Lawrence B. Wallis has traced the spectacular rise and fall in *Fletcher, Beaumont & Company* (New York, King's Crown Press, 1947), pp. 3–125.

3. The corpus consists primarily of the plays published in the Second Folio (see Bibliographical Note). No one has satisfactorily determined the exact shares of the various collaborators, and since the editors of the Second Folio mentioned only the two authors, the plays are usually referred to collectively as the "Beaumont and Fletcher" plays. I shall use this designation hereafter without quotation marks; it must be understood as a general collective term, implying nothing about authorship.

4. I use the adjective "Fletcherian" in this study as a convenient shorthand term for what pertains to the several authors of the Beaumont and Fletcher plays. The choice of Fletcher's name is not entirely arbitrary, since his contributions were quantitatively greater than those of any other collaborator, but I do not imply that Fletcher was solely responsible for the pattern.

ties of the individual plays stand out more clearly when the distinctive identity of the group is perceived. And since the characteristics of the inherent pattern are more crudely obvious in the early plays than in the later ones, there is a great advantage in looking first at the formative period of Beaumont and Fletcher's career. Surprisingly enough, the pattern which brought them to the pinnacle of their popularity is pre-figured in the unsuccessful *The Faithful Shepherdess.* In *Philaster* it is partly achieved, but it appears for the first time in its full development in *A King and No King.* The emergence of the pattern during this period will be our first concern.

A serious difficulty about this approach is the uncertainty about the dating of the Beaumont and Fletcher plays. Without more facts than we now have no strictly chronological account of development can be given. One fact to which we can cling, however, is the date of *A King and No King,* which was licensed in 1611 and acted at court on December 26 of that year. It is rather generally agreed that the eight other plays which I have selected for discussion in this chapter precede *A King and No King;*[5] beyond this point there is no general agreement. The order of my discussion follows the dating of Harbage, which corresponds to what seems to me a logical order of development: *The Woman-Hater* (1606), *The Knight of the Burning Pestle* (1607-10), *The Faithful Shepherdess* and *Cupid's Revenge* (1608), *Philaster* and *The Coxcomb* (1609), *The Maid's Tragedy* (1610), *The Woman's Prize* and *A King and No King* (1611). But whether or not the plays appeared in this precise sequence, it remains true that they reveal in various stages of development the pattern which tends to conceal itself in the most successful tragicomedies.

Before the public had damned *The Faithful Shepherdess* Beaumont had written at least one play and possibly two. *The Woman-Hater,* printed in 1607, may have been performed the preceding year. *The Knight of the Burning Pestle* was probably performed sometime between 1607 and 1610. The main plot of *The Woman-Hater* concerns

5. The following critics consider that these plays were performed before the end of 1611: Ashley H. Thorndike, *The Influence of Beaumont and Fletcher on Shakspere* (Worcester, Mass., O. B. Wood, 1901); E. K. Chambers, *The Elizabethan Stage* (Oxford, Clarendon Press, 1923), *3;* E. H. C. Oliphant, *The Plays of Beaumont and Fletcher* (New Haven, Yale University Press, 1927); Henry W. Wells, *A Chronological List of Extant Plays Produced in or about London, 1581-1642* (New York, Columbia University Press, 1940); and Harbage, *Annals.* There are no other plays which these five critics agree to date earlier than the end of 1611. Charles M. Gayley, *Beaumont, the Dramatist* (New York, Century, 1914), assigns all of them to dates earlier than the end of 1611 except for *The Woman's Prize,* which he dates 1610-14. In this chapter I do not discuss *Wit at Several Weapons,* which Thorndike, Oliphant, Wells, and Harbage put with the early plays, because it is not typical of Beaumont or Fletcher, neither of whom seems to have had an important share in the composition; it resembles strongly the comedies of Middleton, who probably wrote most of it. I shall refer to it briefly in a later chapter.

Gondarino, whose savage hatred of the other sex is punished by fate when Oriana, a virtuous and determined woman, takes refuge in his house from a storm. In the subplot the parasite Lazarillo pursues a great culinary delicacy, the head of a fish called the umbrana, which changes hands three times during the course of the play, finally coming into the possession of a pander; Lazarillo is last seen as he agrees to marry one of the pander's girls in the hope of eating the umbrana's head.

Even this brief account of the play suggests its satirical quality, which appears unmistakably in the following description of life at court.

> I'll tell you what you shall see, you shall see many faces of mans making, for you shall find very few as God left them: and you shall see many legs too; amongst the rest you shall behold one pair, the feet of which, were in times past, sockless, but are now through the change of time (that alters all things) very strangely become the legs of a Knight and a Courtier; another pair you shall see, that were heir apparent legs to a Glover, these legs hope shortly to be honourable; when they pass by they will bow, and the mouth to these legs, will seem to offer you some Courtship; it [will] swear, but [it] will lye, hear it not.
>
> I, iii; Cam., *10, 77*

In passages such as this and in the exposition and punishment of the humors of Lazarillo and Gondarino, Beaumont's debt to the Jonsonian comedy of humors has long been recognized. One of the means by which Oriana plagues Gondarino is similar to a device of satire which Jonson uses in *Every Man out of His Humor*. This is Oriana's affectation of wantonness in the first scene of the third act, as the "Physick that is most apt to work upon him." Jonson's virtuous Asper, of whom I shall have more to say in a later chapter, affects the cynicism of an envious malcontent in order to put the foolish characters of the play out of their humors. The juxtaposition of opposites within one character is a striking effect for which both Beaumont and Fletcher show great fondness in their later plays.

The general tone of *The Woman-Hater* is light, but the situation of Oriana in the last two acts is serious enough to make this part of the play tragicomic rather than purely comic. In revenge for her feigned pursuit of him, Gondarino has Oriana locked in a room of a brothel (a most piquant situation) to which he brings the Duke, her lover, and Valore, her brother. When they remain unconvinced by a view of her in the window, Gondarino tries to prove that her virtue is a sham by sending a man to her with the news that she is to be executed for her unchastity and that her only means of escape is to give herself to him. However, Oriana proves to everyone's satisfaction that her virtue is genuine and heroic when she instantly chooses death. She is rewarded by an offer of marriage from the Duke. A happy outcome is not long in doubt, and never seriously so, yet the scenes with Oriana in the brothel are far from comic and the heroine is, however momentarily, threatened with death. The prologue states the case accurately in these words:

> I dare not call it *Comedy* or *Tragedy;* 'tis perfectly neither:
> A Play it is, which was meant to make you laugh,
>
> Cam., *10, 71*

It is plain that Beaumont departs knowingly from the accepted norms of tragedy and comedy, even though he does not specifically call his play a tragicomedy, as Fletcher does *The Faithful Shepherdess.*

Beaumont's first play is a spirited and well-written piece which should have had a considerable appeal, but so far as we know it was not a success, and neither was his second play, *The Knight of the Burning Pestle.* The publisher of the 1613 Quarto states that the world "utterly rejected" this play and suggests that it may have been "for want of judgement, or not understanding the privy marke of *Ironie* about it . . ." (Cam., *6,* 412.) From a literary point of view it is superior to *The Woman-Hater* in every way, notably in originality, but since it is a satire of the immensely popular Palmerin romances, of the readers who delighted in them, and of the naivete of theater audiences drawn from such readers, it may have been unwelcome to the audience at Blackfriars. Even in the private theater there may have been many admirers of these popular tales, or many spectators whose response to the drama was as naive as that of the Citizen and his wife in the play. *The Knight of the Burning Pestle* is too well known to necessitate any further general rehearsal of it, and it is too special—too far from the main stream of Beaumont's or Fletcher's development—to warrant a discussion of details. It stands by itself as a literary burlesque.

Beaumont's two plays are satirical in their inspiration and one of them obviously inclines toward tragicomedy. Both of them reflect with some accuracy the manners of the familiar world and are in this respect very different from the first play of Beaumont's future collaborator. Fletcher's pastoral tragicomedy *The Faithful Shepherdess* is as stiffly artificial as a seventeenth-century masque or a modern ballet. Its many characters are introduced in the first act singly or in pairs as if to dance their *pas seul* or *pas de deux.* In speeches as formal as the movements of a dancer they exhibit their diverse natures and establish the themes of the play. Then follows a series of regroupings—variations on the opening themes—continuing to the end of the last act. The plot, like the story of a ballet, is less important than the component situations in which an idea, a relationship, or an emotion is given a brief, vivid actuality. A markedly symmetrical structure takes the place of a tight narrative sequence; the characters, rigidly typed and artfully disposed, are almost allegorical. Yet, obvious as this artificiality is, the failure to penetrate its significance may lead to misunderstanding the play. Fletcher blamed its unkind reception on the failure of the audience to understand the conventions of pastoral and tragicomedy.[6]

The Faithful Shepherdess presents a gamut of love extending from spiritual devotion to bestial sensuality. The play opens with a poetic statement of the ideals of fidelity and chastity in the hymn of Clorin, the "faithful shepherdess," to the "holy earth," where she has buried the shepherd she loved and still loves. We are immediately transported to a world where everything exists in an absolute state: the buried shepherd was "the truest man that ever fed his flocks"; Clorin's devotion to him is so pure that she utterly abjures "all insuing heats and fires of love" (1, i; Cam., *2, 372*) for a life of unalloyed grief.

In marked contrast to the solemnity of Clorin's speech are the first words of the Satyr, who now runs on stage:

> Through yon same bending plain
> That flings his arms down to the main,
> And through these thick woods have I run,
> Whose bottom never kist the Sun
> Since the lusty Spring began,
> All to please my master *Pan,*
> Have I trotted without rest
> To get him Fruit;
>
> 1, i; Cam., *2, 373*

Clorin's blank verse is as different from the Satyr's rhyming octosyllabics as her mourning is different from his rude—even coarse—gaiety. Here is natural man, part beast, to be sure, and neither corrupt nor deliberately good.[7] Like the satyrs in *The Faerie Queene* he instantly

6. In the address to the reader prefixed to the First Quarto; see below, chap. ii. W. W. Greg, *Pastoral Poetry and Pastoral Drama* (London, A. H. Bullen, 1906), pp. 264–82, concludes from Fletcher's remarks on decorum in the pastoral that his interest lies "in a more or less realistic representation" (p. 271) and then berates him for "the unconvincing conventionality of the patterns of chastity" and "the unreality of the characters which serve them as foils" (p. 274). Greg's impatience with literary and moral conventions other than his own makes him wholly unsympathetic to the purpose of the play as he understands it: "For some reason unexplained . . . the author deemed it necessary that the whole should redound to the praise and credit of cloistral virginity and glozing 'honour,' and whatever else of unreal sentiment the cynicism of the renaissance had grafted on the superstition of the middle age" (p. 273). This is not the place to speculate at length about the reasons for Greg's feelings about "cloistral virginity," but in giving the impression that it is not quite well-bred for a character to proclaim her purity as Clorin does, Greg is applying standards which Fletcher's conventions invalidate. Clorin is neither a society woman nor a country girl; she is the embodiment of chastity.

7. V. M. Jeffery, "Italian Influence in Fletcher's *Faithful Shepherdess*," MLR, *21* (1926), 148–9, has pointed out a resemblance between Fletcher's Satyr and one in the *Mirzia* of Antonio Epicuro dei Marsi.

recognizes in the supremely virtuous woman something divine, to which he pays homage by presenting Clorin the fruits he has gathered for Pan. This symbolic gesture establishes the main theme of the play, the power of chastity. It is restated in ritualistic action as four young couples march in to be blessed by the Priest of Pan and purged with holy water of their wanton desires.

The remaining scenes in the first act present a series of love relationships which are to be judged by reference to the ideal already set forth. First we see Perigot and Amoret, two of the lovers who have just been blessed by the Priest of Pan, making a tryst at which, as Perigot is careful to explain, there is to be only the interchange of chaste kisses and garlands—a ritual of noble love. But as Amoret leaves the stage she is succeeded by Amaryllis, who also loves Perigot and is not to be satisfied with ritual. Her love, though constant, is uncontrolled, and she meets with a firm rebuff. Perigot is now succeeded by the Sullen Shepherd, a lover as incontinent as Amaryllis, but cynically inconstant. With him Amaryllis plots to be revenged on her rival and obtain the love of Perigot. She clearly demeans herself by association with one who is in every respect the antithesis of the admirable Clorin.

A final sequence of scenes presents Cloe, the female counterpart of the Sullen Shepherd, an embodiment of enthusiastic and indiscriminate lust. She first approaches Thenot, an idealistic lover, devoted to Clorin. When Cloe sees that he is not her match, she tries Daphnis, who is a faithful lover but so extremely simple that he is easily lured into a rendezvous. Cloe has misgivings about him, however, and, in order to be on the safe side, makes another rendezvous with Alexis, a congenial sensualist. When the act closes Fletcher has his whole gamut. It is a far cry from Clorin's first words, "Hail, holy Earth," to the last lines of Cloe:

> My grief is great if both these boyes should fail:
> He that will use all winds must shift his sail.
>
> I, i; Cam., 2, 387

Guarini's *Il Pastor fido*, from which Fletcher probably took the title of *The Faithful Shepherdess*, though not the plot, is also a highly artificial play, but the artifice is quite different. The characters of *Il Pastor fido* are modeled on conventional pastoral types, but they are not fitted into the elaborate and rigid ethical scheme which provides the pattern for Fletcher's first act. To be sure, Corisca is a wanton shepherdess, rather like Amaryllis; she is in love with a good shepherd who doesn't love her, and she tries by various means to revenge herself. Mirtillo is a faithful shepherd, Silvio a shepherd who prefers hunting to love but is pursued and finally won by a loving nymph, Dorinda. But these are not the nice gradations of Fletcher's gamut of love; Guarini's characters are not strictly delineated, as are Fletcher's, according to ethical bent. Nor does Guarini depend so heavily upon dramatic contrast in the exposition of character. The eccentricities of Silvio or Corisca are described by themselves or others as in a non-dramatic pastoral, and there are no scenes to compare with the revealing opposition of Clorin and the Satyr or Perigot and Amaryllis.

The main action of *The Faithful Shepherdess* grows out of the opposition of the lustful to the chaste characters, whose final triumph demonstrates the power of their ideal. The didactic purpose, however, is less important than the separate scenes of conflict which constitute variations on the play's main theme. The scenes dealing with the extraordinary misadventures of Perigot and Amoret illustrate the dramatic entertainment provided by *The Faithful Shepherdess*. To further her designs on Perigot, Amaryllis persuades the Sullen Shepherd to transform her into the likeness of Amoret. In this guise she accosts Perigot and commences to make love to him, but he, as a chaste lover, can only love Amoret so long as she behaves with a modesty suiting her chastity. The spectacle of Amoret wooing him with ever diminishing delicacy is an appalling novelty which he first interprets as a trial of his constancy, but this illusion is shattered when Amaryllis replies cynically to his anguished protestations of purity. Unable either to accept or reject Amoret as the nymphomaniac she now seems to be, Perigot draws his sword and threatens to kill them both. Before he can do so Amaryllis escapes and is restored to her own shape by the Sullen Shepherd.

In the scenes that follow Fletcher presents every conceivable complication resulting from Amaryllis' deception of Perigot. The true Amoret encounters him and, to her bewilderment, finds him so enraged against her that he strikes her with his sword. Somewhat later, when his mood has changed from anger to sorrow, Amaryllis finds him and is moved by repentance to confess her trick. To prove her story she offers to disguise herself again. While she is doing so Perigot is plunged in even deeper sorrow, for he believes he has killed Amoret, whom he now knows to be innocent. At this moment Amoret herself appears, but Perigot of course believes her to be Amaryllis in disguise. Amoret, puzzled by his distant manner with her, tries to please him by repeated assurances of her love. To Perigot this behavior seems to be a horrible travesty of Amoret. His passion rises again to a peak, and in the name of his injured lady he plunges his sword for the second time into her body.

To the Perigot-Amoret-Amaryllis situation there is a close parallel in the story of Thenot's love for Clorin. Since his professions of love, noble as they are, conflict with her vow of utter fidelity, she decides to rid herself of his attentions and at the same time to cure him of passionate love. She therefore pretends to abandon herself to him and in this way so disgusts the chaste lover that, after expressing his disillusionment in stirring phrases, he leaves her. Clorin's behavior, like Oriana's in *The Woman-Hater*, recalls the device of Jonson's satirical reformer Asper.

The intense emotion of the characters is the most conspicuous feature of these scenes. This intensity is due to Fletcher's ingenuity in straining the relations between his characters to the last degree of tautness. The dilemmas of Perigot and Thenot resemble the dilemmas of many a romantic hero—of Spenser's Red Cross Knight or Sidney's Pyrocles —though the emotional disturbance of the hero receives more emphasis here than in *The Faerie Queene* and the ethical contrasts are more marked than in the *Arcadia*. In every scene the characters are (or, in some cases, imagine themselves to be) moral opposites, and the disguising of vice as virtue or the appearance of virtue as vice merely heightens the implicit contrasts in these situations by the irony of the juxtaposition. The basis of all the most dramatic scenes in *The Faithful Shepherdess* is an apparent antithesis between such abstractions as lust and chastity, fidelity and infidelity.

In an episode of *Il Pastor fido* (IV, viii, ix) which might be compared to Perigot's wounding of Amoret, Silvio shoots an arrow into Dorinda, who has unhappily disguised herself as a wolf. The emotion of this scene arises from Silvio's recognition of his mistake and is conveyed first in a long soliloquy, then in a dialogue between the lovers in which, rather than opposition or strain, there is repentance and forgiveness. The effect is totally different from that of the mental torture of Perigot. Since much of the emphasis of *Il Pastor fido* falls upon the fulfillment of a cryptic prophecy, the climatic scene is the one in which the true identity of the hero is revealed and the misunderstanding of the prophecy thus removed. The effect of the scene is again derived from recognition. The denouement of *The Faithful Shepherdess* is the reconciliation of the chaste lovers Perigot and Amoret, the punishment of the Sullen Shepherd, and Clorin's healing of the lustful lovers Cloe, Alexis, and Amaryllis; it presents a final contrast and a final demonstration of the power of chastity.

The Faithful Shepherdess is neither the mechanical combination of tragedy and comedy that many an earlier English tragicomedy had been, nor is it truly like the pastoral tragicomedy on which it appears to be modeled. The effect of each scene is a fusion of certain effects of tragedy and comedy—what Ellis-Fermor singles out as the distinguishing characteristic of Fletcherian tragicomedy—a "middle mood."[8] But this mood is dependent upon a treatment of character unlike that of *Il Pastor fido*. One feels sympathetically the torment of Perigot and Amoret, or to a lesser degree of Thenot; yet the very element of exaggeration in these characters which makes their torments acute simultane-

8. Ellis-Fermor, *The Jacobean Drama*, p. 205.

ously places Perigot, Amoret, and Thenot in a world remote from
one's experience. The conflict is moving; yet it is a conflict between
hypothetical persons—near abstractions. The formal balance of these
abstractions removes them still further from reality. What is compelling
in *The Faithful Shepherdess* is a distillation of emotion related only in-
cidentally to character or plot and thus, as it were, freed from the laws
of cause and effect which govern the narrative and determine the most
obvious meaning of the play. Fletcher's new sort of tragicomedy is
the product of a refined sensationalism.

The Faithful Shepherdess is not entirely successful, however. In spite
of many effective moments, in spite of passages of poetry which Milton
honored by imitation in *Comus,* and in spite of a remarkably individual
character, the play does not carry conviction; it fails to make its artifice
persuasive. At times the expression of character is too nakedly direct
for so formal an occasion and is merely ludicrous, as in Cloe's flat statement, "It is impossible to ravish me, / I am so willing." (III, i; Cam.,
2, 405.) At such moments the artifice collapses. The speech is unconvincing not because it is extravagant but because it is prosaic in a context of stylized poetry. The most successful scenes are those which are
sustained by formal, highly rhetorical verse, like that of the speeches
of Perigot and Amoret at the height of their misunderstanding:

> *Per.* Thou art not worthy of that blessed name,
> I must not know thee, fling thy wanton flame
> Upon some lighter blood, that may be hot
> With words and feigned passions: *Perigot*
> Was ever yet unstain'd, and shall not now
> Stoop to the meltings of a borrowed brow.
>
> .   .   .
>
> *Amo.* . . . I am that maid,
> That yet untainted *Amoret,* that plaid
> The careless prodigal, and gave away
> My soul to this young man, that now dares say
> I am a stranger, not the same, more wild;
> And thus with much belief I was beguil'd.
>
> IV, i; Cam., *2,* 423–4

The fact that such scenes occur chiefly in the stories of Perigot,
Amoret and Amaryllis, or of Clorin and Thenot suggests another weakness. The scenes presenting the affairs of Cloe are deficient not only in
poetic texture but in dramatic momentum. One lover follows another
in a kaleidoscopic succession which permits of no development and no
intensity, as if Fletcher were presenting a scenario rather than fully
written scenes. Here the artificiality offends because the artifice is crude.
All in all, the defects of the play are what might be expected from a

youthful playwright; they are due to Fletcher's failure to realize fully an artistic conception.

Probably the first play on which Beaumont and Fletcher collaborated was the tragedy of *Cupid's Revenge* (1608?),[9] inspired by Sir Philip Sidney's pastoral romance, the *Arcadia*. Two stories in the second book are combined to form the plot. One (from chap. xiii) concerns a princess who causes all the statues of Cupid to be destroyed and is punished by falling in love with a man far below her in station. In the other (from chap. xv) a king marries his son's mistress, who then wants to continue her affair with the prince; when he rebuffs her, she revenges herself by bringing about his exile. Beaumont and Fletcher make Leucippus, the prince of the second story, the brother of Hidaspes, the princess of the first story, whereas in Sidney he is her chief enemy.[1] Since the sufferings of Leucippus are motivated by the responsibility he shares with his sister for the destruction of the images of Cupid, he appears not as a man corrupted by the force of his passions but as a puritanical zealot, like his sister, guilty of sacrilege. Her punishment, ending in her death in the second act, serves chiefly as a foreshadowing of his. Both stories conform to one scheme, and the cause of the dual tragedy is defiance of the god of love.

In this play the character of the hero is not only less accountable for the tragedy than supernatural forces but is scarcely even definable as an entity, so greatly does it alter from scene to scene. In the beginning Leucippus is a prude, offended by the naked statues; in the second act (owing to Cupid's ministrations) he is a young man-about-town with a mistress whom he is keeping secret from his father; throughout the remainder of the play he is the innocent man plagued by an evil woman. Ellis-Fermor says of him: "he is not a homogeneous and continuous human being, but a series of imperfectly associated groups of responses to the stimulus of carefully prepared situations."[2]

The situations to which Leucippus and the other characters are made to respond are as highly schematized as those of *The Faithful Shepherdess*. As in Fletcher's pastoral, the theme of the play is introduced in the opening scenes. Hidaspes is presented as a fairy-tale princess, beautiful and virtuous, who is promised on her birthday the fulfillment of one wish. When she announces that it is the destruction of the statues of Cupid, her naive opposition to the god is contrasted with the ribald

9. The earliest known performance was at court, January 5, 1612 (Chambers, *Elizabethan Stage, 3,* 225), but it very likely was performed before that date. James E. Savage argues persuasively that it preceded *Philaster* and may have been given as early as 1607, "Beaumont and Fletcher's *Philaster* and Sidney's *Arcadia*," *ELH, 14* (1947), 194–206; "The Date of Beaumont and Fletcher's *Cupid's Revenge*," *ELH, 15* (1948), 286–94. Harbage, *Annals,* gives 1608. If Fletcher had any share in *The Woman-Hater* or *The Knight of the Burning Pestle*, it was very slight.
1. The names of the characters in Sidney are different.
2. *Jacobean Drama,* p. 208.

cynicism of the courtiers, much as Clorin's chastity in *The Faithful Shepherdess* is given the foil of the Satyr's animal spirits. But instead of the Priest of Pan purifying four young couples, we now have the Priest of Cupid encouraging "four young men and Maids" to

> Kiss again, and in your kissing,
> Let no promises be missing:
>   i, i; Cam., 9, 226

Thus the power of love, which corresponds to the power of chastity in *The Faithful Shepherdess,* is dramatized by an exactly comparable ritual. Next Cupid descends, as in a masque, and threatens the impious with revenge. No such things occur in the *Arcadia.* Beaumont and Fletcher greatly augment the artificiality of the original stories by working them into a formal pattern and by exploiting the conventions of the masque.

There is also an alteration in the punishment of the princess. Hidaspes falls in love, not with a man who is simply her social inferior but with a dwarf. The contrast is more striking and the power of Cupid all the more apparent. None of the many contrasts in *The Faithful Shepherdess* is more extreme or more improbable. When the dwarf is put to death because of the impropriety of the affair, Hidaspes sickens and dies, and Cupid has gained his first revenge.

In the meantime he has begun his second revenge by causing Leucippus and then Leontius, his father, to become infatuated with Bacha. She is a combination of two characters in the *Arcadia*—of the mistress in Chapter xv, a hypocrite who knows how to "make shamefastnes the cloake of shamelesnes," and a character in another story (chap. xxii), described as the "most impudentlie unchaste woman of all *Asia.*" Beaumont and Fletcher's Bacha is the ultimate in unchastity, but she poses as the ultimate in chastity, like Amaryllis disguised as Amoret. Bacha's effect upon Leucippus is shown when his father bursts in upon the lovers, and Leucippus swears solemnly that his mistress is the chastest woman alive. The parallel between the stories of Hidaspes and Leucippus now becomes plain, for the moral deformity of Bacha corresponds to the dwarf's physical deformity, and Cupid's revenge on Leucippus is moral corruption instead of the physical humiliation visited upon Hidaspes.

In the latter part of the play when Bacha is queen, two situations are worth analysis. One is the sensational scene in which the repentant and now irreproachable Leucippus is ardently courted by his lustful stepmother. Like Perigot and Thenot he manfully repels her advances and accepts imprisonment rather than dishonor. As markedly as in any scene of *The Faithful Shepherdess,* virtue confronts and triumphs over vice, and the combat is made unusually lurid (for a seventeenth-century mind) by the threat of incest in addition to lust. The scene is highly moral but far from dull. It reveals clearly that, early in their careers, Beaumont and Fletcher learned how to make dramatic capital out of virtue triumphant.

The second of the two situations is brought about by the unprepared introduction of Bacha's daughter Urania, who has been brought up in the country (as she shows by speaking a rustic dialect) and is as free of vice as Bacha is of virtue. Urania immediately falls in love with Leucippus and follows him into exile, disguised as a page.[3] She is killed when she rushes between Leucippus and a wicked envoy sent by Bacha to murder him. Only then does he discover her identity. This romantic incident seems to be included solely for the sake of its emotional appeal. Here, as in the scene of Bacha's immodest overtures, the effect depends upon the depiction of Leucippus as the noble hero, regardless of what he may have been earlier in the play. To such effects consistency of character is sacrificed.

The structure of *Cupid's Revenge* rests on the power of love. Different sorts of love are displayed (though not so many as in *The Faithful Shepherdess*), all of which are fatal: the infatuation of Hidaspes and of Leucippus, the lust of Bacha, the doting of gullible Leontius, and the pure, unrequited love of Urania. At the end of the play each lover has died as a direct or indirect consequence of his love. This ingenious scheme is very nearly as contrived as that of *The Faithful Shepherdess,* and the sporadic appearances of Cupid, let down from the "heavens," emphasize the artificiality.

Once again the workmanship is crude. The patchwork by which the story of Leucippus has been fastened to the story of Hidaspes is glaringly apparent when Hidaspes is disposed of in the second act; more patchwork is seen when Urania makes her unexpected appearance in the fourth act. The artifice is not uniformly persuasive.

In one respect *Cupid's Revenge* is conspicuously different from *The Faithful Shepherdess*. The language of Fletcher's pastoral never recalls the language of every day (the baldness of Cloe's speeches is fully as unfamiliar as the formality of the others). *Cupid's Revenge* contains excellent examples of the imitation of the "conversation of gentlemen," for which Dryden praised Beaumont and Fletcher,[4] and of the even more familiar language of citizens. In a style innocent of rhetorical elaboration the courtiers discuss the improbable happenings at the court of Lycia as courtiers in London might discuss the events of the day. They view with alarm the project of granting the princess any wish she may make; they greet her defiance of Cupid with leering comments on

---

3. This situation may have been suggested by the story of Zelmane in *Arcadia,* II, xxii, xxiii.

4. "An Essay of Dramatic Poesy," Dryden, *Essays, I,* 81.

the threat of chastity; they crack jokes about the beheading of the
dwarf; when Bacha becomes queen they observe cynically:

> *Doria*[*lus*]. We live to know a fine time, Gentl[emen].
> *Nis*[*us*]. And a fine Duke, that through his doting age
> Suffers him to be a child again
> Under his Wives tuition.
> *Agen*[*or*]. All the Land holds in that tenor too: in womans
> service? sure we shall learn to spinn.
> *Dor.* No, that's too honest: we shall have other
> Liberal Sciences taught us too soon;
> Lying, and flattering, those are the studies now:
> And Murther shortly I know, will be humanity, Gent[lemen].
> If we live here we must be knaves, believe it.
>
> III, i; Cam., *9*, 257

The political observations and rough jokes of the citizens in the first
scene of Act IV are pure English homespun.

The world of romance is never a familiar place. Its conventions emphasize its remoteness from the everyday world rather than the resemblance which the two worlds bear to each other. Henry James describes the experience which is projected in fiction as a captive balloon;
when the cable is cut and the experience is disengaged to float "at
large and unrelated," the result is romance.[5] In *The Faithful Shepherdess* the cable is cut, but in *Cupid's Revenge* the conversation of courtiers
and citizens constitutes a link between the earth and the experience of
the play. The familiar language and tone, unlike anything in *The
Faithful Shepherdess,* hold the balloon in check and make the world of
actuality seem nearer than it is. In succeeding plays the remoteness of
the experience of the play is even less apparent: the captive balloon
seems never to have left the surface of the earth.

Though related closely to Fletcher's tragicomedy and to the tragicomedies which succeed it, *Cupid's Revenge* is a tragedy. Because of
the discontinuity of Leucippus' character, however, and because of the
sort of exaggeration which produces the middle mood of *The Faithful
Shepherdess,* the tragic feeling of *Cupid's Revenge* is not great. The
most memorable scene is Bacha's attempted seduction of Leucippus,
where intense emotion is generated by the dilemma of the innocent
hero. Another striking scene is that in which Urania risks her life to
save Leucippus. If all the characters were saved from death and if the
play ended in repentance and reconciliation, its total effect would be very
little different. Even as it stands, with five deaths, *Cupid's Revenge* is
more like tragicomedy than tragedy.

5. Henry James, *The Art of the Novel* (New York, Charles Scribner's Sons, 1934),
pp. 33–4.

The tragicomedy of *Philaster* was Beaumont and Fletcher's first undoubted success. By no means a radical departure from *The Faithful Shepherdess* and *Cupid's Revenge* (both of which may have been performed the year before *Philaster*), it is enough better to make the success understandable. Although no one source for the play can be proved beyond a doubt, the material of *Philaster* certainly derives from pastoral romance. One is aware instantly of the romantic atmosphere of the scenes in which Philaster pursues Arethusa and is pursued by Euphrasia, disguised as a page. Critics who have studied the play have found striking resemblances to situations in Shakespeare's romantic comedies, to Montemayor's *Diana*,[6] and to Sidney's *Arcadia*. Savage's theory that in *Philaster* Beaumont and Fletcher reworked the material from the *Arcadia* which they had used in *Cupid's Revenge* has the great advantage of accounting for the romantic atmosphere of the play and also for its dramatic superiority.[7] If he is right, *Philaster* represents a logical advance in the emergence of the pattern of tragicomedy from the material of pastoral romance.

The pseudohistorical setting provided by Beaumont and Fletcher notably counteracts the remoteness of the romantic story. In the opening scene the gentlemen of the court reveal that Philaster, the rightful heir to the throne of Sicily, is being kept from his inheritance by the King of Calabria, who has deposed Philaster's father and now rules over both kingdoms. The spectacular history of Sicily was recent enough to be well known in the early seventeenth century. It is discussed by Paulus Jovius in the *Historiae sui temporis* published in the same volume[8] with his *De Romanis piscibus*, from which Beaumont got the story of the umbrana for *The Woman-Hater*. It is also given in great detail by every sixteenth-century historian of France, Italy, or Spain, the three countries which at one time or another controlled the destiny of Sicily. Thomas Danett's translation of *The Historie of Philip de Commines* (1596), which Fletcher certainly knew,[9] gives a circumstantial account of the French adventure in Naples and, in a footnote (pp. 24–5), a brief summary of the whole complicated story of Naples and Sicily from the time of the Normans to the death of Charles VIII of France. The events described in *Philaster* do not correspond exactly to any one situation in Sicilian history, but they sufficiently resemble several situations to suggest historical authenticity. More than one king of Sicily had been a duke of Calabria; the throne was continually seized by force; several of the kings were as unprincipled as Beaumont and Fletcher's King; and the support of a foreign alliance was often

6. With regard to *Diana* see T. P. Harrison, Jr., "A Probable Source of Beaumont and Fletcher's *Philaster*," *PMLA, 41* (1926), 294–303.
7. *ELH, 14,* 194–206.
8. Paulus Jovius, *Opera quotquot extant omnia* (Basel, 1578).
9. It is one of the sources of *The Double Marriage* and possibly of *A Wife for a Month*.

sought, just as the King in the play seeks to marry his daughter Arethusa to Pharamond,[1] prince of Spain. But there was also another Sicily—the Sicily of Theocritus with its famous spring Arethusa, which seems to have given its name to the daughter of Beaumont and Fletcher's King. In *Philaster* the court scenes, reflecting the Sicily of political upheavals, alternate with woodland scenes, reflecting pastoral Sicily, to form a combination of pseudo-history and romance.

The opening dialogue of the courtiers delineates the evil atmosphere of the court and sets off Philaster as an innocent victim. The moral situation at court is then suggested in another way in the "characters" given by these courtiers to three ladies who come in together. One is "a wise and modest Gentlwoman"; the second is "one that may . . . simper when she is Courted by her Friend, and slight her Husband"; and Megra, the third, the most thoroughly evil character in the play, is described in these words:

> Marry I think she is one whom the State keeps for the Agents of our confederate Princes: she'll cog and lie with a whole army before the League shall break: her name is common through the Kingdom, and the Trophies of her dishonour, advanced beyond *Hercules*-pillars. She loves to try the several constitutions of mens bodies; and indeed has destroyed the worth of her own body, by making experiment upon it, for the good of the Common-wealth.
>
> I, i; Cam., *I, 77*

Amoret, Amaryllis, and Cloe are similarly distinguished, though they are not presented in descriptive speeches. The epigrammatic "character" often appears as an introduction on the Jacobean stage, but as Beaumont and Fletcher use it here it is especially reminiscent of the comedies of humor in which satirical commentators present the "humor" characters. In the comedies of humor such comments perform the accepted comic function of holding a mirror up to society, and the use of the same device here tends to equate Philaster's world with the everyday world of comedy. Thus the setting and the satirical comment reinforce each other in this regard.

Though the courtiers in the instance I have cited speak familiarly, like the courtiers of *Cupid's Revenge,* the evil atmosphere of the Sicilian court is sometimes presented in a more formal rhetoric, as in the following declamatory passage:

1. It is odd that Beaumont and Fletcher call the Spanish prince Pharamond, the name given by many sixteenth-century historians to the partly legendary first king of France. A possible explanation is Comines' reference to Pharamond (p. 378 of the edition cited) within nine pages of a part of his discussion of Sicily and Calabria (p. 369). His venomous account of King Ferrand (pp. 293 ff.), which provided the character of the tyrant in *The Double Marriage* and perhaps Frederick in *A Wife for a Month,* might have suggested the wicked King in *Philaster,* too.

> Is it not a shame
> For us, that should write noble in the land;
> For us, that should be freemen, to behold
> A man, that is the bravery of his age,
> *Philaster,* prest down from his Royal right,
> By this regardless King; and only look,
> And see the Scepter ready to be cast
> Into the hands of that lascivious Lady,
> That lives in lust with a smooth boy, now to be
> Married to yon strange Prince, who, but that people
> Please to let him be a Prince, is born a slave,
> In that which should be his most noble part,
> His mind?

> III, i; Cam., *I, 103*

Here the evils of the world acquire an extraordinary intensity from the passion of virtuous denunciation. Philaster himself displays a similar bitterness when the slander of Megra has made him believe that Arethusa is deceiving him with his page (the disguised Euphrasia):

> Oh, that I had been nourished in these woods
> With Milk of Goats, and Acorns, and not known
> The right of Crowns, nor the dissembling Trains
> Of Womens looks; but dig'd my self a Cave,
> Where I, my Fire, my Cattel, and my Bed
> Might have been shut together in one shed;
> And then had taken me some Mountain Girl,
> Beaten with Winds, chast as the hardened Rocks
> Whereon she dwells; that might have strewed my Bed
> With leaves, and Reeds, and with the Skins of beasts
> Our Neighbours; and have born at her big breasts
> My large course issue. This had been a life free from
> vexation.

> IV, i; Cam., *I,* 119

These lines, as Dyce pointed out many years ago, are an imitation of the opening of Juvenal's sixth satire, the famous satire on women, though the predominant imagery is as bucolic as that of an eclogue. Philaster has fled from the court to the woods, from historical Sicily to pastoral Sicily, and his speech is a brilliant illustration of how the two are related in the play, one implying the other. The world of the play is not entirely the world of pastoral romance, nor is it a true reflection of the world of actuality. The woods echo Philaster's worldly disillusionment, and the court is, after all, only pseudohistorical.

Philaster has been compared to Hamlet and Othello, but he is a much simpler character than either of these Shakespearian heroes. He is created to respond to the chief situation with which he is confronted, the apparent guilt of Arethusa, but his attitude toward her, both before and after Megra's accusation, lacks the implications which give Hamlet's attitude toward Gertrude or Othello's attitude toward Desdemona moral significance outside the world of the play. Although Philaster is the epitome of honest love confronted by what appears to be immoderate lust, his response, unlike theirs, is merely a display of violent feeling from which there is only the slightest radiation of universal meaning. He threatens to "preach to birds and beasts, / What woman is":

> How heaven is in your eyes, but in your hearts,
> More hell than hell has; how your tongues like Scorpions,
> Both heal and poyson; how your thoughts are woven
> With thousand changes in one subtle webb,
> And worn so by you.
>
> .   .   .
>
> These sad Texts
> Till my last hour, I am bound to utter of you.
> So farewel all my wo, all my delight.
>
> III, i; Cam., I, 115

This is more reminiscent of *The Faithful Shepherdess* than of *Hamlet* or *Othello*. The situation of Philaster is exactly comparable to that of Perigot when Amaryllis impersonates Amoret. There is the same appearance of wantonness in a chaste woman and the same horror on the part of the virtuous man. Philaster stabs Arethusa and Euphrasia as Perigot stabs Amoret.

In *Philaster* the middle mood of the play is borne out by a happy ending. When the romantic entanglement has reached the point where Philaster, Arethusa, and Euphrasia are all threatened by death, the denouement is effected by means of a revolution in favor of Philaster; the King repents, Euphrasia reveals herself, and the evil Megra is banished. The dark atmosphere of the play is dissipated, and Philaster is shown that the evil which most affected him, the supposed treachery of Arethusa and Euphrasia, was no more than a false hypothesis.

The world of seeming evil, typical of Fletcherian tragicomedy, begins to take its characteristic shape in *Philaster*. It is a world of pseudo-history and romance, where happenings as fantastic as any in *The Faithful Shepherdess* have the deceptive appearance of actuality; evil, though unsubstantial, is more bitterly persuasive than in Fletcher's early play. The threat of tragedy is more immediate, and yet this tragicomic world is so constituted that the happy resolution is brought about without impropriety. The skill of Beaumont and Fletcher is seen in the successful uniting of contradictory elements, the achievement of a precarious blend of remoteness and familiarity.

I have pointed out certain resemblances between *Philaster* and *The Faithful Shepherdess* and have suggested that *Philaster* represents a progression from the earlier tragicomedy. But according to the verse tests, Beaumont wrote by far the larger portion of *Philaster* and had no share in *The Faithful Shepherdess*. I see no reason to change these traditional ascriptions, nor do I suggest, what can never be proved, that Fletcher was responsible for the plan of *Philaster* and other tragicomedies in which he and Beaumont collaborated. Whatever was the division of labor between the collaborators,[2] the pattern developed in their plays is prefigured in *The Faithful Shepherdess* and not in *The Woman-Hater* or *The Knight of the Burning Pestle*. For the study of the pattern it is relatively unimportant whether Beaumont or Fletcher was primarily responsible for it, but something of its nature is revealed by its relationship to Fletcher's unsuccessful play.

The Coxcomb is a comedy—probably the first on which Beaumont and Fletcher collaborated. It may have been performed in the same year with *Philaster* (1609?). Here the relation to satirical drama is almost as plain as in *The Woman-Hater,* for Antonio, who gives the play its title, is a preposterous character, so absurdly generous with his friend Mercury that he insists on gratifying Mercury's passion for his wife. Unlike the fools of Jonsonian comedy, he is never put out of his humor and at the end of the play, generous as ever, is unaware that he is a cuckold. He is presented throughout as a thoroughly ridiculous character. Mercury, who never wanted to be disloyal to his friend, is quite cured of his passion by the desperate expedient of the wife, who gives in to him in order to make him see what a beast he is. Her strategy saves the marriage and brings about a dubious victory for morality. She describes herself accurately as "the honestest woman . . . that ever lay with another man."

With this satirical farce is a subplot of romantic comedy which borders on tragicomedy. The romantic lovers Ricardo and Viola plan an elopement, but before the appointed time Ricardo is lured by his friends into a drinking bout, in the course of which he forgets Viola. This situation suggests a treatment as satirical as that of the main plot, but Viola is portrayed as a pathetic character, the victim of a series of misfortunes considerably more appalling in their entirety than those faced by Shakespeare's Viola or Rosalind. She is insulted by Ricardo (who doesn't recognize her) and his drunken friends, is refused shelter by Antonio, who suspects her of being a thief, is robbed and bound to a tree, rescued

2. For theories of their methods of collaboration see Louis Wann, "The Collaboration of Beaumont, Fletcher, and Massinger," *Shakespeare Studies by Members of the Department of English of the University of Wisconsin* (Madison, University of Wisconsin Press, 1916), pp. 147–74; Wallis, *Fletcher, Beaumont & Company,* pp. 195–8.

by a man who then tries to seduce her, rescued again by milkmaids (virtuous countryfolk contrasted with the vicious city dwellers), and taken to Mercury's house, where she is hired as a slavey by his mother and is berated for breaking the glassware. The pathos of her situation is constantly brought out by the contrast between her naive innocence and the cynical cruelty of her persecutors. The best example is the scene in which she is robbed by a tinker and his "trull," who insist on believing that she is a "gentlewoman whore," while she continues with unbelievable patience to address them as "good sir" and "good woman." Her outburst when they leave her tied to the tree is typical of her:

> O Heaven, to what am I reserv'd, that knew not
> Through all my childish hours and actions,
> More sin, than poor imagination,
> And too much loving of a faithless Man?
>
> II, i; Cam., 8, 331

Viola never rises above the pathetic, partly because of the run-of-the-mill speeches she is given and partly, perhaps, because of the rather haphazard sequence of horrors to which she is subjected. She is too obviously devised as a victim. The final scene of the subplot is her reconciliation with Ricardo, who abases himself and is magnanimously forgiven.

The comparison of Viola with Euphrasia, another lovelorn maiden, is instructive. Euphrasia's story is also a sentimental one but more compellingly so, not, certainly, because it is more credible but because it belongs to the world of romance projected in *Philaster,* and Euphrasia's virtue, like Arethusa's, is enhanced with a heroic nobility worthy of the misfortunes which befall her. In that remote world perfect innocence is more convincing than in the mean surroundings of *The Coxcomb.* Viola's story needs the climate of romance. While Fletcher and his collaborators succeed better in later comedies in combining farce with romance and satirical humor with pathos, the significant thing about *The Coxcomb* is the attempt to make the combination. Within a brief period, perhaps little more than a year, Beaumont and Fletcher wrote *Cupid's Revenge,* their first tragedy; *Philaster,* their first tragicomedy; and *The Coxcomb,* their first comedy. Both the tragedy and the comedy show the influence of tragicomedy, the form which from the first asserts its hegemony over the Beaumont and Fletcher plays.

The Maid's Tragedy, one of the best known and most successful of all their productions, is a far better tragedy than *Cupid's Revenge.* The atmosphere of the play is more compellingly evil, dominated by more virulent forms of lust and ambition. The setting of a corrupt court is established more firmly and the illusion of actuality is not marred by the intrusion of gods into the action. One indication of this sort of change is that the masque introduced into the first act is made part of the court entertainment of the bride and groom. At first sight, then, this play does not seem so remote or contrived as *Cupid's Revenge.*

As in the earlier tragedy, however, two plots have been joined, the "maid's tragedy" of Aspatia, whom Amintor deserts at the King's command in order to marry Evadne, and the tragedy of Amintor, who discovers that Evadne is the King's mistress but is too loyal a subject to take any revenge. Though the joining of the two plots is more skillful than in *Cupid's Revenge,* the relations of Amintor, Evadne, and the King provide so much of the drama that Aspatia's tragedy seems almost irrelevant. Basing his expectations on the title, Rymer, who treated the play in his usual rough fashion, demanded querulously: "If *Amintors* falshood and its fatal consequences are to be noted, what occasion have we for a King in this Tragedy? cannot *Corydon* deceive his *Amarillis* (for such is *Aspatia*) but the King must know of it, the King must be murder'd for't?"[3] The action of the play does not form an entirely coherent whole.

As a tragic hero Amintor does not conform to any of the familiar Elizabethan types. He is a more satisfactory, because a more consistent, character than Leucippus in *Cupid's Revenge,* but compared to other Elizabethan heroes he does not seem altogether tragic. Unlike most of them he has not been led to commit a grave sin by the perversity of fate or by a flaw of character. He is punished, presumably, for his disloyalty to Aspatia, as Rymer thought, but this is not presented as an indubitable fault. Amintor has been confronted by a choice between his duty to Aspatia and his duty to the King. At the opening of the play he has made his decision, and though he regrets the injury he has done to Aspatia, he believes that he has chosen the higher good. The choice between vengeance and dishonor, which is central to the play, is in effect the same choice in a different guise. In this instance he places his duty to the King higher than his personal honor and accepts the infamy of being the nominal husband of the King's mistress. But since his actions are presented as consistently noble, a tragic punishment is not the logical necessity that it is for the usual Elizabethan hero. The evil of the world remains largely external to him. A victim of circumstance, he suffers for his nobility, physically crushed but morally triumphant. Amintor is in this respect the precursor of the supermen of Restoration heroic drama, who are infinitely more noble than erring. One feels that his plight, like many of theirs, might have a happy resolution without any inconsistency.

When Waller prepared the play for production after the Restoration, he rewrote the last act so as to bring about a happy ending. Although

3. Thomas Rymer, *The Tragedies of the Last Age . . .* (1678), in Spingarn, *2,* 194. Rymer noted that this tragedy is closely affiliated with pastoral romance. It has been suggested that the source of the incident of Aspatia fighting in male attire with Amintor may have been the fight of Parthenia and Amphialus in the *Arcadia,* iii, xvi, though the parallel is not exact.

his alteration is unsatisfactory because of its miserable verse, his idea
is not shocking as is the idea of contriving happy endings for the
tragedies of Shakespeare. The chief objection to such a change is the
loss of two situations which are indisputably good theater. The first is
the combat between Amintor and Aspatia when she impersonates her
brother, challenges Amintor to a duel, and dies on his sword. The second
is the moment of Amintor's horrified reply to Evadne when she announces that she has avenged him by killing the King:

> Why, thou hast rais'd up mischief to his height,[4]
> And found out one to out-name thy other faults;
>
> .   .   .
>
>   thou hast toucht a life,
> The very name of which had power to chain
> Up all my rage, and calm my wildest wrongs.
>   v; Cam., *1, 70*

Scenes such as these are the lifeblood of the play. To take any of them
away is to lose what is most characteristic of *The Maid's Tragedy*.

The contrivance of certain spectacular scenes in the second and third
acts shows clearly a trick of characterization which becomes one of the
outstanding features of the Fletcherian pattern. Evadne's relation to the
King is first revealed in the second act; up to the moment of revelation
the secret is jealously guarded. Like the writers of detective fiction,
Beaumont and Fletcher deliberately falsify their point of view and
write the first scene of the act as if Evadne were what Amintor and the
audience imagine her to be. As her maids prepare her for the bridal night,
she behaves with becoming modesty to Dula, whom she scolds for her
indecent jokes, and with dignity and sympathy to Aspatia, whose grief
is a jarring note in the joy of the occasion. In this scene the strong contrasts tend to enhance one's opinion of Evadne. Next there is a brief
interchange between Aspatia and Amintor in which she unselfishly
wishes him joy and he is momentarily struck with repentance, a foil
to the joy he anticipates. Then comes the main business of the act, the
scene between Amintor and Evadne, which goes counter to the carefully developed expectations. The first surprise is Evadne's refusal to
come to bed. Amintor ascribes her behavior to coyness or to anger at
some wrongdoer, and she leads him on by playing the part of a mysterious
heroine of romance:

> Now I shall try thy truth; if thou dost love me,
> Thou weigh'st not any thing compar'd with me;
> Life, Honour, joyes Eternal, all Delights

---

4. I have preferred the reading "his height" of the early quartos to "this height" in
the Second Folio.

This world can yield, or hopeful people feign,
Or in the life to come, are light as Air
To a true Lover when his Lady frowns,
And bids him do this: wilt thou kill this man?
Swear my *Amintor,* and I'le kiss the sin off from thy lips.

II; Cam., I, 19

But when he suggests that she has taken a vow to preserve her maidenhead for one night, she catches up the word with the cynicism of a
hardened prostitute: "A Maidenhead *Amintor* at my years?" The surprise of the *volte-face,* far more shocking than the first surprise, leads
by gradual stages to the revelation that Evadne is the King's mistress.
Her cynical question is the turning point of the scene. Up to this time
the relationship of Amintor and Evadne rests upon the misconception
that she is an innocent girl and the reason for her strange behavior is
sought in a series of hypotheses based on this misconception. A mounting tension results from Amintor's failure to understand Evadne's aloof-
ness. When it becomes clear to him that she is thoroughly corrupt, his
injured nobility is expressed by a rage as passionate as Perigot's when
he believes that Amoret is unchaste, or as Philaster's when he succumbs
to Megra's slander. The moment this rage has been fully expressed it is
turned to despairing resignation by the knowledge that the King is the
source of all the corruption. In the hope of concealing his humiliation
from the world, Amintor makes a last request of Evadne, as surprising,
perhaps, as anything else in the scene:

Come let us practise, and as wantonly
As ever loving Bride and Bridegroom met,
Lets laugh and enter here.

II; Cam., I, 23

Like the dancers of a *pas de deux* Amintor and Evadne assume a
variety of postures and constantly change their positions, but always in
such a way as to set each other off to the maximum advantage. Each is
a foil to the other; the relationship is one of contrast. At all times some
real or apparent opposition produces tension between the two characters,
whether Evadne appears as her hardened and cynical self or whether she
plays a part quite contrary to her true nature, though having no motive
for concealing the truth from Amintor. Dryden's comment on the characters of Beaumont and Fletcher applies perfectly to Evadne: "you know
not whether they resemble vice or virtue, and they are either good, bad,
or indifferent, as the present scene requires it."[5] The consistency of
Evadne's character is sacrificed not simply for surprise, as is sometimes
suggested, but for the sake of the antitheses which compose the pattern

---

5. "Preface to *Troilus and Cressida,*" Dryden, *Essays, I,* 217.

of emotional tensions. The play acting of Amintor when the scene closes
does not alter the relationship of the two characters, but it produces one
final effect by the ironic contrast between his feelings and his behavior.

The stormy interview of Amintor and Melantius, Evadne's brother,
in the third act is another illustration of the manipulation of character
and situation. Here the two characters are firm friends, and although
Amintor at first tries to conceal his grief, his pretense is so transparent
that Melantius is not deceived. Nevertheless, a series of oppositions keeps
the two friends at a high emotional pitch. At first Melantius is so offended by Amintor's refusal to confide in him that he threatens to end
their friendship, but this prospect is so horrible that Amintor's delicacy
vanishes in an instant and he tells Melantius in so many words that his
sister is a whore. The insult almost provokes Melantius to a duel, from
which he refrains at the last moment in the name of friendship, accepting his sister's guilt and offering to avenge his friend. Amintor is so
scandalized by the thought of revenge on the King that he attempts to
dissuade Melantius and, in his turn, challenges his friend to a duel.
Once more friendship wins out, however, and the scene ends in reconciliation. It is an extraordinary tour de force of contrived antipathies.

A suggestion of psychological truth makes such scenes momentarily
credible on the stage, but another factor is even more important in making them acceptable within the framework of the play. The reiteration
of heroic struggles, of extreme positions, of characters who pose, deceive, are untrue to themselves creates a world apart. There are links
between this world and the world of actuality, but once we have been
introduced to the world of the play, we discover that it has its own laws
and decorum to which the characters and situations conform. The unique
quality of this world is projected by a brand of emotional rhetoric which
is perfectly adapted to the artifices of character and situation. Amintor,
for instance, laments his dilemma in the following speech:

> I know too much, would I had doubted still;
> Was ever such a marriage night as this!
> You powers above, if you did ever mean
> Man should be us'd thus, you have thought a way
> How he may bear himself, and save his honour:
> Instruct me in it; for to my dull eyes
> There is no mean, no moderate course to run,
> I must live scorn'd, or be a murderer:
> Is there a third? why is this night so calm?
> Why does not Heaven speak in Thunder to us,
> And drown her voice?
>
> II; Cam., *I*, 20–1

"There is no mean, no moderate course" in verse, character, or situation in *The Maid's Tragedy*. It is a sequence of brilliantly executed scenes in which each component element is pushed to an extreme.

Amintor has sometimes been compared with Hamlet, and though their resemblance is superficial, the comparison is instructive. No one has the slightest doubt that Hamlet is by far the more impressive tragic hero. More relevant to this analysis of *The Maid's Tragedy* is the fact that Hamlet's dilemma ultimately engages the spectator's emotions more completely than does Amintor's dilemma. Even when judged on the basis of emotional appeal, therefore, *Hamlet* is more successful than *The Maid's Tragedy*. But this quantitative difference is less significant than the difference between the methods by which an emotional response is elicited. The response to Hamlet's dilemma is cumulative, depending upon the continuous, logical presentation of his interlocking attitudes toward Claudius, Gertrude, the world, and the problem of revenge. The response to Amintor's dilemma is in reality a series of responses to several successive dilemmas, each one equally compelling. And whereas Shakespeare's famous soliloquies reveal many aspects of his hero's character and relate Hamlet's problems to many fundamental human concerns, Beaumont and Fletcher strictly limit the character of their hero and by the shocking nature of the situations emphasize what is special and extraordinary in his problems. Thus, while the spectator is progressively aroused by *Hamlet* to a greater emotional response, his emotions are immediately engaged by *The Maid's Tragedy* and are subjected to a rapid succession of unexpected stimuli which maintain but only slightly increase the original intensity. Beaumont and Fletcher achieve a high pitch of emotion by the manipulation of character and plot and by a special rhetoric which I shall discuss at greater length in succeeding chapters. Since this kind of manipulation and this kind of poetry destroy the continuity of character or of thought found in Shakespeare, *The Maid's Tragedy* may well seem to provide a more emotional experience than *Hamlet*. The truth is that it is more exclusively emotional.

Another result of Beaumont and Fletcher's methods in this tragedy is that the spectator comes to relish the very means by which his emotions are appealed to. For however inferior *The Maid's Tragedy* may be when compared to *Hamlet,* it is an amazing piece of dramatic contrivance. Admiration for the sheer virtuosity of the play is an important part of the spectator's response.

The artistic success of the play, which is considerable without being complete, is dependent in large measure upon a special kind of consistency. Though no one idea informs the tragedy and no one group of images dominates the poetry; though the characters are altered to fit the situations and the situations do not evolve by an inevitable logic, the play is remarkably homogeneous. All the component elements obviously belong together. This virtue does not make the play a better tragedy than Rymer thought it, for judged by the conventional standards of tragedy it is far from convincing. Only when it is judged as another sort of dramatic entertainment does the virtue of *The Maid's Tragedy* appear.

The Woman's Prize,[6] written by Fletcher alone, is essentially a comedy of trickery, as is Beaumont's *The Woman-Hater.* The alternate title, *The Tamer Tamed,* and also another title, *The Taminge of the Tamer,* used by Sir Henry Herbert in his *Office Book,* recall *The Taming of the Shrew,* as do the names of some of the characters and several allusions.[7] Petruchio, who is a widower "famous for a woman-tamer," has married his second wife, Maria, who is much pitied by her friends for the ordeal which she is about to undergo. To the amazement of everyone, however, she gets the upper hand by refusing to have anything to do with him until he agrees to give her her own way; she is an able successor to Alice of Bath. The humor of the play derives from the reversal of Shakespeare's situation and from the means by which a woman gains the "maistrye" over a willful man.

Fletcher's treatment of this situation is characteristic of him. The central opposition of Maria to Petruchio furnishes the design of the whole play, so that, instead of the single combat between two individuals, we have the war between the sexes. Maria and her militantly feminist cousin Bianca barricade themselves in Maria's room, where they are joined by Maria's sister Livia and a revolutionary band of City and Country Wives. In other words, the comedy is developed along the lines of a rigid scheme. While Shakespeare's subplot of the wooing of Bianca, borrowed from *The Supposes,* has no direct bearing on "the taming of the shrew," Fletcher's subplot of the mutual love of Rowland and Livia and of Livia's method of getting rid of Moroso, the old suitor favored by her father, is treated as a parallel to the main plot. So compelling is the structural scheme that, although there is not the slightest disagreement between Livia and Rowland, he is made to think that he has been abominably treated by her and behaves throughout the play as if he had a common cause with Petruchio. As for Livia, she

6. There is wide disagreement about the date of *The Woman's Prize.* Thorndike places it in 1604, making it earlier than any other play by either Beaumont or Fletcher. Baldwin Maxwell, *"The Woman's Prize, or The Tamer Tamed," Studies in Beaumont, Fletcher, and Massinger* (Chapel Hill, N.C., University of North Carolina Press, 1939), pp. 29-45, argues convincingly for a date of 1611 on the basis of topical allusions and the apparent reminiscences of Jonson's *Epicene* (1609) and *The Alchemist* (1610). Harbage accepts the date of 1611.

7. In the article referred to above Maxwell points out that Fletcher's play is not, strictly speaking, a continuation of Shakespeare's. Not only is the scene altered but many of Fletcher's characters do not fit with those of *The Taming of the Shrew.* There can be little doubt, however, that the initial situation is meant to recall Shakespeare.

matches her sister's exploits by her victories over her father and Moroso. Certain details in this play, as in Beaumont's *The Woman-Hater,* recall Jonsonian comedy. Not only has Maria the satirist's aim of changing Petruchio from a monster into a man by teaching him to control his passions but, like Oriana in *The Woman-Hater* or like Jonson's Asper, she deliberately assumes a nature contrary to her own in order to effect her purpose. Livia comments on her disobedience,

> Which yet I cannot think your own, it shews
> So distant from your sweetness.
>
> <div align="right">I, ii; Cam., <i>8, 9</i>[8]</div>

At the end of the play, when Petruchio is "born again" with a better nature, she resumes her own.

The Woman's Prize resembles the earlier plays in Fletcher's persistent use of contrast. Most of the scenes are battles between men and women, and in those where the women are alone their sexual solidarity is destroyed by disagreements and misunderstandings between Maria and Livia. As usual all the contrasts are heightened to the utmost, as when Petruchio's first interview with Maria is preceded by a scene in which he is swaggering with his friends, urging them to lay bets on his sexual prowess. This is a comic equivalent of the preparation for Amintor's wedding night. Serious or farcical, these situations are similarly conceived to achieve the effect of startling contrast.

The plight of Rowland, hero of the subplot of *The Woman's Prize,* is not altogether in keeping with the farcical spirit of the rest of the play. Livia's plot to get rid of Moroso obliges her to encourage him somewhat, and in so doing she mortally offends Rowland, who concludes that she is untrue to him, rails against women, and makes a bet that he will never love again. Though his troubles are never seriously presented they sometimes suggest the situations of tragicomedy. When Livia tempts him to relent toward her, he is torn between her appeal and his bet—a comic dilemma. He is more painfully racked at the end of the play when Livia, pretending to be very ill, asks him and her father and Moroso to witness a document which she says is her repentance for her wild conduct. Rowland is tormented by the thought that though she loves him after all, she is now about to die, but when he examines the document, which has been signed in the dark, he discovers that it is a marriage contract between Livia and himself. As in tragicomedy the unlooked-for happy ending suddenly appears. It is one more piece of evidence, though a small one, that Fletcher's technique in this farce is related to the emerging pattern of tragicomedy.

In *A King and No King,* the joint work of Beaumont and Fletcher

---

8. It is clear from the scansion and from the context that "disobedience" is meant here, though the folio text reads "obedience."

performed December 26, 1611, the pattern is finally established. Of the plays considered so far, four are of special importance because of their contributions to this pattern. In *The Faithful Shepherdess* an elaborate and highly artificial scheme is most apparent. The characters are moral abstractions, strikingly contrasted with each other in a series of surprising situations. The emphasis is more upon emotional tensions than moral significance or individual character as such. The mood of the play is neither comic nor tragic but something in between, and results from a presentation of hypothetical characters in hypothetical situations. The world of the play is far removed from actuality. In *Cupid's Revenge,* although the scheme is again formal and elaborate, the remoteness of the world of the play is less apparent because of certain links with actuality. As a tragedy the play is not persuasive, since the character of the hero is an unconvincing combination of two or three abstractions, such as those of *The Faithful Shepherdess. Cupid's Revenge* has much in common with the tragicomedies. Many of the characteristics of *The Faithful Shepherdess* appear again in *Philaster,* though in a somewhat different form: the characters are not so obviously abstract, the situations not outwardly schematic. The link with actuality, more successfully executed than in *Cupid's Revenge,* takes the dual form of a clever imitation of familiar manners and an illusion of historical veracity. Romantic fantasy appears less contrived than in either *The Faithful Shepherdess* or *Cupid's Revenge.* An important advance toward artistic unity is made in *The Maid's Tragedy,* where a remarkable homogeneity of language, character, and situation is achieved. However, consistency of character is often sacrificed to the brilliant contrasts on which this play, like its predecessors, is based. Not a conventional tragedy, it is a series of sensational situations. These various characteristics of the earlier plays are amalgamated in *A King and No King.*

In one of the commendatory verses prefixed to the First Folio Herrick referred to "that high designe / Of *King and no King*" (Cam., *1,* xli), and Dryden wrote that "the best of their designs . . . is the *King and no King.*"[9] He was not sure how to justify his preference, for Rymer had thoroughly damned the play on neoclassic principles of which Dryden generally approved. In this critical dilemma he fell back upon his experience that the play was moving in spite of "faults of the plot" such as Rymer had lengthily pointed out.[1] The peculiar combination of characteristics which produced Fletcherian tragicomedy explains why the emotional power of *A King and No King* is independent of its improbabilities and breaches of decorum.

---

9. "Preface to *Troilus and Cressida*," Dryden, *Essays, 1,* 212.
   1. Arthur Mizener, "The High Design of *A King and No King,*" MP, *38* (1940–41), 133–54, shows how astute Dryden's comments were and gives a most valuable account of the pattern of emotional responses in the play.

The blend of remoteness and immediacy is at its most paradoxical. The story of the king who falls in love with his sister and is rescued from tragedy by the eventual discovery that she is not his sister and that he is no king is romantic and improbable in the extreme. Yet, as in *Philaster,* many passages of conversation, referring casually to everyday matters, recall the familiar world as, in a very different way, do certain passages of satirical comment on the failings of the flesh. The relation of the play to history is another indication of the blend. Although no complete source is known, the names of many of the characters are taken from the history of Cyrus the Younger, which may also have suggested some of the situations. But Xenophon, whose account of this history in his *Cyropaedia* Beaumont and Fletcher seem to have known,[2] often introduces fictitious matter, and Beaumont and Fletcher have not even followed Xenophon closely. For example, their Tigranes, King of Armenia, is in Xenophon, but not his conqueror Arbaces, King of Iberia, the hero of the play, though in Eutropius we read of another Tigranes of Armenia and an Arthaces of Iberia. (*Brief Chronicle,* tr. Nicolaus Haward [1564], fol. 65 ff.) It is even possible that the suggestion for using these two kingdoms came from the story in the *Arcadia* from which the plot of *Cupid's Revenge* was taken, for the kings of Iberia and Armenia figure prominently there. History and romance seem to be inextricably tangled in *A King and No King.*

The poetry of some of the intensely emotional speeches is the best illustration of the delicate adjustment of the familiar and the remote. It is formal, declamatory verse, remote from the language of conversation, and yet the structure of its sentences is simple, the vocabulary familiar, and there is none of the stiff elaborateness of Sidney's Arcadian prose. Berkenhead said of Fletcher in a commendatory verse:

No savage Metaphors (things rudely Great)
Thou dost *display,* not *butcher* a Conceit;
Thy Nerves have *Beauty,* which Invades and Charms;
Lookes like a Princesse harness'd in bright Armes.
 Nor art Thou Loud and Cloudy; those that do
Thunder so much, do't without Lightning too;
Tearing themselves, and almost split their braine
To render harsh what thou speak'st free and cleane;

                                    Cam., *1,* xliii

These qualities may be seen in a speech of Arbaces':

Why should there be such musick in a voyce,
And sin for me to hear it? All the world

2. See R. Warwick Bond's introduction to *A King and No King* in *The Works of Francis Beaumont and John Fletcher,* ed. A. H. Bullen (Variorum ed., London, G. Bell & Sons, 1904–12), *1,* 246–7.

> May take delight in this, and 'tis damnation
> For me to do so: You are fair and wise
> And vertuous I think, and he is blest
> That is so near you as [your] brother is;
> But you are nought to me but a disease;
> Continual torment without hope of ease;
> Such an ungodly sickness I have got,
> That he that undertakes my cure, must first
> O'rethrow Divinity, all moral Laws,
> And leave mankind as unconfin'd as beasts,
> Allowing 'em to do all actions
> As freely as they drink when they desire.[3]
>
>   III; Cam., *1*, 181–2

The insistent rhythm and the periods of varying length are perfectly planned for the actor as a vehicle of emotional declamation, yet the surface appears most "free and cleane."

It is an easy transition from verse such as this to the more obviously patterned verse of the following impassioned rebuke. Even here, where there are many more rhetorical devices, there are no "savage metaphors" and no "butchering of conceits":

>   Thou art false, false Prince;
> I live to see it, poor *Spaconia* lives
> To tell thee thou art false; and then no more;
> She lives to tell thee thou art more unconstant,
> Than all ill women ever were together.
> Thy faith is firm as raging over-flowes,
> That no bank can command; as lasting
> As boyes gay bubbles, blown i'th' Air and broken:[4]
>
>   IV; Cam., *1*, 199

An occasional homely phrase such as the "boyes gay bubbles" in some measure contradicts the impression made by the formal rhetorical pattern.

The design of the play is implicit in the treatment of the character of Arbaces. He is first described by the faithful captain Mardonius: "he is vain-glorious, and humble, and angry, and patient, and merry and dull, and joyful and sorrowful in extremity in an hour." (I, i; Cam., *1*, 151.) A combination of opposite characteristics, and all "in

---

3. Although this passage contains the qualities ascribed by Berkenhead to Fletcher, the versification indicates that it was probably written by Beaumont. It is doubtful whether seventeenth-century critics had any clear idea of which poet wrote any given speech. The "your" in square brackets is the reading of the first quartos and seems preferable to the "my" of the Second Folio.

4. The speech is probably Fletcher's.

extremity." The characters paired together in *The Faithful Shepherdess* are not more opposed to each other than the contrary humors of Arbaces. When he first appears he gives an excellent demonstration of them by behaving toward his captive Tigranes with the utmost politeness and at the same time with insufferable arrogance:

> Thy sadness brave *Tigranes* takes away
> From my full victory, am I become
> Of so small fame, that any man should grieve
> When I o'recome him?
>
> I, i; Cam., *I, 152*

He graciously offers the hand of his sister Panthea to Tigranes with the insulting observation that her beauty is such as to make the women of Tigranes' country blush for shame at their foulness. The unsympathetic egotism of this behavior is not even made glorious as the *hubris* of a hero; it is presented in a ridiculous light to which a hero is seldom exposed. Arbaces' vainglory is the target for a running fire of satirical comment from Mardonius, who stands aside and observes, like Macilente in *Every Man out of His Humor*. His comments range from ironical humor to such sober criticism as: " 'Tis pity that valour should be thus drunk." (I, i; Cam., *I, 153*.) "Thy valour and thy passions sever'd, would have made two excellent fellows in their kinds: I know not whether I should be sorry thou art so valiant, or so passionate, wou'd one of 'em were away." (I, i; Cam., *I, 154*.) The satirical effect of this presentation of Arbaces is accentuated by its context, for it immediately follows the comic opening scene of the play, in which Mardonius makes sport of the bragging coward Captain Bessus. When we are introduced to the drunken valor of Arbaces, we realize that Bessus, in all his gross absurdity, is a distorted reflection of the King—a caricature of his worst side.

To make Arbaces a sympathetic character after such an introduction is a remarkable feat. The process by which it is accomplished consists in revealing the more pleasing characteristics of his paradoxical nature. First of all Mardonius, the satirical commentator, is shown to be also so devoted a follower of the King that he braves Arbaces' fury to make him see the folly of his behavior with Tigranes and, when everyone else has run away in terror, kneels before the King to say: "Sir, that I have ever lov'd you, my sword hath spoken for me; that I do, if it be doubted, I dare call an oath, a great one to my witness; and were you not my King, from amongst men, I should have chose you out to love above the rest." (I, i; Cam., *I, 158*.) This touching speech pulls the characterization of Arbaces back from the verge of farce by hinting at qualities which make him an appealing human being. In a later speech Mardonius enumerates them:

were you no King, and free from these moods, should I choose a companion for wit and pleasure, it should be you; or for honesty to enterchange my bosom with, it should be you; or wisdom to give me counsel, I would pick out you; or valour to defend my reputation, still I should find you out; for you are fit to fight for all the world, if it could come in question:

I, i; Cam., I, 159

The tribute is weighty because it comes from a severe critic. It also causes Arbaces to shift to his other tack: he now manifests his better nature by promising amendment and humbly thanking Mardonius for telling him the truth. At the same time the suggestion that, were Arbaces no king, he might be a better man prepares for the happy ending of the tragicomedy.

Arbaces' patient treatment of his mother Arane, when she plots against his life, is another factor tending to make him sympathetic. But most important in this process is the attitude of his sister Panthea, the paragon of virtue and beauty. Though she has not seen him since she was nine years old, her devotion to him is complete:

> My Lord, no maid longs more for any thing,
> And feels more heat and cold within her breast,
> Than I do now, in hopes to see him.

II; Cam., I, 170

In the eyes of this romantic heroine Arbaces is the embodiment of the noble hero.

When we come to the palpitations of Panthea, the mood of the play has changed radically from the satire of the first scenes to full-blown romance. The meeting of Arbaces and Panthea is conceived in a thoroughly romantic mode. Panthea's first words when she is led to her brother are extravagant protestations:

> Now let me die, since I have seen my Lord the King
> Return in safetie, I have seen all good that life
> Can shew me;

III; Cam., I, 178

Both Arbaces and Tigranes fall in love with her at first sight: "she is a thing / Both to be lov'd and serv'd" says Tigranes. (III; Cam., I, 179.) Arbaces is paralyzed by the discovery of his passion, and while the court waits for him to speak he expresses his inner torment in the following soliloquy:

> Speak, am I what I was?
> What art thou that dost creep into my breast,

And dar'st not see my face? shew forth thy self:
I feel a pair of fiery wings displai'd
Hither, from hence; you shall not tarry there,
Up, and be gone, if thou beest Love be gone:
Or I will tear thee from my wounded breast,
Pull thy lov'd Down away, and with thy Quill
By this right arm drawn from thy wonted wing,
Write to thy laughing Mother i'thy bloud,
That you are powers bely'd, and all your darts
Are to be blown away, by men resolv'd,
Like dust; I know thou fear'st my words, away.

III; Cam., *1*, 178–9

Satiric fury and cruel humor mingle here with the conventional lover's protest against the power of Cupid. Other speeches might be cited in which satire and romance exist side by side. In general, the less admirable Arbaces is presented satirically, the nobler Arbaces romantically. The romantic mood of his lines,

Why should there be such musick in a voyce,
And sin for me to hear it?

is soon followed by another display of his violent passions, and his folly is immediately underlined by terse, satiric comments from Mardonius. These alternations are a striking development of the mixtures of satire and romance in *Philaster*.

Several tense situations evolve in rapid succession from the incestuous infatuation of Arbaces. He tells Mardonius that he loves Panthea, and Mardonius, although he has already guessed the truth, pretends not to understand until Arbaces turns from hints to a bald statement of what he wants. Then the contrast between his vice and Mardonius' probity is made explicit in a dignified rebuke which reduces the King to abject self-contempt. This interview is balanced by the immediately succeeding one with Bessus, who cheerfully agrees to procure Panthea or Arane or anyone else. Arbaces is so scandalized by this distorted reflection of his own evil that he beats and curses Bessus and resolves to resist his temptation. After a scene in which he displays violent jealousy of Tigranes, whom he suspects Panthea of loving, the high point of the play is reached in an interview of brother and sister. It is a scene of great emotional tension based upon the contrast between sexual depravity and ideal love, both of which are kept constantly before us. Arbaces, as in his previous appearances, is simultaneously the best and worst of men, a hero and a beast. As he confesses his passion to Panthea, he implores her to reject him. She does so, and the tension begins to relax as he bids her farewell. Rymer was much shocked by what follows, as he had reason to be. For now, most unexpectedly, Panthea begins to take the initiative, to delay Arbaces' departure with protestations of her affection, and finally to suggest that "Brothers and Sisters lawfully may kiss." (IV; Cam., *I*, 213.) They embrace and then leave the stage in horror, having increased the emotional tension to its maximum.

Rymer's comment was: "Had *Panthea* been some *Wastcoatteer* of the Village, that had been formerly *Complaisant* with him beyond discretion, more vile submissions she could not devise . . ."[5] Evadne was made inexplicably modest to prolong the tension between herself and Amintor; Panthea, for a comparable reason, is made unexpectedly bold. The consistency of her character is sacrificed to the undeniable effectiveness of a situation. The character of Arbaces not only is a paradoxical combination of opposites but is presented from two points of view. Sometimes Arbaces is seen from the outside as an object of satire and at other times from the inside as the hero of romance. This shifting of the point of view, like the inconsistency in the presentation of Panthea, makes a continuous response to the characters impossible. We respond to the relationships between them in a given situation, but the response does not depend on our having looked at these characters in the same way in preceding scenes. It is a response to the emotion itself—a response which may even be heightened when the characters are presented in a strange new light.

What Dryden admired about *A King and No King* was its "lively touches of passion."[6] The fact that they are achieved through a discontinuity of characterization explains why his judgment of the play does not square with Rymer's damnation of it. If *A King and No King* ended tragically, the inconsistency of Panthea's character would prevent her from being wholly pathetic; heroic she never is. And Arbaces would be even more unsatisfactory as a tragic hero because he has appeared too often as a fool whose excesses clearly merit humiliation. The intrusion of the satirical point of view is a serious deterrent to tragedy. Thus the response which this play demands is not really one response but a series of different responses to shifting relationships between the characters. In this way discontinuity helps to establish a middle-mood like that of *The Faithful Shepherdess*. Even before the denouement has rescued Arbaces and Panthea from moral disaster, the treatment of their characters, and especially the presentation of Arbaces, shows that the design of the play is not tragic.

As in most of the Beaumont and Fletcher plays, the central situa-

5. *The Tragedies of the Last Age* (1678), p. 69. This portion of Rymer's essay is not included in Spingarn.
6. "Preface to *Troilus and Cressida*," Dryden, *Essays, I*, 212.

tion is surrounded by secondary situations to which it is formally related. The clowning of Bessus is a caricature of Arbaces. A serious parallel to his agonizing dilemma is the plight of Tigranes, which forms a subplot much better united to the main action than is the subplot of *The Maid's Tragedy*. Tigranes manages to have Spaconia, an Armenian woman with whom he is in love, brought to Iberia as a servant for Panthea, whom Arbaces has ordered him to marry. His initial dilemma is like Amintor's but when Tigranes discovers that he is falling in love with Panthea against his will, his simultaneous attraction and repulsion make him very like the unfortunate Arbaces. Like the central situation, this secondary one proliferates in still further situations, such as the King's jealousy of Tigranes and the ironic accusation of Spaconia's father that she is a shameless camp follower. Lust and chastity are juxtaposed here as they are, in a different way, in Arbaces' interview with Panthea.

Situations from the two plots alternate in such a way that one emotional crisis succeeds another with only an occasional scene of comic relaxation, so that the temporal sequence consists in artful manipulations of the emotional tension. But the similarities and differences between these scenes, emphasized in many cases by their temporal sequence, suggest that their most significant relationships correspond to a spatial pattern. The dilemmas of Arbaces and Tigranes, of Panthea and Spaconia, take shape in the imagination like the forms of which a painting is composed. The eye travels from one to another, perceiving their interrelations. What happens next is not so important as how one happening corresponds to another. In this sense, then, the design of *A King and No King* is static, determined not so much by the laws of cause and effect as by the rules of artful arrangement. This peculiarity of the design may be another reason why, even before the happy ending, tragedy does not seem inevitable.

Largely by the anguished statements of Arbaces ("I wade in sin . . . Darkness is in my bosom,") an atmosphere of encompassing evil is created in *A King and No King* and increases in density until the end of the last act, when it is dispelled by the discovery that Arbaces is the son of an old counselor and was adopted by the Queen when she thought herself barren. She later gave birth to Panthea, who is consequently the heir to the throne and is free to marry Arbaces.[7] His incestuous passion becomes legitimate romantic love, and (illogically) his other objectionable traits disappear, as if they were functions of the false position in which he was placed. Since Arane has already re-

---

7. This solution of the problem did not in the least please Rymer, for whom it was an offensive impropriety. "For whether a Lady may better marry her Brother or her Groom, is a question more easily decided in Divinity, than in Poetry." *The Tragedies of the Last Age*, p. 70.

pented of her plots against Arbaces, and Tigranes has repented of his momentary infidelity to Spaconia, the evil of the play seems in retrospect to have been nò more than a bad dream. It is a hypothesis which provides the play with the basis of its plot and with its most sensational appeal, for the emotional aura of an abnormal passion is made intensely real.

The pattern of tragicomedy whose emergence we have been tracing is complete in *A King and No King*. For the sake of clarity its characteristics, which determine the distinctive nature of the later plays, may be listed under eight separate headings, though we must bear in mind that no single characteristic exists independently of its fellows.

1. *Imitation of the manners of the familiar world.* G. Hills, one of the writers of commendatory verses for the 1647 Folio, wrote of Fletcher:

> *Proteus* of witt! who reads him doth not see
> The manners of each sex of each degree!
>
> Cam., *1,* xlvi

And Dryden, confining the scope of his praise more narrowly, wrote of Beaumont and Fletcher: "they understood and imitated the conversation of gentlemen . . . whose wild debaucheries, and quickness of wit in repartees, no poet can ever paint as they have done."[8] The accuracy with which the surface of life is reflected in Beaumont and Fletcher pleased and astounded many seventeenth-century critics, and even in the twentieth century, when the literary conventions and the life of the Jacobean era are equally unfamiliar, readers often have the same response, more especially if they come to Beaumont and Fletcher from Jonson, Marston, Chapman, and certain other contemporary dramatists. The first impression is of a certain naturalness, of verisimilitude. The world of the play seems to be our world. The phraseology of Dryden's comment points to the source of this impression—the ease, and frequently the familiarity, of the language. It is at the opposite pole from the language of Chapman, whose tortured sentence structure and arresting imagery emphasize the distance separating us from Bussy D'Ambois or Charles, Duke of Byron. The language of Beaumont and Fletcher seems "free and cleane," as Berkenhead said of it, "Nor *swoln* nor *flat,* a True Full Naturall veyne . . ." (Cam., *1,* xliii.) Largely because of this sort of language *A King and No King* appears to imitate the manners of the familiar world—in particular, the manners of the "gentlemen" to whom it was addressed.

2. *Remoteness from the familiar world.* As we have already seen, the impression of familiarity is somewhat deceptive. In contrast to the critics just cited, Ellis-Fermor emphasizes the remoteness of the world of Beaumont and Fletcher. Her phrase, "the moonlit stage of an exquisite opera-

8. "An Essay of Dramatic Poesy," Dryden, *Essays, 1,* 81.

set,"[9] admirably describes the artificiality which more truly characterizes the conception of such a play as *A King and No King*. For, in spite of its reflections of the surface of life, this is a highly stylized play, whose formal movements are reminiscent of the court masque. The first impression is not entirely wrong, but the link with actuality is slighter than it seems at first. The world of the play is neither so immediate as the world in which we live nor so remote as the world of romance. It is a theatrical world, which imitates life to some extent but, like an ingenious stage set, calls attention to its own virtuosity in doing so. Again the language of the play is indicative; it is framed, more obviously than the language of many other plays, to be spoken by an actor, and often, while conforming somewhat to the norm of conversation, abounds in the devices of oratorical rhetoric and the rhythms of declamation. The pattern is not truly lifelike nor completely formalized. It is neither and both. All the other characteristics of the pattern are to some extent dominated by the combination of the first two.

3. *Intricacy of plot*. The plot of *A King and No King* is given some semblance of actuality by the smooth transitions which make the most implausible developments momentarily acceptable, but the most striking feature of this plot is its capacity to surprise. As Henry Harington wrote of *The Wild-Goose Chase*,

> And for thy *Plot*
> When ere we read *we have, and have it not,*
> And glad to be deceiv'd, finding thy Drift
> T'excell our guess at every turn, and shift.
> Cam., *4,* 410

Actuality is distorted not only by continual surprises but by symmetrical contrasts and parallels—the plights of Panthea and Spaconia, of Arbaces and Tigranes. Without shocking by outright contradiction of the familiar laws of cause and effect, the plot imposes upon experience a formal and intricate scheme.

4. *The improbable hypothesis*. The situations which compose the plot are as unusual as they are sensational. Dilemmas like those of a nightmare confront the chief characters: Tigranes must choose between his duty to Spaconia and his new love for Panthea; Arbaces and Panthea between incest and the renunciation of their love. These are the most characteristic situations of the play. They provide its best scenes. Each of them is a challenge to the reader or spectator to imagine what it would be like to experience such conflicting emotions. The appalling hypothesis is advanced: "Let us suppose that a king of great nobility has conceived an instantaneous and consuming passion for his sister"; and as one such hypothesis follows another, we come to ac-

9. *Jacobean Drama*, p. 201.

cept them as properly belonging in a world that is neither impossible nor quite probable—a world of hypotheses.

5. *The atmosphere of evil.* The horror felt by Mardonius, Panthea, and Arbaces himself at the passions which have engulfed him creates an atmosphere of overwhelming evil, scarcely relieved by the bitter clowning of the despicable Bessus. When Arbaces first appears on the stage he is like a man possessed by some evil spirit which is counteracting his native goodness. By the time of his fatal interview with Panthea he is tortured by the sense of an almost tangible power forcing him toward sin—a power which he describes as flame and venom and plague. And yet, miraculously, he remains unconsumed by the evil atmosphere which surrounds and penetrates him. Despite its terrifying imminence, it is never truly manifested in his actions, and in the end it vanishes, leaving no traces. Unreal yet compelling, contrived yet life-like, this atmosphere is one of the characteristics which make the most lasting impression.

6. *Protean characters.* Though the leading characters of *Philaster,* *A Maid's Tragedy,* and *A King and No King* speak in a comparatively familiar idiom, they are strange, unpredictable creatures, who belong to a world of theatrical contrivance. They are monsters and saints, living abstractions and combinations of irreconcilable extremes. And often, like Proteus, they elude our grasp by changing shape from moment to moment. Their changes are of several different sorts. Many of the characters are experts in what Bacon called "dissimulation" and "simulation." That is, they sometimes conceal what they are beneath disguises and sometimes pretend to be what they are not. Thus within the play these characters assume different roles. In certain cases, where there is no question of disguise or pretense, the behavior of some characters is utterly inconsistent with what has gone before, their accustomed shapes unexpectedly distorted. The Protean changes of Beaumont and Fletcher's characters, whether brought about by disguise, pretense, or unexplained distortion, serve to support and prolong important situations. At all times the characters confront each other as opposites—faithless Tigranes and faithful Spaconia, lustful Arbaces and chaste Panthea—and by their intense reactions exploit to the full the possibilities of some fantastic situation. But if the customary behavior of the characters does not make them opposites, or if one conflict between them has been resolved, a sudden change creates the all-important tension. When Arbaces has temporarily mastered his passion for his sister, the situation is prolonged and even intensified by her inexplicable change from saintly compassion to provocative affection. Sometimes, when no real change in the character occurs, a seeming distortion is produced by a conspicuous shift in the point of view. Arbaces, for example, seems at first a ridiculous object of satire, while later he closely re-

sembles a pitiable romantic hero. In every case the character, conceived as an extreme type, is subordinate to the situation and often changes radically to suit the requirements of the intricate plot.

7. *"Lively touches of passion."* The passions, of which Beaumont and Fletcher's characters have an inexhaustible store, have more real solidity than the characters themselves. In the most unlikely situations the most extravagant characters react to each other with emotional outbursts which have, as it were, a life of their own. They are literally "vivid" or, as Dryden put it, "lively." Because they are so, a play like *A King and No King* may be genuinely moving, as it was for Dryden, in spite of being in many respects unbelievable. Thomas Stanley's praise of Fletcher in the 1647 Folio is noteworthy for its emphasis on the verisimilitude not of the characters but of their emotions:

> He to a Sympathie those soules betrai'd
> Whom Love or Beauty never could perswade;
> And in each mov'd spectatour could beget
> A reall passion by a Counterfeit:
> When first *Bellario* bled, what Lady there
> Did not for every drop let fall a teare?
> And when *Aspasia* wept, not any eye
> But seem'd to weare the same sad livery;
>
> .   .   .
>
> Thus he Affections could, or raise or lay;
> Love, Griefe and Mirth thus did his Charmes obey:
> He Nature taught her passions to out-doe,
> How to refine the old, and create new;
> Which such a happy likenesse seem'd to beare,
> As if that Nature Art, Art Nature were.
>
> Cam., 1, xxvii

When Spaconia, a character of little substance, rebukes Tigranes for a fault of which he has already repented, her theatrical speech "Thou art false, false Prince . . ." is a valid projection of the emotions of a wronged woman, even though we are aware that she is not wronged. Often in Beaumont and Fletcher, as in this instance, the emotion even gains intensity by its exact inappropriateness to the situation.

The middle mood of which Ellis-Fermor writes is due not only to the fact that tragedy threatens without materializing. Most of all it is due to the independent life of the emotions of the play—to the communication of the feelings of a tragic situation where the treatment of plot and character do not convey the sense of inevitable tragedy and where evil is more an atmosphere than a real force. In other words, the middle mood is achieved by the combination of the last four characteristics I have mentioned.

8. *The language of emotion.* A dramatist's language can less well be isolated than any other aspect of his technique, for, strictly speaking, it is from the language of the play that we receive every impression. We have already seen that the language of Beaumont and Fletcher is largely responsible for our sense of contact with the familiar world and also of remoteness from it. The combination of ease and rhetorical formality in the language cannot be separated from the first two characteristics of the pattern. However, the suitability of Beaumont and Fletcher's verse for the expression of emotion is so important that it merits separate consideration. T. S. Eliot objects to the superficiality of this poetry: "Their words have often a network of tentacular roots reaching down to the deepest terrors and desires." However,

> Looking closer, we discover that the blossoms of Beaumont and Fletcher's imagination draw no sustenance from the soil, but are cut and slightly withered flowers stuck into sand. . . . the evocative quality of the verse of Beaumont and Fletcher depends upon a clever appeal to emotions and associations which they have not themselves grasped; it is hollow. It is superficial with a vacuum behind it;[1]

It is true that the emotional power of the speeches of Arbaces and Spaconia is derived from a context of associations which remain exterior to the play and hence almost irrelevant; there is an appeal to conventional moral attitudes, such as disapproval of incest or approval of loyalty, about which Beaumont and Fletcher have nothing to say. Not only do the incest and disloyalty of the play prove to be nonexistent but even while they appear to exist they are not treated with the insight of Shakespeare, Webster, or Tourneur. The poetry does nothing to give these moral problems fresh significance. A part of Eliot's criticism is therefore just, but the implications of his flower metaphor lead away from the nature of the Beaumont and Fletcher plays. The blossoms of their imagination are artificial flowers which cannot wither. Their conspicuous artificiality suits them to the plays, but there is no more deception here than in any artistic convention, nor does this verse imitate the kinds of dramatic verse which Eliot admires. The verse of Beaumont and Fletcher, which does not deal seriously with life, as does the verse of some of their contemporaries, is exactly what it appears to be and exactly what the situations demand, a means of eliciting the maximum emotional response. The poetry of every major scene is a brilliant solution to a rhetorical problem.

Because this kind of poetry emphasizes emotion rather than signifi-

1. "Ben Jonson," *Selected Essays, 1917–1932* (New York, Harcourt, Brace, 1932), p. 135.

cance, it tends to isolate moments of powerful feeling and hence to reinforce the impression that they have a sort of independent existence. The high points of *A King and No King* are these dramatic moments, whose vitality is given them by declamatory rhetoric.

When these eight characteristics are seen together, certain conclusions about the pattern can be drawn. One of the most important is that *A King and No King,* as Eliot once said perversely of Shakespeare's drama, has no meaning. It says nothing about incest, pride, jealousy, or wrath, but it presents an arrangement of dramatic moments in which these passions are displayed. Each moment has its meaning, but the whole has none that can be readily defined. Release from the bondage of a total meaning which connects and controls each detail of the pattern not only gives the moment of powerful feeling a greater relative importance (as the comparison of *Hamlet* and *The Maid's Tragedy* has shown) but also facilitates the contrivance of such moments. An isolated phrase is free to evoke its response by means of associations which may be quiet irrelevant to the context—by a rhythm, a sequence of sounds, or an allusion which may suggest something slightly different to every listener. Many phrases in Beaumont and Fletcher operate in this way. A good example is one from *The Faithful Shepherdess* which Eliot chose to illustrate the verse:

> Your hair wove into many a curious warp,
> Able in endless errour to infold
> The wandring soul,
>
> ii, i; Cam., *2, 392*

The image is compelling for reasons which would be difficult to explain and which do not lie mainly in the relevance of Thenot's words to Clorin, whom he is describing. In fact the strong suggestions of sexual attraction are made here only to be dismissed a few lines later as antithetical to Clorin's true nature. Yet, having once been conjured up, they linger on with almost a life of their own; and an important part of their lasting quality is due to their vagueness—another important part to the pattern of sounds. A more rigorous poetic control would have eliminated such lines from a scene defining the pure love of Thenot for "the faithful shepherdess."

The renunciation of meaning is no mere relaxation of control, however. It can better be described as one of the strategies by which Beaumont and Fletcher achieve their superbly calculated succession of dramatic moments. Theirs is a deliberate playing with the most serious issues. To make much of every relationship becomes a kind of game which is most successfully when most daringly played. The sudden change, the unexpected revelation, the disappearance of one issue to make way for another are all parts of an intricate pattern of feeling which is fundamental to Fletcherian tragicomedy. The game is played with consummate skill.

The pattern of tragicomedy in *A King and No King* is an experiment in a new and sophisticated form of dramatic entertainment. The most radical departure from the familiar forms is the abandonment of the meanings of tragedy and of comedy, though many of their techniques and some of their effects are retained. Beaumont and Fletcher's tragicomedy bears somewhat the relation to the older drama that abstract painting bears to the more conventional schools of painting. The emphasis is upon the formal pattern, to which everything else is sacrificed. Imitation of the familiar world is counteracted by extreme improbabilities and distortions. The appeal is made directly to an emotional and aesthetic response.

In a sense, then, this drama represents a refinement, or possibly an abstraction, of older dramatic practices, giving us the design but not the body of drama. The shape of the conflict which is essential to all dramatic action is preserved, proliferating in endless oppositions, even though the conflict signifies nothing beyond itself. The passions remain though character is warped beyond recognition. The language indicates the final stage of this process of abstraction. By the operation of a rhetoric to be discussed in later chapters, the dramatic conflict becomes almost exclusively verbal, so that language in some measure supplants rather than expresses the action. The pattern of the Beaumont and Fletcher plays takes from earlier drama only what is necessary to make them at all times eminently effective in the theater.

II

Satyr and Shepherd

THE SIGNIFICANCE OF the pattern just described is partially obscured by two layers of difficulty. The first is that the term "tragicomedy" was applied in the Renaissance to many dramatic works which do not greatly resemble each other.[1] But even when we know what various works were called tragicomedies, Fletcherian tragicomedy remains something of an anomaly—almost another genre. The chief difficulty is to understand and criticize something which is unique.

In dealing with this kind of critical problem it is often helpul to begin by noting what the new form has in common with established forms. Critics in the sixteenth and seventeenth centuries followed this procedure when they emphasized the obvious relationships of tragicomedy with tragedy and comedy. They occasionally sought to explain the anomalous genre by referring to the Greek satyr play, about which very little was known. They did not discuss the less apparent relationships with satire and pastoral romance, though they often, sometimes confusedly, associated tragicomedy with one or the other. Since these two forms have an important bearing on the unique quality of Fletcherian tragicomedy, this chapter will be concerned mainly with their salient characteristics. Satire and pastoral romance will aid us in overcoming our major difficulty. First, however, we shall glance briefly at some Renaissance theories of tragicomedy, which will enable us to surmount the more general difficulty of what the term meant when Beaumont and Fletcher were beginning to write.

Fletcher himself prefixed some well-known remarks on tragicomedy to the First Quarto of *The Faithful Shepherdess* (undated, but probably 1609–10) after the dismal failure of the play on the stage. Sarcastic and brief as they are—the self-justification of an unappreciated young man—they provide some important indications for a modern reader.

1. For a general treatment of the subject see F. H. Ristine, *English Tragicomedy, Its Origin and History* (New York, Columbia University Press, 1910).

TO THE READER

If you be not reasonably assurde of your knowledge in this
*kinde of Poeme, lay downe the booke or read this, which I would
wish had bene the prologue. It is a pastorall Tragic-comedie,
which the people seeing when it was plaid, having ever had a
singuler guift in defining, concluded to be a play of coñtry hired
Shepheards, in gray cloakes, with curtaild dogs in strings, sometimes laughing together, and sometimes killing one another: And
mis[s]ing whitsun ales, creame, wasiel & morris-dances, began
to be angry. In their error I would not have you fall, least you
incurre their censure. Understand therefore a pastorall to be a
representation of shepheards and shephearddesses, with their actions and passions, which must be such as may agree with their
natures at least not exceeding former fictions, & vulgar traditions:
they are not to be adorn'd with any art, but such improper ones
as nature is said to bestow, as singing and Poetry, or such as experience may teach them, as the vertues of hearbs, & fountaines:
the ordinary course of the Sun, moone, and starres, and such like.
But you are ever to remember Shepherds to be such, as all the
ancient Poets and moderne of understanding have received them:
that is, the owners of flockes and not hyerlings. A tragie-comedie
is not so called in respect of mirth and killing, but in respect it wants
deaths, which is inough to make it no tragedie, yet brings some
neere it, which is inough to make it no comedie: which must be a
representation of familiar people with such kinde of trouble as no
life be questiond, so that a God is as lawfull in this as in a tragedie,
and meane people as in a comedie. This much I hope will serve to
justifie my Poeme, and make you understand it, to teach you more
for nothing, I do not know that I am in conscience bound.

Cam., *2, 522*

The playful petulance of Fletcher's last thrust is understandable but
also exasperating: a fuller explanation is held out only to be snatched
away. Yet the comments bear on two important problems: the nature
of pastoral tragicomedy and the principles of decorum derived there-
from. Fletcher distinguishes tragicomedy from the dramatic monsters
to which Sidney scornfully refers as "mungrell" tragicomedies that
"match Horn-pypes and Funeralls."[2] For Fletcher tragicomedy is not
a mechanical combination of the attributes of tragedy and comedy but
a subtle fusion in which each loses its identity. Nevertheless he shows
which elements of these familiar forms are involved.

2. Sir Philip Sidney, "An Apologie for Poetrie," G. G. Smith, *1, 199.*

Fletcher's concern with the decorum of the pastoral and the tragi-comedy seems exaggerated to the contemporary critic because he, un-like the critics of the Renaissance, is not much interested in making nice distinctions between the various types of literature. With Shake-speare to afford him a respectable precedent, he is apt to guffaw at pedantic classifications: "tragedy, comedy, history, pastoral, pastoral-comical, historical-pastoral, tragical-historical, tragical-comical-histori-cal-pastoral." But though Shakespeare has his laugh at the Poloniuses of literary criticism, Fletcher seems to care about such distinctions, and the student who ignores the theories of pastoral tragicomedy will miss a clew to the understanding of the Fletcherian pattern.

1. *Tragicomoedia, Satyr, Pastor*

An iconographical representation of tragicomedy appears on the title page of the 1616 Folio of Ben Jonson's *Workes*. Although there is no tragicomedy among the plays in this volume, the figure of *Tragi-comoedia* stands at the top of the page on the highest level of a baroque façade which seems to symbolize the drama. At the base are the *plaustrum,* the cart in which the first actors are said to have traveled, and the *visorium,* where they acted; higher up is the more modern *theatrum.* In niches to the left and right of the title stand *Tragoedia* and *Comoedia,* each attired in her traditional robes, and in much smaller niches above are the diminutive figures of the tutelary gods Bacchus and Apollo. Tragicomoedia, in an incongruous assortment of the clothes of her elder sisters, seems to preside over the entire fabric of the drama, as she faces eagerly forward, poised on a scroll in front of a niche which she has clearly outgrown. Seated below her, to the left and right of the theatrum, are two figures who turn toward her as if in token of some special relationship. One has goat's legs and a long stave and plays on a syrinx; the other, dressed with the rustic elegance of sixteenth-century Arcadia, has a crook and plays on a shepherd's pipe. These attendants of Tragicomoedia would easily be recognized even without their labels of *Satyr* and *Pastor.*

The presence of Tragicomedy on this title page is not so surprising as it seems at first glance. That Jonson was not the rigid classicist he is sometimes thought to be, and did not view with alarm such relatively new forms as tragicomedy, is shown by a familiar passage from the Induction to *Every Man out of His Humor,* where Cordatus, after referring to the innovations of Menander, Plautus, and others, con-cludes with these words: "I see not then, but we should enjoy the same licence, or free power, to illustrate and heighten our invention as they did; and not bee tyed to those strict and regular formes, which the nicenesse of a few (who are nothing but forme) would thrust upon

GOSHEN COLLEGE LIBRARY
GOSHEN, INDIANA 46526

us." (ll. 266–70.)[3] Furthermore, Jonson not only read and criticized Guarini's pastoral tragicomedy *Il Pastor fido* but commented to Drummond that Fletcher's *The Faithful Shepherdess* was "a Tragicomedie well done."[4] It is possible that Fletcher's play was responsible for Jonson's interest in this form, or that Jonson, following his own critical principles, urged his young friend to experiment. Thus the title page may be one slight indication of the important relationship between the older and the younger dramatist.

From Tragicomedy's lofty position on the title page we may legitimately conclude that for some critics in 1616 this hybrid was the highest achievement of the drama. We see also that a definite relationship is assumed between Tragicomedy and certain other allegorical figures. The clothing, a combination of what Tragedy and Comedy wear, shows —what Fletcher implies—that the nature of Tragicomedy is a blend of the natures of these two; at the same time the figure of Tragicomedy has an expression, a stance, a gesture all her own. As for the serenading Satyr and Shepherd, they are traditional characters in pastoral, whose conventions often enter into tragicomedy, as they do in *Il Pastor fido* and *The Faithful Shepherdess*. It is obvious that this gaily dressed Shepherd is, as Fletcher says, no mere "hireling" but a gentleman-shepherd, such as "all the ancient poets" portray. The Satyr, of whom Fletcher says nothing, belongs not only in pastoral but also in the Greek satyr play. Satyr and shepherd are fully as important as tragedy and comedy in determining the nature of Fletcherian tragicomedy. The significance of the satyr, never properly appreciated, can best be approached through Renaissance critical theory.

2. Guarini and the Satyr Play

Many of the general ideas implied by Jonson's title page are explicitly stated in an essay which is probably the source of Fletcher's comments on pastoral tragicomedy—*Il Compendio della poesia tragicomica,* first published in 1601 by Guarini in defense of his own pastoral tragicomedy *Il Pastor fido,* written in 1585. Guarini objects strenuously to the idea that tragicomedy is a mechanical combination of tragedy and comedy: "for he who makes a tragicomedy does not intend to compose separately either a tragedy or a comedy, but from

---

3. All references to Jonson's writings are to *Ben Jonson,* ed. C. H. Herford, Percy Simpson, and Evelyn Simpson (Oxford, Clarendon Press, 1925–). For further comment on Jonson's attitude see Freda L. Townsend, "Ben Jonson's 'Censure' of Rutter's *Shepheards holy-day,*" *MP, 44* (1947), 238–47.

4. *Ben Jonson's Conversations with William Drummond of Hawthornden,* 4.64–5; 18.611–2; 12.227–8.

Reproduced from the title page of the 1616 Jonson
Folio in the Elizabethan Club, Yale University.

SATYR

PASTOR

LOCVM TENEANT SPITA IDEN

TRAGŒDIA

COMŒDIA

THE

WORKES

OF

Beniamin Jonson

— neque, me vt miretur turba,
laboro:
Contentus paucis lectoribus.

LONDON
printed by W:
Stansby, and are
to be sould by
Rich: Meighen.

PLAVSTRVM

VISORIVM

Chorus

An. D. 1616.

the two a third thing that will be perfect of its kind . . ."[5] It is as different from tragedy and comedy as the mule is from the horse and the ass (this is not the happiest of Guarini's comparisons), or bronze from copper and tin, or gunpowder from sulphur, niter, and carbon. Tragicomedy has a nature and (as the last comparison suggests) a potency of its own.

Guarini anticipates Fletcher in stating that the decorum of tragicomedy permits a mixture of social classes, which, as he points out, results in a more truthful imitation of life than either comedy or tragedy. His account of how the author of tragicomedy is indebted to tragedy and comedy is more detailed and more illuminating than Fletcher's: "from the one he takes great persons but not great action; a plot which is verisimilar but not true; passions, moved but tempered; the delight, not the sadness; the danger, not the death; from the other, laughter which is not dissolute, modest amusement, a feigned complication, a happy reversal, and above all, the comic order . . ."[6]

After giving this account of the concoction of tragicomedy Guarini rises to a most ecstatic claim for his chosen form:

> And truly if today men understood well how to compose tragicomedy (for it is not an easy thing to do), no other drama should be put on the stage, for tragicomedy is able to include all the good qualities of dramatic poetry and to reject all the bad ones; it can delight all dispositions, all ages, and all tastes—something that is not true of the other two, tragedy and comedy, which are at fault because they go to excess.[7]

Thus tragicomedy is the ultimate refinement of drama, the one form for truly civilized and well-bred men.

The *Compendio* is a reply to the critics who blamed Guarini for writing a sort of drama never sanctioned by Aristotle. But while he, like Jonson, defends his right to use forms unknown to the ancients, he is still careful to cite classical precedents for his experiments. He leans most heavily on Aristotle's reference to tragedies with happy endings; on the *Amphitryon,* which Plautus himself called a tragicomedy; and on the curious, so-called "satyr play," the *Cyclops,* in which Euripides "mixed grave danger for the life of Odysseus, a tragic character, with the drunkenness of the Cyclops, which is a comic action."[8] The satyr play is Guarini's stoutest prop. He quotes the description of satyr

5. "The Compendium of Tragicomic Poetry," in Allan H. Gilbert, *Literary Criticism: Plato to Dryden* (New York, etc., American Book Co., 1940), p. 507.

6. Translated from Giambattista Guarini, *Il Compendio della poesia tragicomica,* printed with *Il Pastor fido* (Bari, Gius. Laterza & Figli, 1914), p. 231. I am indebted to Professor Thomas Bergin of Yale University for checking this translation.

7. "The Compendium of Tragicomic Poetry," in Gilbert, *Literary Criticism,* p. 512.

8. *Ibid.,* p. 508. See also Ristine, *English Tragicomedy,* pp. 33–45 and *passim.*

plays given by Horace in the *Ars poetica* as the best description of tragicomedy ever given:

Hee too, that did in Tragick Verse contend
For the vile Goat, soone after, forth did send
The rough rude Satyres naked; and would try,
Though sower, with safetie of his gravitie,
How he could jest, because he mark'd and saw,
The free spectators, subject to no Law,
Having well eat, and drunke (the rites being done)
Were to be staid with softnesses, and wonne
With something that was acceptably new.
Yet so the scoffing Satyres to mens view,
And so their prating to present was best,
And so to turne all earnest into jest,
As neither any God, were brought in there,
Or Semi-god, that late was seene to weare
A royall Crowne, and purple, be made hop,
With poore base termes, through every baser shop:[9]

This description of satyr plays coincides in several respects with Guarini's conception of tragicomedy: comic matter follows upon tragic, novelty is used as an appeal to sophisticated spectators, and characters of different milieux are judiciously mixed without infringing the sacred code of decorum.

The naked and scoffing satyrs have a special fascination for Guarini. He explains that they are taken from the satyr play into the pastoral drama, where they join the shepherds and nymphs derived from the eclogue. *Il Pastor fido,* which is a pastoral tragicomedy, boasts a satyr whose presence there is doubly justified, if we accept Guarini's theories, for the form of drama to which the satyr gave his name not only influenced the pastoral drama but was the closest analogue in classical literature to tragicomedy. Thus, according to Guarini a satyr such as we see on Jonson's title page plays a major role in the development of tragicomedy.

The satyr play, known in the sixteenth century through only one example, the *Cyclops* of Euripides, and through the tantalizingly brief references of Horace and others, interested Renaissance writers immensely. Cinthio wrote one, called *Egle,* and discussed the genre in an essay where he stated that the emotional effect of the satyr play should be a combination of the effects of tragedy and comedy.[1] One can say of him, as Guarini does of Horace, that he gives an excellent

9. I give Jonson's translation; *Horace His Art of Poetrie,* ll. 319–34.
1. Giovambattista Giraldi Cintio, *Discorso . . . sopra il comporre le satire atte alle scene,* in G. Daelli, *Biblioteca rara, 53* (Milan, 1864), 134–5.

description of tragicomedy. Both his essay and his play reveal that to him the satyr play is a sort of pastoral drama, whose aim is to evoke laughter, pity, and terror by a story of the loves of satyrs and nymphs.

Thomas Lodge gives a different impression of the satyr play in explaining the origins of the drama in his *Defence of Poetry, Music, and Stage Plays* (1579):

> for sonnets in prayse of the gods, they did set forth the sower fortune of many exiles, the miserable fal of haples princes, the reuinous decay of many countryes; yet not content with this, they presented the lives of Satyers, so that they might wiselye, under the abuse of that name, discover the follies of many theyr folish fellow citesens. And those monsters were then as our parasites are now adayes: suche as with pleasure reprehended abuse.[2]

Though the "lives of Satyers" seem to occupy an intermediate position here between tragedy and comedy, as in Cinthio's account, Lodge is referring not to pastoral drama but to dramatic satire, aimed at reprehending abuse. Thus in the Renaissance the satyr play was claimed as the ancestor of tragicomedy, pastoral drama, and satire.

The behavior of the satyr in pastoral drama and tragicomedy reflects this critical confusion, for he often retains characteristics which associate him with satire. In this way Renaissance theories of the origin of satire enter into our study of the nature of tragicomedy. The appearance in several of the early Beaumont and Fletcher plays of the methods of dramatic satire suggests that in practice as well as in theory some sort of relationship existed between satire and Fletcherian tragicomedy.

3. The Satyr and Renaissance Theories of Satire

Lodge's description is the product of a misconception which haunted literary criticism for a long time. Because of the verbal similarity between "satire" and "satyr" many critics believed that the form of literature written by Lucilius, Horace, Persius, and Juvenal was an outgrowth of the satyr play of the Greeks or of some Latin equivalent of the satyr play. In one respect they were not far wrong, for Roman satire presumably derives from a crude form of drama known as *satura,* described by Livy in the seventh book of his Roman history.[3] The word "satura," however, denotes a "mixed" form and has nothing to do with satyrs. William Webbe provides another example of the common confusion in the comments on "Satyres" in his *Discourse of Eng-*

---

2. G. G. Smith, *1,* 80.
3. For a detailed account of Renaissance theories of satire see Campbell, *Comicall Satyre and Shakespeare's Troilus and Cressida,* pp. 1–14, 24–34.

lish Poetrie (1586): "In a *Satyr* the clownish company and rurall Gods are brought in to temperate the Heavinesse of Tragedies wyth some myrth and pastyme. . . . The olde manner of Commedies decayde by reason of slaundering which therein they used against many, for which there was a penaltie appointed, least their bitternes should proceede to farre: In place of which, among the Latines, came the *Satyres*."[4] The first sentence is a reflection of Horace's description. The second, which shows that Webbe is thinking of satire, presents another idea, common to many Renaissance critics—that satire was a means of mitigating the effect of the harsh censure contained in Old Comedy. The theory was that after a period in which living people were ridiculed by name on the stage (as in the plays of Aristophanes) this practice was forbidden by law and was succeeded by the introduction of actors dressed as satyrs, who could castigate the vices and follies of the times with an impunity guaranteed by their disguise. It was not so offensive to hear harsh or coarse abuse from the lips of an outlandish creature who was known in legend to be harsh and coarse by nature. The satire could be accepted, like the licensed insults and ribaldry of the Saturnalia or the Feast of Fools, as a part of a ritual or game. The connection between the fool and the satirist's role is illustrated by the title pages of several editions of Juvenal,[5] on which the satyr and the fool confront each other. And Jaques in *As You Like It* says:

O that I were a fool!
I am ambitious for a motley coat.

. . .

I must have liberty
Withal, as large a charter as the wind,
To blow on whom I please;[6]
II, vii, 42–3, 47–9

Aelius Donatus, the fourth-century grammarian and commentator on Terence, was probably responsible for the wide dissemination of this theory, for it is contained in his essay "De Tragoedia et comoedia," which was prefixed to most sixteenth-century editions of Terence. George Puttenham, in his *Arte of English Poesie* (1589), is explicit about the importance of the role of the satyr, though he differs from several of his contemporaries in his account of the order in which the dramatic forms evolved and also in the austerity of his conception of satyrs (for the various shadings of opinion on these matters provide eloquent testimony to the fecundity of the critical imagination):

4. G. G. Smith, *I*, 294–5.
5. See, for example, those of Amsterdam, 1647 and 1650.
6. All references to Shakespeare are to *The Complete Works of Shakespeare*, ed. G. L. Kittredge (Boston, etc., Ginn, 1936).

And the first and most bitter invective against vice and vicious men was the *Satyre:* which, to th'intent their bitternesse should breede none ill will, either to the Poets, or to the recitours (which could not have bene chosen if they had bene openly knowen), and besides to make their admonitions and reproofs seeme graver and of more efficacie, they made wise as if the gods of the woods, whom they called *Satyres* or *Silvanes,* should appeare and recite those verses of rebuke, whereas in deede they were but disguised persons under the shape of *Satyres,* as who would say, these terrene and base gods, being conversant with mans affaires, and spiers out of all their secret faults, had some great care over man, & desired by good admonitions to reforme the evill of their life, and to bring the bad to amendment by those kinde of preachings; whereupon the Poets inventours of the devise were called *Satyristes.*[7]

For several centuries those in search of the origins of satire wandered through woods infested with satyrs. It seems clear enough now that the woods and their inhabitants were a trick of semantic magic, but in the sixteenth century they were real and solid; they must still be treated as such in discussions of Renaissance literary theory. In 1605 Casaubon in his edition of Persius gave the correct explanation of satire, but the old misunderstandings could not be banished from one day to the next. For the study of Fletcherian tragicomedy it is particularly useful to understand this confusion, which entered into the education of Beaumont and Fletcher and their contemporaries.

What might be called the satyr theory of satire had the virtue of explaining the dramatic nature of much Roman satire. Horace, Persius, and Juvenal abound in imaginary conversations, carefully planned scenes, situations which serve as the basis of the poet's feeling. Horace writes an essay on his methods of satire as a dialogue between himself and Trebatius (*Satires* ii.1) or presents the scene of the banquet of Nasidienus in a conversation between himself and Fundanius (*Satires* ii.8); Juvenal opens his first satire with the impassioned protest, "Must I always be a hearer only? Shall I never retaliate?" and then by his railing descriptions fixes in the mind of his reader the intolerable situation which, in his famous phrase, makes it "difficult not to write satire."

The satyr also served to support the decorum of the satire, for the railing of Juvenal and the quieter familiarity of Horace could both be considered as characteristic of "the terrene and base gods." John Marston writes: "I will not deny there is a seemely decorum to be observed and a peculier kinde of speech for a Satyres lips . . ."[8] The

---

7. G. G. Smith, *2*, 32–3.

8. "To those that seeme judiciall perusers," *The Scourge of Villanie,* ed. G. B. Harrison (London, John Lane, 1925), p. 10. All references to *The Scourge of Villanie* are to this edition.

English satirists debated hotly whether or not it was essential to be as obscure as Juvenal and Persius were then thought to be, and in the course of the debate the distinction between an obscure style and a "rough" one was sometimes lost; everyone agreed that the appropriate effect to achieve was a sort of roughness. The familiarity of style recommended and practiced by Horace did not become the subject of controversy, but the practice of Marston, Donne, and the rest reveals their awareness of this aspect of satirical decorum. In discussing the decorum of satirical drama Puttenham relates its low style to the character of the satyr and to the woodland setting where he imagines "the *Satyres* were first uttered" (a setting faithfully recreated by Serlio in his "satyrical scene") : "the *Satyre* was pronounced by rusticall and naked *Sylvanes* speaking out of a bush . . ."[9] The character of satire accorded miraculously with the whole mythology of satyrs.

Since the delimitations of satire have never been clear, the satyr was particularly useful in determining for the Renaissance satirist what his role should be. I use the word "role" deliberately, not only because of the widely accepted idea that the satyr provided a convenient disguise for the satirist but because the English satirists of the late sixteenth century seem to have been constantly aware of playing a part. The special character of the satyr and the very idea of assuming a role inevitably affect the tone, the attitude, the vocabulary, the rhetoric of the satirist.

The satires, both dramatic and nondramatic, which thus evolved at about the turn of the century, supposititious descendants of the satyr play, exerted an important influence upon that other supposititious descendant of the satyr play, tragicomedy. There was never anything so explicit as a well-defined theory of the relation between tragicomedy and satire; in fact the perusal of critical comments on both forms or of the literary productions to which the names of "satire" and of "tragicomedy" were given is convincing proof that in these fields nothing was well defined. It is, rather, the very confusion of genres, of which I have given examples, which made it possible for a writer who was aware of the decorum of literary forms to borrow from satire in writing tragicomedy. Because Fletcher and his collaborators were in some respects, as I shall show, followers of the satirists Jonson and Marston, an understanding of the role of the satirist leads toward an understanding of Fletcherian tragicomedy.

4. *The Satyr as a Role in Juvenalian Satire*

The deliberate assumption of a special role by the satirist is emphasized in the first words of the Prologue to *Virgidemiae* (1597) by Joseph Hall:

9. G. G. Smith, *2,* 35, 37.

I First adventure, with fool-hardie might
To tread the steps of perilous despight:
I first adventure: follow me who list,
And be the second English Satyrist.

.   .   .

Goe daring Muse on with thy thanklesse taske,
And do the ugly face of vice unmaske:
And if thou canst not thine high flight remit,
So as it mought a lowly Satyre fit,
Let lowly Satyres rise aloft to thee:
Truth be thy speed, and Truth thy Patron bee.
                  Virgidemiae, I, Prologue, ll. 1–4, 19–24[1]

As if to accustom his victims gradually to the full force of satire, Hall
unmasks "the ugly face of vice" somewhat gently in the first half of
Virgidemiae, but at the end of these "Toothlesse Satyrs," as he calls
them, he gives a sinister warning to the guilty to prepare their sides for
his scourge. The second half of *Virgidemiae,* published the following
year, contains "byting Satyres." These "luck-lesse Rymes" are presented in "The Authors Charge to His Satyres" as the children whom
"not unkindly spight / Begot long since of Trueth and holy Rage,"
and the first of them fully lives up to its pedigree in the moral fervor of
its extravagant denunciations of the "disguised *Messaline,*" "the close
adultresse," the "stale *Bacchis.*" It is no accident that Hall echoes Juvenal
when he protests:

Should I endure these curses and dispight
While no mans eare should glow at what I write?
                  Virgidemiae, IV, i, 35–6

The imitation is deliberate, as he explains in a postscript: "I thinke my
first Satyre [i.e., the first of the "byting satyres"] doth somewhat resemble the soure and crabbed face of Juvenals . . ." ("A Post-script
to the Reader," ll. 90–2.) The indebtedness is also acknowledged in
the first satire of the fifth book and is everywhere apparent. The
vehement and bitter spirit of the "renowmed Aquine" is constantly at
Hall's side:

The *Satyre* should be like the *Porcupine,*
That shoots sharpe quils out in each angry line,
And wounds the blushing cheeke, and fiery eye,
Of him that heares, and readeth guiltily.
Ye Antique *Satyres,* how I blesse your daies,
That brook'd your bolder stile, their owne dispraise,
                  Virgidemiae, v, iii, 1–6

1. All references to Hall's satires are to *The Collected Poems of Joseph Hall,* ed.
A. Davenport (Liverpool, University Press of Liverpool, 1949).

Hall presumes to be different from his model only in being "packe-staffe plaine," for like his contemporaries he considers Juvenal obscure. Thus Hall sets out to be an English Juvenal. But his role is not simply the impersonation of another writer; it is the reproduction of the role which he thought Juvenal had assumed. If Satire was derived from some kind of satyr plays, then presumably the Roman satirists imagined themselves as "rusticall and naked Sylvanes"—Juvenal more than the others because of his bitterness and emotional intensity (though it is most unlikely that he did so imagine himself). These same qualities are conspicuous in Hall and his followers, who have rather little of the wit and detachment of Horace. The Juvenalians adopt a role which has the support of contemporary critical theory and which seems to be exemplified by their illustrious model.

Another aspect of Hall's role as a satirist is his notable self-righteousness. In his references to satire he projects his conception of himself as a mighty champion of the good life, defying Mammon with a crazy disregard of his own safety. Fearlessly he tells the unvarnished and unwelcome truth and scourges iniquity wherever he finds it. Marston, Guilpin, Lodge (to a lesser extent), and Wither[2] present the same self-dramatization.

Marston bears "the scourge of just *Rhamnusia,* / Lashing the lewdnes of *Britania*" (*The Scourge of Villanie,* Proemium to Bk. 1, p. 11); like Juvenal he "cannot hold," his "rage must freely runne" in a satire (Satyre II, p. 17) to which he affixes Juvenal's *"Difficile est Satyram non scribere."* He asks himself whether the vicious shall be allowed to continue on their way without reproof and boldly replies:

> No gloomy *Juvenall,*
> Though to thy fortunes I disastrous fall.
> Satyre II, p. 36

The first satire of Everard Guilpin's *Skialetheia* (1598) echoes Juvenal in presenting the familiar figure of the satirist unable to keep silence, and elsewhere Guilpin calls the "Satyre" not only the strappado and rack but the *"Tamberlaine* of vice" (*Skialetheia,* sig. C^v).

George Wither, writing more than ten years later, furnishes a brilliant illustration of how the satirist's aggressive morality is combined with his role as satyr. In an address to the reader prefixed to *Abuses Stript and Whipt* (1613) he protests, "I neither feare nor shame to speake the Truth" (sig. B^v), and in "The Scourge" at the end of the volume he threatens the guilty with these words:

2. In Francis Meres' *Palladis Tamia* (1598) Hall, Marston, Guilpin, and Lodge are chosen, along with Langland, as the English equivalents of the Roman satirists. G. G. Smith, *2,* 320.

Ile send abroad a Satir with a scourge,
That to their shame for this abuse shall strip them,
And being naked in their vices, whip them:

Sig. T7

In some later editions an illustration of this satyr is placed opposite the
poem, and over the satyr's head in the 1620 edition of *The Workes of
Master George Wither* appears the redundant inscription "Vices Executioner: OR *The Satyr's selfe-description of himselfe*," which serves
as the title of a poem introduced here between the illustration and "The
Scourge." In spite of their artistic crudity (or perhaps because of it),
both illustration and poem present an unusually vivid portrait of the
satirist as satyr. The explicitness of the "self-description" warrants its
quotation in full:

Though in shape I seeme a Man,
Yet a Satyr wilde I am;
    Bred in Woods & Desert places,
    Where men seldome shew their faces;
Rough and hayrie like a Goate,
Clothed with Dame Natures coate;
    Eagle-sighted, quick of hearing,
    Spying Vice at first appearing;
Barefoot like a silly Fry'r
Such a shaveling was my Sy'r;
    Chaste & holy as was that Nun,
    Of whom the Pope begat a Son;
Ape-like-fac't, Spaniell tayl'd,
Fawning till I have prevayl'd;
    My pleasing left hand hath a pipe,
    On which I play till Folly's ripe;
To carelesse Fooles in a Trance,
I doe pipe and they doe Dance;
    Like mirth-full Syrens that doe charme,
    Delighting those they meane to harme;
Teaching men to hold their way,
Not from their right course to stray:
    The other hand a whip doth beare,
    With which (provok't) I surely teare
Skin from flesh, and flesh from bone
Of such as I hap upon:
    I'me sent abroad the World, to purge
    Mans vile Abuses with my scourge;
Oft I make my Master sport,
When men sinne to lash them for't.

An Execut'oner am I,
Of Lust, and wanton Venery.
Thus are vices scourg'd by mee,
Yet my selfe from vice not free;
  Like to Sumners that cite others,
  When themselves defile their mothers.
They have warning had before,
Yet they'l not amend; therefore,
  Such-ones as take delight in sin,
  The bloud Ile drawe from out their skin:
Great and small are one to mee,
None shall bribe me with a Fee;
  But if the Greatest dare offend,
  Ile lash them still, till they amend.

Pp. 306–08

Vices Executioner:

O R

The Satyr's selfe-description of himselfe.

Reproduced from the 1620 edition of *The Workes of Master George Wither* in the Yale University Library.

This satyr is a rather elaborate iconographical development of the ancient woodland deity, especially adapted to the conception of satire held by the Juvenalians. No longer a simple compound of man and goat, he has characteristics of man, goat, eagle, ape, and spaniel, and to his pipe has been added a whip. The interpretation in the poem of these incongruous characteristics calls attention to the paradoxical nature of satire, a logical corollary of the conception of the satirist as satyr. He "seems a man" but is a "satyr wild"; he fawns, pleases, pipes for fools to dance, then whips them and tears their flesh; he is a fearless executioner of lust, who is, however, lewd and vicious himself.

The ambivalent symbol of the wanton satyr lashing vice denotes perfectly a kind of poetry which has the undeniable appeal of any sensational exposé. The Juvenalian satirists outdo each other in their denunciations of scurrility, but their satires contain descriptions which are literally, if not legally, pornographic. Once again they are following in the footsteps of the master, whose vivacity of phrase drives even contemporary translators to euphemism and omission. Nor does the patently moral intention of the satires counteract their scandalous appeal, for in Juvenal and his imitators the reformer's zeal seems to add spice to an already tasty potpourri.

The satirist disavows any such appeal. He will have it that the lewdness of the satyr, an integral part of the assumed role, is merely a means to his moral end. The antagonists of satire naturally choose to regard such self-righteousness as pure hypocrisy. Thus the Duke in *As You Like It* rebukes Jaques:

> Most mischievous foul sin, in chiding sin.
> For thou thyself hast been a libertine,
> As sensual as the brutish sting itself;
> And all th'embossed sores and headed evils
> That thou with license of free foot hast caught,
> Wouldst thou disgorge into the general world.
>
> II, vii, 64–9

Marston shifts from one role to another in such a way as to make even a sympathetic reader question his sincerity. In 1598 he published *The Metamorphosis of Pygmalion's Image. And Certain Satires.* The highly erotic nature of the poem about Pygmalion fits the poet's reference to his "wanton Muse" in an introductory poem "To His Mistress," but following the *Metamorphosis* comes a poem in which the author congratulates himself with heavy irony upon the "Salaminian titillations, / Which tickle up our lewd Priapians."[3] In *The Scourge of Villanie* Marston returns to the subject with the forthright statement:

3. *The Works of John Marston,* ed. A. H. Bullen (London, 1887), *3,* 250, 261.

Hence thou misjudging Censor, know I wrot
Those idle rimes to note the odious spot
And blemish that deformes the lineaments
Of moderne Poesies habiliments.

Satyre VI, p. 60

In other words, Marston maintains that *The Metamorphosis of Pyg-malion's Image* was really a satire of the kind of poem it seemed to be, though within the poem there is no indication that this is so. Few readers have been willing to take Marston at his word.

Whether or not Marston was sincere, it is plain that he was aware of assuming various roles. He strikes an attitude like that of Wither's satyr, pipes his wanton tune, and threatens with a whip. Not only does he make the abrupt change from the style of the *Metamorphosis* to that of the satires but he writes at the end of *The Scourge of Villanie:*

Here ends my rage, though angry brow was bent
Yet I have sung in sporting merriment.

Satyre X, p. 118

The pose is adopted like the exaggerated severity of a prosecuting attorney in order to put a damning case. It is part of the dialectic of satire. For the development of the sort of characterization we have observed in *The Faithful Shepherdess* or *The Maid's Tragedy* Marston's delight in ambiguity, his reinterpretations, his assumption of contrasting roles are vitally significant.

5. The Satyr's Language

The quotations I have given illustrate the tone of these satires—the bitter fury of outraged virtue, borrowed from Juvenal and related to the satirist's attitude toward himself and toward satire. A special rhetoric also evolved out of the satirist's conception of his role. Guilpin's phrase "the Tamberlaine of vice," which fits well with Wither's portrayal of the wicked satyr sent to scourge the world, suggests the declamatory style of the famous stage-Tamburlaine, and the comparison is not farfetched. Jonson's scornful description of Tamburlaine's language could be applied with only slight alterations to that of the Juvenalian satirists: "And though his [the "true Artificer's"] language differ from the vulgar somewhat; it shall not fly from all humanity, with the *Tamerlanes,* and *Tamer-Chams* of the late Age, which had nothing in them but the *scenicall* strutting, and furious vociferation to warrant them to the ignorant gapers." (*Discoveries,* ll. 775–9.) There is certainly "furious vociferation" in the opening stanza of Marston's dedication of *The Scourge of Villanie:*

Foule canker of faire vertuous action,
Vile blaster of the freshest bloomes on earth,
Envies abhorred child *Detraction,*
I heare expose, to thy all-taynting breath
The issue of my braine, snarle, raile, barke, bite,
Know that my spirit scornes *Detractions* spight.
                              "To Detraction," p. 1

This is the soaring style of oratory, which might well be said to "fly
from all humanity." Its remoteness from familiar speech is apparent in
the extensive use of alliteration, the abundance of metaphors (which
shift at bewildering speed), the artful variation of the rhythm with a
series of monosyllabic commands. It is a vehicle formed to convey the
powerful pent-up emotions which traditionally burst from the Juvenalian
satirist.

The vocabulary of these blasts includes "wild outlandish terms," such
as Jonson ridiculed in *Poetaster* (v, iii, 275–92, 465–527), some of
Greek and Latin, some of native origin. Marston seeks out the unusual word or devises new ones, and he studs his pages with allusions
to classical mythology. But side by side with the exotic is the familiar
—more often than not, the disgustingly familiar. Marston's style in
The Scourge of Villanie is distinguished by the steep climb from vernacular to pedantry and the sudden plunge from the sublime to the revolting.

Who would not shake a Satyres knottie rod?
When to defile the sacred seate of God
Is but accounted Gentlemens disport?
To snort in filth, each hower to resort
To brothell pits; alas a veniall crime,
Nay, royall, to be last in *thirtith* slime.
                              Satyre ii, pp. 19–20

            ô stay, thou impious slave,
Teare not the lead from off thy Fathers grave,
To stop base brokage, sell not thy fathers sheete,
His leaden sheete, that strangers eyes may greete
Both putrefaction of thy greedy Sire,
And thy abhorred viperous desire.
But wilt thou needs, shall thy Dads lacky brat
Weare thy Sires halfe-rot finger in his hat?
                              Satyre iii, pp. 26–7

Shall cock-horse, fat-paunch'd *Milo* staine whole stocks
Of well borne soules, with his adultering spots?

Shall broking pandars sucke Nobility?
Soyling faire stems with foule impurity?
Nay, shall a trencher slave extenuate,
Some *Lucrece* rape? and straight magnificate
Lewd *Jovian* lust? Whilst my satyrick vaine
Shall muzled be, not daring out to straine
His tearing paw? No gloomy *Juvenall*,
Though to thy fortunes I disastrous fall.

Satyre III, p. 36

The shock of the juxtapositions in these passages is increased by the fact that the rhetorical structure which supports Marston's affected vocabulary works against the use of vernacular. Marston is quite aware of exceeding the familiar vein in which the satyr traditionally speaks; in the following passage he comments on his combination and provides a further example of it:

Grim-fac'd *Reproofe*, sparkle with threatning eye
Bend thy sower browes in my tart poesie.
Avant yee curres, houle in some cloudy mist,
Quake to behold a sharp-fang'd Satyrist.
O how on tiptoes proudly mounts my Muse,
Stalking a loftier gate than Satyres use.
Me thinks some sacred rage warmes all my vaines,
Making my spright mount up to higher straines
Then wel beseemes a rough-tongu'd Satyres part,
But Art curbs Nature, Nature guildeth Art.
Come downe yee Apes, or I will strip you quite,
Baring your bald tayles to the peoples sight
Yee Mimick slaves, what are you percht so hie?
Downe Jack an Apes from thy fain'd royaltie.
What furr'd with beard, cas'd in a Satin sute
Judiciall Jack? how hast thou got repute
Of a sound censure? O ideot times,
When gawdy Monkeyes mowe ore sprightly rimes!
O world of fooles, when all mens judgment's set
And rests upon some mumping Marmoset!

Satyre IX, pp. 92–3

These twenty lines contain all the distinguishing characteristics of Juvenalian satire and also those of Marston's individual style. The dramatic nature of this satire comes out in the second paragraph, where the poet harangues the vicious and inveighs against the intolerable situation which they have created. In the first paragraph is the "rough-tongu'd Satyre," the ancestor of satire, whose character determines its traditional decorum. The satirist's conception of his role is apparent in his solemn appeal to Reproof and in his railing at the apes: he is a man dedicated to the nasty but necessary task of exposing and punishing the vices of the times; he is equipped with Juvenal's scourge. Incorruptible righteousness exudes from each line, and yet the imagery of exposé is decidedly indecent—while lashing others, the satyr may himself be lewd. The satirist seems quite aware that he is playing a part, for the intensity of his fury and the unbelievable depravity of the objects of his attack can only be taken as deliberate exaggeration. The style is an extraordinary blend attributable to the diverse requirements of the satirist's role and also to Marston's unusual taste. It is the style of oratorical denunciation, using a rhetoric which calls attention to itself by its startling comparisons and its formal apostrophes, but the echo of a Ciceronian "O tempora, o mores" gives way unexpectedly to the almost slangy "mumping Marmoset," and "grim-fac'd *Reproofe*" is not far from "Judiciall Jack." Nothing could be more typical of Marston than the concatenation of "sacred rage" and "bald tayles." The paradoxical mixtures of his language have something in common with the alternations of the familiar and the remote, the simple and the elaborate, in the language of Fletcherian tragicomedy. But it was probably in the theater that Beaumont and Fletcher encountered the satyr and his special rhetoric.

6. The Satirist on the Stage: Jonson and Marston

In the years between 1599 and 1608 (when *The Faithful Shepherdess* probably made its ill-starred first appearance) the role of the satyr was projected on the London stage in a form almost identical with that which I have been describing. For example, the Induction to *Every Man out of His Humor* (1599) opens explosively with the impassioned reply of Asper, the presenter, to the critics Cordatus and Mitis, who have been urging him to restrain himself:

> Away.
> Who is so patient of this impious world,
> That he can checke his spirit, or reine his tongue?
> Or who hath such a dead unfeeling sense,
> That heavens horrid thunders cannot wake?
> To see the earth, cràckt with the weight of sinne,
> Hell gaping under us, and o're our heads
> Blacke rav'nous ruine, with her saile-stretcht wings,
> Ready to sinke us downe, and cover us.
> Who can behold such prodigies as these,
> And have his lips seal'd up? not I: my language
> Was never ground into such oyly colours,

To flatter vice and daube iniquitie:
But (with an armed, and resolved hand)
Ile strip the ragged follies of the time,
Naked, as at their birth . . .
                    and with a whip of steele,
Print wounding lashes in their yron ribs.
                                    Ll. 3–18, 19–20

This Juvenalian outburst is followed, just as one would expect it to be, by an angry description of some of the evildoers and fools who make life intolerable for an upright man. "Well I will scourge those apes" (l. 117), says Asper, his fury mounting in spite of the renewed attempts of his friends to calm him, for he is as fiercely bent on castigation at his predecessor, the grim ape-scourger of Marston's poem. To effect his purpose Asper disguises himself as Macilente (literally "lean") and contrives a series of situations which put the various characters of the play out of their foolish or vicious "humors." Thus the chief intriguer of *Every Man out of His Humor* is the satirist Asper-Macilente, a character with a dual role. As Asper he is, in the words of Jonson's description following "The Names of the Actors," "of an ingenious and free spirit, eager and constant in reproofe, without feare controuling the worlds abuses. One, whom no servile hope of gaine, or frosty apprehension of danger, can make to be a Parasite, either to time, place, or opinion." As Macilente he is "A Man well parted, a sufficient Scholler, and travail'd; who (wanting that place in the worlds account, which he thinks his merit capable of) falls into such an envious apoplexie, with which his judgement is so dazeled, and distasted, that he growes violently impatient of any opposite happinesse in another." That one part of the satirist's role should be depicted as the envious malcontent is consonant with the opinion of Jonson's contemporaries,[4] who held that envy was the motivating force of satire and often spoke of the satirist, as Puttenham does of Langland,[5] as a malcontent. The special character of Macilente is both a psychological explanation of Asper's ruling passion and a means by which his goal may be reached; it is not neatly divisible from Asper's own character. When Macilente comments on Sogliardo, the would-be courtier, for instance, the accents of Asper's bitterness are clearly heard, mingled with the envy of Macilente:

Torment and death! breake head and braine at once,
To be deliver'd of your fighting issue.
Who can endure to see blinde *Fortune* dote thus?
To be enamour'd on this dustie turfe?

---

4. See Campbell, *Comicall Satyre*, pp. 59 ff.
5. "The Arte of English Poesie," G. G. Smith, *2*, 64–5.

> This clod? a whorson puck-fist? O god, god, god, god, &c.
> I could runne wild with griefe now, to behold
> The ranknesse of her bounties, that doth breed
> Such bull-rushes; these mushrompe gentlemen,
> That shoot up in a night to place, and worship.
>
> I, ii, 155–63

In tone and content this passage is very like Asper's initial outburst. Asper's disguise as Macilente is part and parcel of his role as satirist.

At the end of the play, since every character has been put out of his humor, there is nothing left for Macilente to envy, and so he too is out of his humor, "emptie of all envie," his "soule at peace." (v, xi, 54–5.) As he steps forward to give the curtain speech he puts off the character of Macilente and presents himself once more as Asper, but even Asper is changed:

> Wel, gentlemen, I should have gone in, and return'd to you, as I was ASPER at the first: but (by reason the shift would have beene somewhat long, and we are loth to draw your patience farder) wee'le intreat you to imagine it. And now (that you may see I will be out of humour for companie) I stand wholly to your kind approbation, and (indeed) am nothing so peremptorie as I was in the beginning:
>
> v, xi, 75–82

Asper's distinguishing harshness is gone because there is no further occasion for it, any more than there is for the envy of his alter ego; the presenter steps out of the role of the satirist and, with all due humility, begs the audience for applause.

In 1599, the year of *Every Man out of His Humor,* Marston wrote the first part of *Antonio and Mellida,* in which there is also a satirist, Feliche, though his part in the play is not so important as Asper-Macilente's. A brief quotation from Feliche's comment on the courtier Castilio will suffice to show that Marston began to make use of the satirical role in his plays at the same time as Jonson:

> O that the stomach of this queasy age
> Digests, or brooks such raw unseasoned gobs,
> And vomits not them forth! O! slavish sots!
>
> II, i, 94–6[6]

The accent of the Juvenalian satirist is once more unmistakable. Another example of this type in Marston's plays is Malevole in *The Malcontent* (1604),[7] who, like Asper-Macilente, determines the outcome of the play by his intrigues. In reality Giovanni Altofronto, the exiled

---

6. All references to Marston's plays are to the edition of A. H. Bullen, cited above.

duke of Genoa, he first appears in his disguise of the malcontent Malevole, shouting insults at the Genoese courtiers to the accompaniment of "the vilest out-of-tune music": "I'll come among you, you goatish-blooded toderers, as gum into taffata, to fret, to fret: I'll fall like a sponge into water, to suck up, to suck up." (I, i, 22-4.) His character is immediately given by Pietro, the usurping duke, and though the description chiefly emphasizes malevolence it is nevertheless a recognizable portrait of the satirist as satyr:

> This Malevole is one of the most prodigious affections that ever conversed with nature: a man, or rather a monster; more discontent than Lucifer when he was thrust out of the presence. His appetite is unsatiable as the grave; as far from any content as from heaven: his highest delight is to procure others vexation, and therein he thinks he truly serves heaven; for 'tis his position, whosoever in this earth can be contented is a slave and damned; therefore does he afflict all in that to which they are most affected. The elements struggle within him; his own soul is at variance within herself; his speech is halter-worthy at all hours.
>
> I, i, 26-37

Like Macilente he is motivated by envy; like the traditional satyr he is a monster, whose "soul is at variance within herself"; like all his fellow scourgers he is a rough and foulmouthed fellow, whose greatest pleasure is in tormenting others for their own good.

The dramatic form evolved by Jonson and Marston in presenting such satirists on the stage[8] is described by O. J. Campbell in his *Comicall Satyre and Shakespeare's Troilus and Cressida.* I have suggested elsewhere that the emphasis in the Beaumont and Fletcher plays upon "the emotions of morally opposed, extreme types" may derive from the technique of Jonson and Marston. In certain scenes, such as the parting of Ovid and Julia in *Poetaster* or Volpone's attempted seduction of Celia, Jonson also anticipates the tone of Fletcherian dilem-

---

7. The date of *The Malcontent* has been disputed but is now usually given as 1604. See Chambers, *The Elizabethan Stage, 3,* 431-2; Harbage, *Annals;* H. R. Walley, "The Dates of *Hamlet* and Marston's *The Malcontent,*" *RES, 9* (1933), 397-409.

8. Of the plays in which the satirist has an important part, those most closely related to the tradition of formal satire are three of Jonson's, which he called "comicall satyres": *Every Man out of His Humor* (1599), *Cynthia's Revels* (1600-01), and *Poetaster* (1601); and three comparable plays of Marston's: *Jack Drum's Entertainment* (1600), *What You Will* (1601), and *Parasitaster* (1605). Here the exposing and punishing of fools by a stage satirist constitutes the main action of the play. But the influence of the satirical tradition is clearly discernible in several other plays of Jonson's and Marston's performed before 1608 (the probable date of *The Faithful Shepherdess*): Jonson's comedies *Every Man in His Humor* (1598) and *Volpone* (1606), Marston's comedy *The Dutch Courtesan* (1604), and his tragicomedies *Antonio and Mellida* (1599) and *The Malcontent* (1604).

mas.[9] Jonson's use of "humors" is reflected in the presentation of character in such tragicomedies as *The Loyal Subject*,[1] and the ingenious contrivance of situations in Jonson's comedies may well have influenced the dazzling shifts of Beaumont and Fletcher's intricate plots.

Marston's use of the role of the satyr in *The Malcontent* is especially significant for Fletcherian tragicomedy. Not only does Malevole as satyr create a special atmosphere, which later appears as one of the distinctive characteristics of the Beaumont and Fletcher plays, but in a sense the tragicomedy itself evolves from his role. The atmosphere of the play may be illustrated by Malevole's speech to the court flatterer Bilioso, who has just announced that he plans to leave his wife at the palace while he goes to Florence. Malevole says:

> At the palace! Now, discretion shield, man; for God's love, let's ha' no more cuckolds! Hymen begins to put off his saffron robe: keep thy wife i'the state of grace. Heart o' truth, I would sooner leave my lady singled in a bordello than in the Genoa palace:
> Sin there appearing in her sluttish shape,
> Would soon grow loathsome, even to blushes' sense;
> Surfeit would choke intemperate appetite,
> Make the soul scent the rotten breath of lust.
> When in an Italian lascivious palace,
> A lady guardianless,
> Left to the push of all allurement,
> The strongest incitements to immodesty,
> To have her bound, incens'd with wanton sweets,
> Her veins fill'd high with heating delicates,
> Soft rest, sweet music, amorous masquerers,
> Lascivious banquets, sin itself gilt o'er,
> Strong fantasy tricking up strange delights,
> Presenting it dress'd pleasingly to sense,
> Sense leading it unto the soul, confirm'd
> With potent examples impudent custom,
> Entic'd by that great bawd, opportunity;
> Thus being prepar'd, clap to her easy ear
> Youth in good clothes, well-shap'd, rich,
> Fair-spoken, promising, noble, ardent, blood-full,
> Witty, flattering,—Ulysses absent,
> O Ithaca, can chastest Penelope hold out?
>
> III, i, 181–207

9. See my "Characterization in John Fletcher's Tragicomedies," *RES*, *29* (1943), 144–53.

1. See my "A Tragicomedy of Humors: Fletcher's *The Loyal Subject*," *MLQ*, *6* (1945), 299–311.

The idea of the palace as the special habitat of sin is a commonplace of Stoic and of Christian philosophy which is given frequent dramatic expression by Seneca and the Elizabethans. And it is well known that the palace—particularly the Italian palace—is the scene for some of the gloomiest of Jacobean tragedies. A similar atmosphere exists in some of the more serious Italian *novelle* which provide the plots for so many tragedies. However, when Marston's predecessors treat the subject of gilded sin they give no such imaginative recreation as he does of the seductions of the palace. Malevole gives Bilioso the piquant details most likely to evoke a convincing and terrifying picture. He exaggerates, he intensifies, he uses suspense, he makes his description palpitate with emotion: he creates the very atmosphere of sin.

This is also the atmosphere of Juvenalian satire. *The Scourge of Villanie* abounds in scenes of "ryot, lust, and fleshly seeming sweetnes" (Satyre VII, p. 67), described with great vividness and emotional intensity. The tone of these satirical descriptions is Malevole's tone, which gives a distinctive quality to *The Malcontent,* for the impassioned disapproval of the Juvenalian satirist gives the life of corruption a vibrancy rarely achieved by the raconteur of the novella. The play opens with "the vilest out-of-tune music," which is followed by Malevole's railing characterization of each vicious courtier. Instantly the spectator finds himself in a world whose outstanding wickedness is projected in the intensely emotional denunciations of the satirist Malevole. It is as if the villainous characters, who are given their identities by his descriptions of them, were creatures of his magic spell. The exaggerated evil of the court of Genoa is largely a feat of satirical rhetoric.

The highly emotional presentation of the blackest evil is somewhat tempered by an element of humor in this opening scene. Malevole is described by Pietro, the usurper, as "one of the most prodigious affections"—a "monster"—"more discontent than Lucifer when he was thrust out of the presence." (I, i, 26–9.) He is tolerated at court as a sort of licensed jester. His first appearance, hurling imprecations from the window of his chamber, is grotesque and, furthermore, his first speeches are characterized by a conscious sardonic humor. The same sort of humor recurs in some of the later scenes, particularly those in which Malevole goads Bilioso. This humor does not dissipate the atmosphere of evil but certainly modifies it, as indeed the humor of Juvenal modifies his fury.

Another feature of *The Malcontent,* counteracting the impression that evil reigns supreme, is the attitude of Malevole toward those who have wronged him. His position vis à vis Pietro is that of the revenger-hero, but as he plans his revenge he is notably unbloodthirsty:

> The heart's disquiet is revenge most deep:
> He that gets blood, the life of flesh but spills,
> But he that breaks heart's peace, the dear soul kills.
>
> I, i, 198–200

To destroy the peace of the usurper's heart Malevole tells him that Mendoza is making him a cuckold, but though Malevole revels in the plots and counterplots set off by this discovery, he takes particular pains, once Mendoza has gained the upper hand, to protect Pietro, the primary object of his revenge. When Mendoza arranges the murder of Pietro, Malevole saves his life and makes an ally of him to undermine the power of Mendoza. To accomplish this purpose Malevole disguises Pietro as a hermit and leads him back into the court over which he recently ruled. The wickedness which he now sees, added to the shock of his narrow escape from death, brings about a reformation of Pietro's character already prefigured by his hermit's disguise. Malevole at this moment reveals his true identity and reconciles himself with his former enemy. The final accomplishment of his revenge on Pietro is not the destruction but the salvation of his soul. Thus Malevole is like the satirist, but unlike the revenger-hero, in making corrective punishment his chief aim. As Macilente finally puts most of the foolish or vicious characters out of their humors, Malevole manages by a series of plots to bring about the reformation of Pietro, his wife Aurelia, and Ferneze, while Mendoza, who is unredeemable, is exiled from a court miraculously transformed. Thanks to Altofronto-Malevole, evil has vanished like a bad dream.

The denouement emphasizes a fundamental contrast between Malevole and Mendoza, who in the earlier scenes of the play resemble each other strongly in their cynical comments on human nature. The following fragments of Mendoza's speeches might easily be ascribed to Malevole, so decidedly do they smack of the satirist:

> Women! nay, Furies . . . Damnation of mankind! . . . their blood is their only god; bad clothes, and old age, are only the devils they tremble at. That I could rail now!
>
> I, ii, 85, 87, 100–02

> Lust's like the plummets hanging on clock-lines,
> Will ne'er ha' done till all is quite undone;
>
> II, i, 9–10

And Mendoza, like Malevole, considers himself aggrieved:

> I'll be reveng'd. Duke, thy suspect;
> Duchess, thy disgrace; Ferneze, thy rivalship;
> Shall have swift vengeance. Nothing so holy,

No band of nature so strong,
No law of friendship so sacred,
But I'll profane, burst, violate, 'fore I'll
Endure disgrace, contempt, and poverty.

II, i, 12–18

The difference between the two men is that Malevole's cynical words
are never matched by cynical actions and that he never even contem-
plates such a revenge as Mendoza's. Malevole clearly respects the "bands
of nature" and the "laws of friendship" and has an underlying faith in
mankind. By means of their similar habits of speech Marston juxtaposes
two entirely different characters, the Machiavellian villain, long familiar
to the Elizabethan audience, and that newer arrival, the malcontent
hero, who assumes in this instance the role of the satyr.

Part of the apparent resemblance of Malevole and Mendoza is due
to the disguise affected by Duke Altofronto, and no study of *The Malcontent* can ignore the special use to which Marston puts the old device
of disguise. To what extent is Altofronto genuinely disillusioned by his
misfortunes, and to what extent is disillusionment part of the disguise
which permits him to return to his court unrecognized? He has reason
enough for bitterness, yet to the audience he disclaims full responsibility
for his railing and bitter jesting:

Well, this disguise doth yet afford me that
Which kings do seldom hear, or great men use,—
Free speech: and though my state's usurp'd,
Yet this affected strain gives me a tongue
As fetterless as in an emperor's.
I may speak foolishly, ay, knavishly,
Always carelessly, yet no one thinks it fashion
To poise my breath;

I, i, 201–08

He obviously disapproves of Mendoza and Pietro, and with good reason, but his extreme language is affected as a means to an end. When
others enter he resumes his disguised manner of speaking, as the stage
direction instructs: "BILIOSO re-entering, MALEVOLE shifteth his
speech." (I, i, 255.) He recognizes harsh, coarse speech, sardonic humor, freedom from inhibition as the decorum of his role, just as the
Juvenalian satirist recognizes those same characteristics as part of his
role. In fact, Malevole's disguise is strikingly like the satirist's: it permits him to express and even to exaggerate his rage in the hope that he
may be able to correct the abuses he sees. It is impossible to say exactly where Altofronto's feelings leave off and Malevole's feelings begin, but when in the course of reforming Pietro (IV, ii, 25–9) Male-

vole voices his utter contempt of the world as "the only region of death, the greatest shop of the devil," where "there's nothing perfect . . . but extreme, extreme calamity," one is aware that his actions presuppose a somewhat more optimistic view of things. His speech is part of his disguise.

The disguise of Duke Altofronto is the basis of Marston's tragicomedy. In relation to the plot it is the means by which Altofronto works to bring good out of evil. With regard to the atmosphere of the play its effect is double, for, as I have shown, the disguise extends to the speeches of Malevole, which insistently portray the evil of the world, and yet, since the audience is in on the secret, the disguise is a warning that the situation may not be so black as it seems. In a sense, then, the evil of the play is no more real than Malevole's disguise. Like a hypothesis, it is assumed for a time only to be disproved. The sins of Pietro and Aurelia are in the past, and their most notable actions on the stage are their conversions; Mendoza's genuine desire to do evil is frustrated. Evil cannot be made actual in the world of *The Malcontent;* it remains an atmosphere—something suggested by "the vilest out-of-tune music" and the harsh tone of a satirical railer. This world in which evil constantly threatens but never materializes is the world of tragicomedy. More specifically, it is the world of *A King and No King,* where once again a false hypothesis makes an unsubstantial evil seem terrifyingly real.

7. The Shepherd in Arcadia

It has long been recognized that another literary form, the romance, exerted a determining influence on Beaumont and Fletcher.[2] Throughout their careers they borrowed freely from the various romances current in the sixteenth and seventeenth centuries, and as we have already seen, one of the first plays on which they collaborated, *Cupid's Revenge,* is based upon Sidney's much admired *Arcadia.* This is a special sort of romance, dominated by the pastoral tradition, which reached Sidney through the pastoral poets and through such Italian and Spanish writers as Sannazzaro and Montemayor, who had combined pastoral and romance. The combination has a direct bearing upon the pattern of tragicomedy in Beaumont and Fletcher.

Just as the satyr is an actor in the satyr play and also a symbol of satire, the shepherd is both a character in pastoral poetry and a symbol of the pastoral ideal. In turning from the satyr to the shepherd we

2. See, for example, Wallis' summary of this influence in *Fletcher, Beaumont & Company,* pp. 142–6. Since the problem of the general influence of romance on tragicomedy is discussed by Ristine and others, I shall confine myself to pointing out the features of pastoral romance which are significant for the development of Fletcherian tragicomedy.

should not forget that the satyr also has his place in the pastoral and thus serves as a kind of link between the two forms. The bucolic simplicity of the shepherd's life has long had a powerful appeal to many people, but most of all to the sophisticated inhabitants of cities; for Theocritus or Virgil or Marie Antoinette it represented the antithesis to the tiresome intrigues of court life. However, as Fletcher contemptuously points out in his remarks on *The Faithful Shepherdess*, it is naive to suppose that the shepherd of pastoral poetry is an ignorant rustic. Owning his flock, he is a gentleman who has had the good fortune to be born free of the toils of urban civilization. His social status is clearly indicated by his dress on the title page of Jonson's *Workes*. This gentleman-shepherd, as he appears in pastoral poetry, becomes associated with the ideal of the Golden Age—with a world uncorrupted by familiar evils.

But Arcadia, even in the idylls of the first pastoral poets, is not without its sorrows of unrequited love and death, and in the pastoral literature of later times, as Greg has noted,[3] a longing for the ideal existence symbolized by the pastoral life exists side by side with the portrayal in Arcadia of conditions obviously similar to those of corrupt Italy or England. Thus the pastoral conventions do two things at once: they embody an imaginative ideal and they present in disguise what is all too familiar. Not all the shepherds in Arcadia subscribe to the Arcadian ideal, and those who do not, like the Sullen Shepherd of Fletcher's *The Faithful Shepherdess,* are prodigiously evil. Since even the good shepherds do not all attain the ideal for which they strive, the Arcadian shepherd properly symbolizes the longing for an ideal rather than its realization.

The satirist, who portrays with awful vividness the very conditions from which the pastoral poet longs to escape, occasionally uses the simple country life as an antithesis to the corruption he satirizes. Juvenal in his eleventh satire invites his friend Persicus to a meal which is to be distinguished by its simplicity. As Juvenal describes the foods to be sent from his farm, the plain dishes in which they will be served, and the country boys who will serve them, each item in his description is symbolic of the good life in the country and is contrasted with the corresponding effete luxuries of Rome—the elaborate banquets, the ornate service, the carefully groomed attendants who have returned from the baths. Thus Juvenal's Stoic ideals are served by the same contrast which is constantly implied in pastoral literature. In a sense, satire and pastoral share not only the satyr but also the shepherd.

The shepherd is again comparable to the satyr in that his characteristics, because of their symbolic value, become useful in literature as a conventional role. Though not explicitly referred to as such, the shep-

3. Greg, *Pastoral Poetry and Pastoral Drama,* pp. 4, 52.

herd with his pipe is often a disguise for a poet and often, less appropri-
ately, for other sorts of characters, as Puttenham suggests:

> the Poet devised the *Eglogue* long after the other *drammatick*
> poems, not of purpose to counterfait or represent the rusticall man-
> ner of loves and communication, but under the vaile of homely
> persons and in rude speeches to insinuate and glaunce at greater
> matters, and such as perchance had not bene safe to have beene
> disclosed in any other sort, which may be perceived by the Eglogues
> of *Virgill*, in which are treated by figure matters of greater im-
> portance then the loves of *Titirus* and *Corydon*.[4]

Sometimes the gentleman-shepherd is clearly revealed as a gentleman
in shepherd's clothes, in which case the role of the shepherd does not
result in allegory ("to insinuate and glance at greater matters") but
forces upon the reader's attention the contrast or the parallel between
the true character and qualities symbolized by the disguise. Florizel's
disguise in *The Winter's Tale* is an important symbolic action. The
role of the shepherd is a convenient shorthand for all the values associated with the pastoral ideal.

8. *Shepherd into Knight*

In *Daphnis and Chloe,* the pastoral romance by Longus, written perhaps in the second century, the shepherd mingles with the pirates and
cruel parents of Greek romance. The Arcadian peace is disturbed though
not destroyed by the wild adventures, the wars, the kidnapings, the
mistaken identities common in Chariton, Xenophon of Ephesus, and
Heliodorus, the writers of the earliest romances. The style of *Daphnis
and Chloe,* like that of the other Greek romances, is largely determined
by the elaborate rhetoric of the Asiatic schools.

In some of the pastoral romances of the sixteenth century the shepherd also participates in the adventures of a group of characters belonging to another and equally important tradition—the medieval
chivalric romance. Certain tenuous connections relate the romance of
the Middle Ages with Greek romance. For example, Dares and Dictys,
upon whom Benoit de Sainte-Maure based his *Roman de Troie,* were
probably Greek contemporaries of Heliodorus, writing in the same tradition with him. And the two types of romance resemble each other in
presenting the numerous extraordinary adventures of their principal
characters. The popular romances of the sixteenth and seventeenth centuries testify to the widespread appeal of this narrative element, which
predominates in them over every other element. The voluminous stories

4. "The Arte of English Poesie," G. G. Smith, *2, 40.*

of Amadis and Palmerin, satirized by Beaumont in *The Knight of the Burning Pestle* and by Cervantes in *Don Quixote* were the adventure stories and the serials of their day.

However, medieval romance, most directly influenced by the epic (both classical and native), had its own form and its own conventions, which do not become thoroughly involved with the Greek romance until the Renaissance. A distinguishing feature of the medieval romance is the code of chivalry, which includes the precepts of Christianity, the idealized rules of warfare between gentlemen, and the equally idealized rules of courtly love by which the knight must govern his relations with ladies. As it has often been pointed out, the glorification—the near sanctification—of women in courtly love is unknown in classical literature and had a lasting effect upon western civilization. For literary tradition the psychological analysis of love and the establishment of the conventions of courtship are only slightly less influential. The chivalric ideal in both love and war is embodied in the character of the knight of medieval romance.

In Sidney's *Arcadia,* where elements of Greek, medieval, and the later popular romance are combined with pastoral, the symbolic figure of the shepherd confronts the no less symbolic figure of the knight. In certain ways their respective ideals are counterparts, even though one is Christian and one pagan, one warlike and one peaceful. The knight and the shepherd represent the same desire to escape from corruption and to achieve an absolute goodness. The knight is a more aggressive champion of good than the shepherd and his quest is a more potent symbol of longing for the ideal; but, like the shepherd, the knight does not always attain it in spite of being manifestly superior to the ordinary run of mortals. Because of these similarities it was possible for the Theocritan and the chivalric symbols to fuse in sixteenth-century romance, shepherd turning into knight and knight into shepherd.

A striking example of the fusion in Sidney's *Arcadia* is the disguise of Musidorus, the Prince of Thessalia, in "sheapperdish apparrel" for the purpose of courting Pamela. Here the knight assumes the role of the shepherd. But even where the evidence is not so plain, the hero of pastoral romance is part shepherd; though he dresses in armor and rides out to do battle, he also sits down beneath a tree to compose a love complaint. The hero of the form of romance which most directly influences the early plays of Beaumont and Fletcher is a complex—in some ways a contradictory—character. His behavior, though always extraordinarily noble, varies with startling rapidity as one or the other of his component elements manifests itself. Philaster and Amintor are obviously his descendants.

9. The Hero's Predicament

In both satire and pastoral romance the contrast between good and bad characters is simplified and heightened, and the situations used to dramatize the conflict are correspondingly acute. In the *Arcadia* the heroes Pyrocles and Musidorus are "excellent young Princes . . . the most accomplished both in body & mind, that the Sun ever lookt upon."[5] Baccha is "the most impudentlie unchaste woman of all *Asia.*" (II, xxii; Sidney, *Works, I,* 290.) It would not be fair to Sidney to suggest that all his characters are entirely one-sided, but in more complicated characters both good and evil elements are exaggerated as in Kalander's description of the Queen of Arcadia, Gynecia: "of most unspotted chastitie, but of so working a minde, and so vehement spirits, as a man may say, it was happie shee tooke a good course: for otherwise it would have beene terrible." (I, iii; Sidney, *Works, I,* 20.) The situations of romance are further complicated by the lavish use of the convention of disguise. A typical situation in the *Arcadia* is the plight of Pyrocles, disguised as Zelmane, an Amazon, in order to court Philoclea, the daughter of the King and Queen, Basilius and Gynecia, both of whom fall in love with him, one thinking him to be the woman he seems, the other suspecting he is not. Pyrocles' behavior in this unusually delicate situation is admirable. His patience and devotion to his lady are quite worthy of the chivalric and, for that matter, of the pastoral ideal. He is plagued, however, by the wandering eyes of a husband and a wife—eyes that one should not meet in Arcadia. Although Basilius and Gynecia are far from being monsters of unchastity like Baccha, the potential evil in them is sufficient to cause exquisite torment for the "excellent young prince" Pyrocles. In fact the entanglement is so extraordinarily unlucky that it is fantastic and becomes laughable the moment one refuses to accept the premise of romance. It is fitting only in a world of extreme good and evil and in a conflict between what ought to be and what is.

This situation is analogous to the extraordinary predicaments in nondramatic satire or the situations fiendishly devised by a Macilente. Since it ends happily with the marriage of Pyrocles and Philoclea and the reconciliation of Basilius and Gynecia, it is also similar to the situations in *The Malcontent,* where evil in an extreme form threatens without precipitating tragedy. Satire and romance, in spite of the great differences between them, both support the presentations of hypothetical evil.

The writer of romance emphasizes the individual situation as does

5. *Arcadia,* II, xiii, in *The Complete Works of Sir Philip Sidney,* ed. Albert Feuillerat (Cambridge, University Press, 1912), *I,* 233. All references to the *Arcadia* are to this edition. I have expanded contractions other than ampersand.

the satirist, but for a different reason. For the satirist the situation is the means of exposing folly and vice; he makes it as dramatic and striking as possible in order to carry his point. For the writer of romance it is the means of exposing the emotions of his characters; the more extreme the situation, the more intense the emotion. Both kinds of writer are ultimately interested in the conflict between the ideal and the actual, but their ways of approaching it are widely different. The satirist deals chiefly with what he hates, dissociating himself from it and partly by this means establishing his conflict. But the writer of romance creates certain ideally good characters, associates himself with them, and portrays the conflict as they feel it. For this reason the typical situation in a romance is a dilemma; the hero or heroine is confronted by a problem to which there seems to be no solution. The acute conflict between the nobility of the protagonist and the vileness of his enemies or the perversity of circumstance is dramatized in the hero's predicament. In *A King and No King* the plight of Arbaces is presented in both ways, sometimes as the result of a repulsive aberration, sometimes as a romantic dilemma.

10. *Arcadian Rhetoric*

Sidney, like the writers of Greek romance, employs a highly artificial style. Abraham Fraunce in his *Arcadian Rhetorick* draws upon Sidney to illustrate all the various devices of rhetoric. Lyly's style in *Euphues* (1578), bursting with alliteration, conceits, and formal antitheses, was one of the important influences upon Sidney, for although euphuism is usually condemned nowadays with the most lofty disdain, it was widely admired and imitated in its day. Sidney's "Arcadianism," as it has been called, is not so extreme but is subject to the same censure. Greg, for example, says that it is "little if at all better than Euphuism. It is just as formal, just as much a trick, just as stilted and unpliable, just as painful an illustration of the fact that a figure of rhetoric may be an occasional ornament, but cannot by any degree of ingenuity be made to serve as a basis of composition."[6] And yet it does precisely "serve as a basis of composition." A typical example of Arcadianism is the soliloquy of Zelmane after she has been passionately importuned by Basilius and Gynecia, the latter making "a piteous war with hir faire haire":

But *Zelmane* being ridde of this loving, but little-loved company, Alas (said she) poore *Pyrocles,* was there ever one, but I, that had received wrong, and could blame no body? that having more then I desire, am still in want of that I woulde? Truly Love, I must needes say thus much on thy behalfe; thou hast imployed

6. *Pastoral Poetry*, pp. 151-2,

my love there, where all love is deserved; and for recompence hast sent me more love then ever I desired. But what wilt thou doo *Pyrocles?* which way canst thou finde to ridde thee of thy intricate troubles? To her whom I would be knowne to, I live in darkenesse: and to her am revealed, from whom I would be most secreat. What shift shall I finde against the diligent love of *Basilius?* what shield against the violent passions of *Gynecia?* And if that be done, yet how am I the neerer to quench the fire that consumes me? Wel, well, sweete *Philoclea,* my whole confidence must be builded in thy divine spirit, which cannot be ignorant of the cruell wound I have received by you.

II, i; Sidney, *Works, I,* 151

Without a doubt, this is formal, tricky, stilted, and unpliable writing, just as Greg says it is, but the situation it expresses is also formal, tricky, stilted, and unpliable. It is useless to single out the style for disapproval, since it is an inseparable part of the literary form.

Sidney's artificial style, in part a function of his artificial situations, is also a means of projecting the fundamental conflict between what ought to be and what is—in the case of Pyrocles, between his ideal love and the apparent impossibility of achieving it. The irony of being frustrated by the more mundane infatuations of Basilius and Gynecia is emphasized by the series of antitheses, culminating in the triple contrast between the "diligent love of Basilius," the "violent passions of Gynecia," and the "divine spirit" of Philoclea. The fact that the conflict is placed within the character is an important aspect of pastoral romance, for in spite of the vast amount of action in the *Arcadia* (an attempt to summarize it shows how much there is) the attention is focused on the feelings of the characters. The psychological analysis, developed so spectacularly by later novelists, is rudimentary here, but it brings to the fore the emotions produced by the basic conflict. The expression of Pyrocles' anxiety is as "formal" and "stilted" as a tenor aria by Mozart, but it is not for that reason an unsatisfactory expression of emotion.

When the passionate outbursts of the romantic hero are compared with those of the satirist, the most striking difference is that the romantic hero ordinarily presents himself as the somewhat passive victim of circumstance, whereas the satirist presents himself as the angry beast, stung beyond endurance and about to inflict punishment upon his enemies. The style, that is, corresponds to the roles of shepherd and satyr which strongly affect the character in each case. Though the major utterances of romance and satire cannot always be neatly contrasted in the manner I am suggesting, the most distinctive speeches of the romantic hero are monologues like that of Pyrocles, in which an internal conflict is expressed by means of a rhetoric of deliberation, while the most distinctive speeches of the satirist are tirades in which the conflict has been externalized and the unambiguous feeling of the speaker is expressed by means of a rhetoric of denunciation.

11. *The Romantic Hero on the Stage: Lyly and Greene*

Some, but not all, of the characteristics of pastoral romance operate in the meaning of "romantic" as it is loosely applied to various Elizabethan playwrights. At its vaguest the term implies something of the remoteness, the adventurousness, or the appeal to the emotions which characterizes the *Arcadia,* but it is obvious that Sidney's deliberate artificiality is present in varying degrees in writers as different as Marston and Greene, and the same sort of qualification would have to be made for other characteristics of pastoral romance. Therefore, in showing briefly how the romantic hero appeared on the stage in the years before Beaumont and Fletcher began to write, I shall make no attempt to deal with all the various sorts of plays which might be called "romantic" but only with a few which were directly affected by the pastoral romance.

The romantic comedies of Lyly, Greene, and Shakespeare introduced to the stage the features of romance which I have emphasized. For example, Lyly's *Endymion* (1588),[7] though it has no explicitly pastoral element, presents a hero similar to the noble young men of Arcadia in a world fully as remote—the world of Greek mythology.[8] Here Endymion is confronted with the choice between the earthly love of Tellus and the heavenly love of Cynthia. When he chooses the ideal in preference to the actual, the seamy side of Tellus' nature is brought out, and she revenges herself by having Endymion lulled into a magic trance. With the hero temporarily removed from the action of the play, its basic conflict is now transferred in a slightly altered form to the mind of Endymion's friend Eumenides, who is in love with the nymph Semele. Promised the fulfillment of one wish, he is uncertain whether to ask for the possession of Semele or the release of Endymion. He grapples with the horns of this dilemma in a speech of central importance to the play and illustrative of Lyly's style:

> Why doe I trifle the time in words? The least minute, beeing
> spent in the getting of *Semele,* is more worth then the whole
> worlde: therefore let mee aske. What nowe *Eumenides?* Whether

7. I am not suggesting any definite connection between Sidney and Lyly, though the *Arcadia* was presumably known to many writers in manuscript before its publication in 1590. Lyly had numerous foreign and domestic romances, including his own, to draw upon.

8. For the influence of the mythological play on pastoral drama see Greg, *Pastoral Poetry,* pp. 215–35.

art thou drawn? Hast thou forgotten both friendship and duetie? Care of *Endimion,* and the commaundement of *Cynthia?* Shall hee dye in a leaden sleepe, because thou sleepest in a golden dreame? I, let him sleepe éver, so I slumber but one minute with *Semele.* Love knoweth neither friendshippe or kindred.

Shall I not hazard the losse of a friend, for the obtayning of her for whome I woulde often loose my selfe? Fonde *Eumenides,* shall the intycing beautie of a most disdainfull Ladie, bee of more force then the rare fidelitie of a tryed friend? The love of men to women is a thing common and of course: the friendshippe of man to man infinite and immortall.

III, iv, 103–16[9]

The carefully elaborated antithéses of this speech correspond exactly to the contrast (typical of Renaissance thought) between love and friendship, which in turn corresponds to Endymion's choice between the two kinds of love. The whole rigid framework of the play rests on the conflict between what is "common and of course" and what is "infinite and immortall." The meaning of the play is expressed in the predicaments of Eumenides and Endymion.

Since action is at a minimum and speech of the sort just quoted at a maximum, the play could suit only a special audience, such as the court of Queen Elizabeth for whom it was written. The characters are as stiff as their speeches and are made no more believable by their allegorical resemblance to persons at court. In fact the allegory is merely another layer of artifice. The chief virtue of *Endymion* is its artistic unity, but as an experiment in the dramatization of romance it must be considered a very limited success. Lyly's methods are too exactly those of the nondramatic form which inspired him.

Greene, who could write as stilted a romance as Lyly when the fit was on him, adapted certain features of the romance to the needs of popular dramatic entertainment in his *Honorable History of Friar Bacon and Friar Bungay* (1589?). The story of Prince Edward, Lacy, and Margaret, the fair maid of Fressingfield, developed from a slight incident in Greene's source, is treated in a manner that immediately recalls the pastoral romance. Greene's setting is domestic but his characters behave like Arcadians. Lacy, disguised "in country apparel," goes to court Margaret for Prince Edward but falls in love with her himself. Clearly he is in a dilemma not unlike that of Eumenides, and in a similar manner he argues with himself, though his conclusion is the opposite of Eumenides':

9. *The Complete Works of John Lyly,* ed. R. Warwick Bond (Oxford, Clarendon Press, 1902), *3,* 49–50.

Daphne, the damsell, that caught Phaebus fast,
And lockt him in the brightnesse of her lookes,
Was not so beautious in Appollos eyes,
As is faire Margret to the Lincolne earle;
Recant thee Lacie—thou art put in trust,
Edward, thy soveraignes sonne hath chosen thee
A secret friend, to court her for himself:
And darest thou wrong thy Prince with trecherie?—
Lacie, love makes no exception of a friend,
Nor deemes it of a Prince, but as a man:
Honour bids thee controll him in his lust,
His wooing is not for to wed the girle,
But to intrap her and beguile the lasse:
Lacie, thou lovest, then brooke not such abuse,
But wed her, and abide thy Princes frowne:
For better die, than see her live disgracde.[1]

Ll. 732–48

Greene's use of question and answer is just as stiff as Lyly's, but the language is not twisted into so formal a design. The antitheses are not so forced; alliteration, after the heavy dosage of the first two lines, is used rather sparingly. These are lines that could be spoken by an actor much more easily than Lyly's.

The comparison of these two situations from *Endymion* and *Friar Bacon and Friar Bungay* suggests what is in the main true, that Greene watered down the elements of the romance for popular consumption. Arcadia becomes the English countryside; the formality of style is considerably relaxed; the characters face problems which are more familiar than those of Lyly's or Sidney's characters. In one respect, however, Greene is closer to the romance tradition and further from the pastoral than Lyly: *Friar Bacon and Friar Bungay* is crowded with action. Apart from the spectacular and comic incidents of the story of Friar Bacon's magic, there is a series of unexpected developments in the love story. Prince Edward discovers Lacy's treachery, threatens to kill him, but repents and begins to further the match when Lacy decides to test Margaret by pretending that he has lost interest in her. At the end this whim is explained just in time to prevent her from taking her final vows as a nun, and, inevitably, the two are married. Greene's play is interesting chiefly because it exemplifies one kind of adaptation of the romance to the stage, in which the artificiality is reduced and the excitement of surprising incident is emphasized. But in spite of these

---

1. *The Life and Complete Work in Prose and Verse of Robert Greene,* ed. A. B. Grosart (London, 1881–83), *13, 37.*

shifts of emphasis, the dilemma of the hero, disguised "in country apparel," is centrally important. The dilemmas of Perigot, Leucippus, Philaster, Amintor, and even Arbaces are clearly related to those of Lyly's and Greene's heroes.

12. Satyr and Shepherd in Shakespeare

In the early plays of Beaumont and Fletcher, where their pattern of tragicomedy begins to take shape, certain characteristics of dramatic satire as it was practiced by Marston and Jonson mingle with characteristics of pastoral romance. The combination is not new but neither is it identical with any previous mixture of satire and romance. Marston, whose *The Malcontent* comes so close to the type of tragicomedy in which Beaumont and Fletcher specialize, fuses romance with satire, but not, in this instance, pastoral romance, and the resulting difference in tone is very great. T. M. Parrott suggested long ago that Chapman's *The Gentleman Usher* (1606), in which there are elements of both satire and romance, anticipates the tragicomedy of Beaumont and Fletcher, but although similarities may be observed, the total effect of the play is not much like *Philaster* or *A King and No King*. One important difference is that Chapman, like Marston in his early plays, combines the satire and the romance mechanically, keeping each separate from the other, as they are not in Beaumont and Fletcher. This maintenance of a clear-cut distinction is characteristic of many other mixtures of satire and romance in dramatic and nondramatic literature. Sidney himself introduces occasional passages of satire into the *Arcadia*—minor incidents, such as the clownish interruptions of Dametas, Miso, and Mopsa, which serve as a sort of burlesque of the main story.

In *The Isle of Gulls* (1606), a play derived from the *Arcadia*, John Day makes burlesque pervasive. The prologue explains that all the characters are "guld in the reach of their hopes" (hence the title) and that Dametas, the rustic of Sidney's romance, is to express "to the life the monstrous and deformed shape of vice." The play corresponds closely to what is promised, for the romantic story of the love of Pyrocles for Philoclea and of Musidorus for Pamela is treated satirically to the point where the lovers themselves are gulled of their sweethearts by two other characters introduced by Day. It is easy to satirize such situations as that of the old Basilius and Gynecia both in love with Zelmane, and in *The Isle of Gulls* each opportunity is duly exploited. The play is scarcely a combination of satire and romance, for not a shred of the romantic original remains intact. Romance here is the object of satire—a target for rotten eggs. Of the early plays of Beaumont and Fletcher which we have considered, only one, *The Knight of the Burning Pestle*, is a satire of romance (and it is far less broad than Day's). In the rest of the plays satire and romance so modify each other that something different from either results.

Although it would be useless to comment on all the combinations of satire and romance which are unlike that of Beaumont and Fletcher, Shakespeare's combination in *As You Like It* must be mentioned because it is so excellent an example of another way of handling the two traditions discussed in this chapter. Certain passages in the play might seem to suggest that Shakespeare, like Day, is chiefly concerned with the satire of romance; others that the two traditions modify each other here as in Beaumont and Fletcher. But neither of these conclusions would be justified. The character of *As You Like It* is distinctive.

In adapting Lodge's romance *Rosalynde* for the stage Shakespeare bases the play upon a series of contrasts between the romantic and satiric modes. Typical of pastoral romance are the good duke exiled by the evil duke, Rosalind disguised as a boy, and Orlando, the lover and innocent victim of oppression. These characters act and speak like the characters of a romance, although Shakespeare replaces the involved euphuistic speeches of his source with witty dialogue which is just as artificial but more appropriate to the stage. In the Forest of Arden a typically romantic entanglement ensues when Phoebe falls in love with Rosalind; Orlando is true to romantic form when he carves love poetry in the bark of trees. A delight in artifice is clearly shown when Rosalind in her disguise obliges Orlando to make love to her as if she were the person she actually is, or when the love complications are finally resolved in a masque of Hymen.

In the good duke's retinue, however, is the melancholy Jaques, who threatens to "rail against all the first-born of Egypt" (II, v, 63) and says belligerently:

> Give me leave
> To speak my mind, and I will through and through
> Cleanse the foul body of th' infected world,
> If they will patiently receive my medicine.
>
> II, vii, 58–61

The satirical railer, unknown to Lodge's *Rosalynde*, is a curious companion for the romantic characters, and Shakespeare insists upon the discrepancy when he makes Jaques chide Orlando for being in love and for marring the trees with his verses. (III, ii, 268–312.) Nor is Jaques the only critic of romantic behavior, for Rosalind is accompanied by the fool Touchstone, also unknown to Lodge's romance. Since the fool, as I have shown, is closely related to the satyr, it is not surprising that Touchstone parodies Orlando's verses (III, ii, 107–18) and provides a farcical contrast to the courtship of Silvius and Orlando by the crude simplicity of his technique in stealing Audrey from William. Touchstone, like other Shakespearian clowns, is a constant exponent of common sense, a habit of mind as startling in the world of romance as the bitterness of the Juvenalian satirist.

Shakespeare subjects the romantic elements in *As You Like It* to the double satirical attack of Jaques and Touchstone, and for Greg "he has in this play revealed his opinion of, and passed judgement upon, the whole pastoral idea."[2] I am not convinced that Shakespeare's judgment is, as Greg states, "appreciation of pastoral, as a delicate colouring, an old-world fragrance, a flower from wild hedgerows or cultured garden, a thing of grace and beauty, to be gathered, enjoyed, and forgotten, unsuited in its evanescent charm to be the serious business of art or life."[3] Greg is suggesting that Shakespeare is gradually emancipating himself from the "trivialities of convention," but it would be more exact to say that he is balancing one convention against another, the romantic against the satiric.[4] It is an oversimplification to suppose that the action of these conventions upon each other consists exclusively or chiefly in an undermining of romance by satire. A great part of the interest of the play lies in the way that the characters associated with each of these conventions make fun of the others and, in turn, are made fun of.[5] The audience laughs both with and at Jaques, Touchstone, and Orlando. The audience of 1599, when the play was first performed, would have found a special point to the Duke's reproof of Jaques for railing at sins of which he himself was guilty (II, vii, 64–9), for this was the year in which a number of satirical works were ordered to be burned and in which stage satirists such as Feliche and Asper were vigorously defending their practice. Jaques does not always have the last word. Even the lovers, who might be expected to suffer most from his cynicism, have the best of him in battles of wit, and ridicule his melancholy. (III, ii, 268–312; IV, i, 1–37.)[6] Touchstone's common sense contrasts not only with the idealism of the romantic characters but also with Jaques' cynicism, while at the same time Touchstone's foolishness, partly affected, partly genuine, is satirized by Jaques. At the end of the play, with the masque of Hymen and the pairing off of the lovers, the romantic con-

2. *Pastoral Poetry*, p. 411.   3. *Ibid.*, p. 413.

4. *The Winter's Tale* (1611) was too late a play to affect the earliest plays of Beaumont and Fletcher and therefore lies outside the province of my discussion, but it seems to me most misleading to state, as Greg does in his discussion of *As You Like It*, that the shepherd scenes in *The Winter's Tale* "owe nothing of their treatment to pastoral tradition, nothing to convention, nothing to aught save life as it mirrored itself in the magic glass of the poet's imagination." *Pastoral Poetry*, p. 411. On the contrary, Shakespeare takes the fullest advantage of the pastoral tradition in his treatment of Florizel and Perdita, whose significance is greatly diminished if they are interpreted realistically.

5. See S. L. Bethell, *Shakespeare and the Popular Dramatic Tradition* (Durham, N.C., Duke University Press, 1944), pp. 111–16.

6. See O. J. Campbell, "Jaques," *Huntington Library Bulletin, 8* (1935), 70–102.

ventions are triumphantly reasserted, but Jaques, after commenting on the conversion of the evil duke, the legitimate concern of a satirist, absents himself from the marriage celebrations, which do not accord with his temperament. If Shakespeare does not fully accept the romantic conventions, neither does he altogether reject them. Rather than passing judgment on the pastoral ideal, he makes drama out of the witty interplay between two sets of conventions.

What emerges most clearly from a study of the elements of satire and pastoral romance in *As You Like It* is Shakespeare's keen awareness of the distinct significance of each set of conventions. Upon this awareness the effect of the comedy depends. But the effect of Beaumont and Fletcher's new tragicomedy depends contrariwise upon the obliteration of all clear lines of distinction, the imperceptible merging of one convention with another. Satyr and shepherd lose their identities here as completely as do tragedy and comedy.

13. *Satyr and Shepherd in Beaumont and Fletcher*

A King and No King measures up to Fletcher's requirements for tragicomedy by presenting characters from more than one social stratum[7] (Arbaces himself being no more than a "groom," as Rymer called him) and by "wanting deaths" though it "brings some neere it" (again Arbaces, plotted against by his mother). These requirements are not complex nor do they determine to an important extent the nature of the play. Most of the elements of Guarini's more detailed formula for tragicomedy are also in *A King and No King*—of the borrowings from tragedy certainly these: "great persons but not great action; a plot which is verisimilar but not true; passions, moved but tempered; . . . the danger, not the death"; and of the borrowings from comedy these: "a feigned complication, a happy reversal, and above all, the comic order." But even Guarini's enumeration accounts for only certain of the qualities of *A King and No King*. Fletcherian tragicomedy is more closely related to the dramatic satire and the pastoral romance of its own day than to *Il Pastor fido*.

The plot of *A King and No King*, abounding in dilemmas in which the characters are most painfully caught, is directly in the tradition of the *Arcadia* and yet recalls Jonsonian dramatic satire by the arrangement of these crucial situations in a series, ingeniously contrived to demonstrate the potentialities of each character. The portrayal of Spaconia, Tigranes, Panthea, and in some scenes Arbaces is influenced

7. It should be noted that Elizabethan tragedy and even, as Guarini points out, Greek tragedy frequently present such a mixture of characters without the sanction of any theory. For this reason it seems useless to stress this feature of the theory of tragicomedy: at most it made legitimate in the newer form what already existed illegitimately in the older.

by romantic archetypes, but the tendency toward moral abstraction implicit in the romantic tradition is strongly reinforced by the tradition of satire, and Jonson's dramatic practice is suggested by the frequent clashes between characters who represent polar extremes. The point of view from which Arbaces is presented is as often satirical as romantic: he is sometimes ludicrous, sometimes noble; sometimes revolting, sometimes appealing. Now the mingling of tragic with comic characters, and of the emotional participation of tragedy with comic detachment, is an analogous process to the one I am describing, and one which is operative in, for example, *The Winter's Tale,* but the peculiar qualities of Beaumont and Fletcher's characters are related to satire and to romance. Arbaces, who seems evil but is not so, who often appears as his own opposite, who is a blend of utterly incongruous qualities, and who is in all things extreme, is both satyr and shepherd.

The satirist's assumption of a role has a special importance for Fletcherian tragicomedy, whose Protean characters constantly disguise, pretend, or change. Though certain of these shifts, such as Euphrasia's pageboy disguise, derive from the romantic tradition and are common in Jacobean drama, others, such as Clorin's affectation of wantonness to cure Thenot, recall particularly the didactic aim of the satirist who speaks as a satyr while he wields a scourge. But these occasional direct reminiscences are less important than the relation between the role of the satirist and the basic assumptions of the new type of tragicomedy. In *The Malcontent* the atmosphere of evil, vivid but not actual, is an extension of this role: at the denouement evil itself seems to have been an assumed role for all the characters except the diabolical Mendoza. In *A King and No King* the consummation of an incestuous passion seems to be an imminent reality up to the last moments of the action. Without knowing it, Arbaces plays an uncongenial part, and all the apparent evil of the play springs from the disguise of his true identity. As in Juvenalian satire and in *The Malcontent,* a concern with sexual vice is pushed to the borders of pornography; the brilliant rhetoric of the play, like Marston's rhetoric, gives life to this evil. Yet, after all, tragedy is averted, because evil never finally materializes. *A Sin and No Sin* would be a fitting alternate title for this play and for many others in the Beaumont and Fletcher canon. To this kind of tragicomedy Marston points the way with his special exploitation of the role of the satyr.

The combination of the conventions of satire and romance produces a genre more formalized and further removed from everyday life than tragedy or comedy or even the kind of tragicomedy Guarini wrote, for the conventions of romance—especially of pastoral romance—tend toward the creation of an ideal world, while the conventions of satire tend to make the portrayal of the familiar world into an exercise in dialectic. Each set of conventions points toward its own sort of abstraction; operating together, they produce the theoretical, the factitious, the hypothetical. But if satire and romance strengthen each other in regard to these tendencies, in certain respects they neutralize each other. The meaning of romance is implicit in the sympathetic portrayal of the forces of good in their eternal heroic fight against the forces of evil. Figuratively speaking, the meaning of romance depends on sharing the feelings of St. George as he tackles the dragon. In the meaning of satire, however, St. George is almost overlooked while we are asked to stand outside and consider the menace of the dragon. The combat is never really fought, for the object is to make the dragon slink away, abashed by our righteous indignation or our laughter. In the two cases, then, our attention is drawn in opposite directions and we are requested to adopt two very different attitudes. To combine these points of view and these attitudes is impossible. They may be alternated as they are in *As You Like It* to achieve a complex meaning, but when the conventions of satire and romance interpenetrate to the extent that they do in *A King and No King,* the result is a denial of the meaning implicit in each. The net effect of the combination of satire and romance upon the pattern of tragicomedy can be described as a major increase in formalization and a corresponding decrease in meaning.

III

The Art of Declamation

ONE OF THE most significant influences upon Fletcherian tragicomedy was a rhetorical tradition which operated both independently and at the same time through the two literary forms discussed in the last chapter. In both Juvenalian satire and Arcadian romance rhetoric plays a conspicuous part. The scourging satirist wields the rhetoric of denunciation:

> ô stay, thou impious slave,
> Teare not the lead from off thy Fathers grave,
> To stop base brokage, sell not thy fathers sheete,
> His leaden sheete, that strangers eyes may greete
> Both putrefaction of thy greedy Sire,
> And thy abhorred viperous desire.[1]

The rhetoric of deliberation provides the hero of romance with eloquent expression for his dilemma:

> But what wilt thou doo *Pyrocles?* which way canst thou finde to ridde thee of thy intricate troubles? To her whom I would be knowne to, I live in darkenesse: and to her am revealed, from whom I would be most secreat. What shift shall I finde against the diligent love of *Basilius?* what shield against the violent passions of *Gynecia?* And if that be done, yet how am I the neerer to quench the fire that consumes me?[2]

The moments of greatest emotional intensity in satire and romance are realized dramatically in passionate utterance—in speech that may accurately be called oratorical. It is not surprising that Marston and Sidney should write in this way, for the sixteenth century had a high regard for oratory. Declamation was a part of every boy's education in England, and orations were culled from Livy and others for separate publication. The admiration for oratory can be traced back to ancient Greece and Rome, where eloquence was the most highly prized of the arts. By the first century A.D. the training of orators in Rome was the culminating point of formal education. The art of declamation as taught

1. Marston, *The Scourge of Villanie,* Satyre III, pp. 26–7.
2. Sidney, *Arcadia,* II, i; *Works, I,* 151.

in these Roman schools exerted a powerful influence upon satire and romance in their formative stages, as much later it was to influence English writers in these and other literary genres.

Most of what we know about the schools of declamation in Augustan Rome comes from Seneca the Elder, who attended one of the schools as a boy, presumably entering, as was customary, between his twelfth and sixteenth years.[3] In his *Oratorum et rhetorum sententiae, divisiones, colores*[4] he records for the benefit of his sons Annaeus Novatus, Annaeus Mela, and Lucius Annaeus, the tragedian and philosopher, what he can remember of the speeches he has heard in the schools. A man of over ninety at the time of writing, he laments the failing of a memory which once enabled him to repeat two thousand names in the order they were given to him and up to two hundred lines of poetry in reverse order.[5] But there seems to be no reason to doubt the accuracy of this fabulous memory even in its decline. Seneca's work is divided into ten books of *Controversiae,* or judicial declamations, and one book of *Suasoriae,* or deliberative declamations. Originally each book of *Controversiae* had a preface dealing with some of the problems of declamation or with the characters of famous orators,[6] but some of these prefaces have been lost and some of the *Controversiae* themselves survive only in the form of *Excerpta* made at a later date. From the books which are complete the procedure in the schools is plain; the master (the *rhetor*) outlined a situation, either historical or more often purely fictitious, and told the students what opinion each of them was to defend. They began with suasoriae, in which they imagined themselves deliberating with Alexander whether to launch his ships on the sea, or with Agamemnon whether to sacrifice Iphigenia. They then came to the more difficult controversiae, in which they imagined themselves in the forum, taking one side or the other in a legal battle. After they had composed their declamations, but before they committed them to memory, the master ordinarily made corrections. Finally he criticized

3. See S. F. Bonner, *Roman Declamation in the Late Republic and Early Empire* (Liverpool, University Press of Liverpool, 1949); Henry Bornecque, *Les Déclamations et les déclamateurs d'après Sénèque le père,* in *Travaux et mémoires de l'Université de Lille,* n.s., *1*[1] (1902); René Pichon, "L'Education romaine au premier siècle de notre ère," *Revue universitaire,* *4*[1] (1895), 156–69; Gaston Boissier, "Les Ecoles de déclamation à Rome," *Revue des deux mondes,* 5th period, *11* (1902), 481–508.

4. The best edition is that of Henri Bornecque: Sénèque le Rhéteur, *Controverses et suasoires* (rev. ed., Paris, Garnier Frères, 1932). The Latin and a French translation appear on alternate pages. The *Controversiae* seem never to have been translated into English, and Bornecque's is, so far as I am aware, the only translation into a modern language since the seventeenth century. The *Suasoriae* were edited and translated into English by William A. Edward: *The Suasoriae of Seneca the Elder* (Cambridge, University Press, 1928).

5. *Controversiae,* Preface to bk. 1 (*1, 2*). The *Controversiae* will be designated by book and number within the book. When, as in this case, a more specific additional reference is necessary, I also give volume and page in Bornecque's edition.

6. Jonson draws upon these prefaces in his *Discoveries.*

their delivery and sometimes declaimed himself in order to provide them an example.

The declamation was a trial flight for orators—the preparation for a career of public speaking in the senate and the forum. Since this training was intended to be eminently practical, it is ironical that the notable characteristic of the declamations which have survived is their remoteness from the actuality for which they were to prepare the student, and yet this perverse development is easily understood. The idea of practice orations seems to have originated in the fourth or third century B.C., when Greek oratory was dominated by the sophistic tradition of the Asiatic School and the School of Rhodes.[7] The hypothetical case of the declamation was fatally well suited for cultivating the virtuosity emphasized by this tradition. From the very beginning there was the danger that the declamation might become a display piece. In Rome this sort of training was apparently unknown until the time of Cicero and was not widespread until after his death. Thus the declamation was established in Roman schools a short time before the divine Augustus ended the political freedom which had made oratory important. When the affairs of state were no longer debated in public, the orator lost his chief function. But oratory was not allowed to wither. Nourished enthusiastically in the hothouse atmosphere of the schools of declamation, it put forth more and more exotic blooms. The cases, instead of imitating contemporary Roman life, presupposed imaginary laws and fantastic circumstances far removed from the actuality of the forum.

At the same time the schools themselves inevitably influenced the character of the declamation. Both Petronius and Tacitus accuse them of debauching the art of oratory by encouraging an ornate and bombastic treatment of the most unrealistic themes.[8] The masters devised cases which should be particularly hard to decide—cases in which two laws were brought into conflict or in which extraordinary circumstances made the law seem unjust—and competition between the schools undoubtedly led the young orators to select a master whose cases would not be dull.[9] It would be more entertaining to debate the fine points of tyrannicide, rape, and piracy than the problems of good and evil or justice and injustice recommended by Tacitus. And then there was the audience to consider, for the declamations were heard not only by the personnel of the schools but by the parents and by friends of the pupils

7. See Bornecque, "Histoire des déclamations," *Les Déclamations et les déclamateurs,* II, i. For more general discussions of the declamation see, in addition to the works already cited, Charles S. Baldwin, *Ancient Rhetoric and Poetic* (New York, Macmillan, 1924), pp. 87–101; Gaston Boissier, "Declamatio," in Ch. Daremberg et Edm. Saglio, *Dictionnaire des antiquités grecques et romaines* (Paris, Hachette, 1873–1919); Martin Schanz, *Geschichte der Römischen Literatur,* 4th ed., rev. Carl Hosius, 2 (Munich, C. H. Beck, 1935), 338–56.

8. Petronius Arbiter *Satiricon* 1, 2; Cornelius Tacitus *Dialogus de oratoribus* 31–5.

9. Petronius *Satiricon* 3.

and of the rhetor. Consequently there was an added incentive to put on a good show. Finally, since many people in the audience were familiar with the case in a given declamation from hearing it debated on previous occasions (the same cases were used year after year), they looked mainly for novelty in the treatment. A tendency in this direction can be sensed even in the sober comments of Seneca: "Porcius Latro treated the subject in this original fashion . . . Cestius Pius used the following witty argument . . ." Thus various features of the school system conspired with the political situation to force the declamation along the path of the sophistic tradition of rhetoric. What was once a practice oration became an end in itself, a vehicle for a clever performer. For years after their schooling was finished Juvenal, Tacitus, and Pliny continued to declaim, and the professional rhetores earned their livelihood in this way. Crowds gathered as at the theater. The declamation became an art form of a very special sort.

The complaints of Petronius and Tacitus are substantiated by the controversiae in Seneca's collection. The fantastic contrivance of the subject matter stands out for anyone to see in the brief narrative summaries which precede the controversiae, outlining the background of the cases. Frequently, as in the first example I shall give, the summary is itself preceded by one or more relevant statutes, though many of these statutes were not Roman, and some were archaic or purely imaginary. Here is the beginning of the fifth controversia in the first book, "The Man Who Raped Two Women":

> A woman who has been raped may choose whether her seducer shall be executed or shall marry her without a dowry.
> In one night a man raped two women; one chooses his death, the other chooses to be married.
>
> *I,* 104

At this point the student orators begin to compose their declamations in favor of one or the other of the unhappy women. They are confronted with a more complicated question by the next controversia, "The Daughter of the Pirate Chief," or "Archipiratae Filia," as the heroine is more beautifully called in Latin:

> A youth, captured by pirates, wrote his father for a ransom; no ransom was sent. The daughter of the pirate chief forced the youth to promise he would marry her if he were freed; he promised. She left her father and followed the young man. He returned to his father and married her. An orphan heiress appears; the father orders his son to marry her, abandoning the daughter of the pirate chief. When he refuses, his father disinherits him.
>
> *I,* 116

Keeping all these interesting circumstances in mind, the students must devise arguments to support either the father or the son. As a final example, the fifth controversia in the second book, "The Woman Tortured by the Tyrant because of Her Husband":

> A woman, tortured by a tyrant to make her confess what she knew of her husband's tyrannicidal plot, continued to deny everything. Her husband later killed the tyrant. He then sent her away on the grounds of barrenness, since in five years she had had no children. She brings action for ingratitude.
>
> *I, 272*

The challenge of these extravagant situations was met with masterpieces of ingenuity. Cestius Pius, arguing for the death of the ravisher in Controversia 5 (bk. i.), suggests that he deliberately took the second woman in order to avoid the death penalty. Cestius goes further and insinuates that the second woman was really quite willing and hence was not raped at all. (*I, 104.*) Pompeius Silon elaborates the same idea: "How cleverly she played her role! With what cries she complained of being 'raped'!" (*I, 106.*) But with equal facility Pompeius Silon imagines another scene as he turns to the defense of this very woman: "The next day, when they told the man what he had done (for he thought he had raped only one woman), it was the second one to whom he knelt, imploring forgiveness with outstretched hands. I suspect that is why the other woman is more angry." (*I, 106.*) Imaginative descriptions are common in the declamations. Seneca especially praises Quintus Haterius for a description which he invents in his defense of the father in the case of "Archipiratae Filia": he pretends to hear a tumultuous din, to see a universal devastation and rapine, farmhouses in flames, the people of the country fleeing. After this terrifying description he adds, "But why should you tremble, young man? It's only your father-in-law arriving." (*I, 126.*) The application here is witty and amusing, as the description unexpectedly becomes a sardonic judgment upon the rashness of the son's marriage. In other instances descriptions are used to evoke pity, as does the torture scene imagined by Papirius Fabianus in defense of the tyrannicide's wife. No gruesome detail is spared in bringing this situation to life. At the end we see the woman, her body broken and weak with pain, thrown from the tyrant's stronghold. (*I, 278.*)

The declamations are liberally sprinkled, as Seneca himself observes, with commonplaces, or *sententiae,* on "fortune, cruelty, the times, riches" (*I, 20*)—observations which can be added to almost any discussion as philosophical decoration, though the relevance to the argument may be slight. Papirius Fabianus, still defending the tortured wife, asks her husband,

What reason have you to send your wife away? [Barrenness is clearly stated as the reason in the opening summary.] Are her expenses a drain on your resources? Moved by the widespread luxury which demeans us all, does her female ambition make her extravagant in rivalry, as is the custom of our times, to the injury of the home and even of the state? Did she rage for precious stones, pearls from distant shores, gold, and such clothes as no matron should wear?

I, 278

However attractive in itself, this commonplace is purely ornamental, and the same might be said of many others. Their arresting and often epigrammatic phraseology is not a means to an end but an end in itself.

Since no judgment was to be handed down on these cases, the orator had comparatively little incentive to stick to cogent argument. His main objective was the applause of the students, parents, and friends, who looked for entertainment. And the applause, we may be sure, was for the ingenious argument, the witty turn, the moving appeal, the effective commonplace, the dramatic scene. Tacitus writes,

> I should find it difficult to say whether the place itself, or the company, or the sort of exercise does more harm to the student's abilities. . . . Ye gods, what *controversiae,* and how incredibly composed! It follows, moreover, that a declamation may be fashioned on material which is abhorrent to truth. Thus it happens that they pursue with great phrases the rewards for tyrannicides, the choices of ravished women, the remedies for plague, or the incests of matrons, or whatever is daily disputed in the schools and rarely or never in the forum.[1]

Critics of the controversiae invariably fasten upon their subject matter, which is so absurdly irrelevant to everyday life. Now that the educational value of these exercises is no longer at stake, their themes are cause for more amazement than alarm, for they are the stuff of a fiction which we associate with later periods. The narrative summaries in Seneca's collection are, in effect, capsule-sized romances, known to every schoolboy at least two centuries before Heliodorus, Xenophon of Ephesus, Longus, and the other early writers of romance. Thus the controversiae, because of their subject matter alone, deserve a place in the history of prose fiction.

The treatment of the material is distinguished by two characteristics which should be borne in mind in the ensuing discussion. One is the frequent use of dramatic scenes, in which all argument is arrested for the sake of recreating a moment in the story. This is standard legal

1. Tacitus *Dialogus* 35.

practice today in certain criminal cases, but it is important to note that these scenes, like the subject matter of the controversiae, make their appeal to the imagination. The other characteristic is rhetorical elaboration, for which progress in the argument is also sacrificed. The declamations are studded with epigrams and unexpected comparisons, daring figures of speech and clever allusions—with all that constitutes the self-conscious style associated with the Asiatic school of rhetoric. One rhetorical device which has long been a staple of oratory merits separate notice because it is used so often in the controversiae: the trick of the repeated word or phrase, used to intensify an emotional appeal. Porcius Latro, arguing for the death of the seducer in Controversia 5 (bk. i), cries: "punish him, fathers, punish him, brothers, punish him, husbands!" (*1*, 104.) In Controversia 5 (bk. ii), he imagines the tortured wife heroically urging her husband on with the words: "Climb up to the fortress! . . . kill the tyrant; otherwise I shall inform against you . . . Now is the time; climb up to the fortress! go if only to have children, for I will not have any except of the man who has killed the tyrant . . . Climb up to the fortress! kill the tyrant! I would go with you if the tyrant had not made me useless. Climb up to the fortress! I, in my way, have already killed the tyrant." (*1*, 272.) The persuasive power of a scene or of an entire declamation may be concentrated in such a rhetorical flourish as this.

The writers of the first Greek romances seem to have profited not only from the subject matter of the controversiae (though this was only one of many sources) but from the style.[2] The *Aethiopica* of Heliodorus is written in a highly ornamented prose, rich in epigrams, philosophical commonplaces, descriptions, and literary allusions, to which the English translator Thomas Underdowne points in marginal comments: "A pretie similitude,"[3] "A very pretty description of an old woman sorceres . . ."[4] More directly related to the declamations are the many orations of the characters, also marginally indicated by Underdowne, some of which occur as pairs of accusations and answers. In the tale of Cnemon in the first book there is "Aristippus Oration against his sonne Cnemon,"[5] followed by Cnemon's defense of himself. In this instance the situation—a father and son put at odds by a vicious stepmother—is also typical of the controversiae. In spite of the multitude of incidents in the *Aethiopica,* the narrative continually stops for the introduction of such oratorical exchanges. Charles S. Baldwin writes that, "Like Alexandrian narrative, sophistic oratory cares little for onward-

2. Erwin Rohde, *Der Griechische Roman und Seine Vorläufer* (Leipzig, 1876), pp. 336–60.

3. Heliodorus, *An Aethiopian History*, tr. Thomas Underdowne (1587), ed. Charles Whibley (London, David Nutt, 1895), p. 62.

4. *Ibid.*, p. 169.   5. *Ibid.*, p. 21.

ness . . ."[6] Centuries later these same characteristics appear in the romances of Sidney, Greene, Lyly, and others: the ornamented style and the formal speech. For, as we shall see, the declamation was still an integral part of education and could influence these writers directly as well as through the early models of romance. The speech of Pyrocles quoted at the beginning of this chapter is in reality a sort of declamation —a suasoria rather than a controversia.

We learn from the early lives of Juvenal that he declaimed until the middle of his life,[7] that is, until he was about forty, and certain features of Juvenalian satire are illuminated by this information. The Senecan *Controversiae* present a galaxy of criminals—tyrants, murderers, seducers, adulterers—and tend to concentrate on the sexual crime. The world of these hypothetical cases is surprisingly like the world cynically observed by Juvenal in his first or his sixth satire. Passages in the *Controversiae,* such as the speeches of Arellius Fuscus and Papirius Fabianus in the first controversia of the second book, setting forth the vices of wealth and the virtues of poverty, are remarkably like Juvenal's tenth and eleventh satires. I have already quoted a most Juvenalian digression on female luxury made by Papirius Fabianus in the fifth controversia of the second book. Nor is the resemblance of Juvenal's satires to the *Controversiae* confined to the prominence of spectacular criminals or the conventional disapproval of materialistic corruption. It is even more a matter of how these criminals are introduced and how the moral condemnation is expressed. Juvenal habitually presents the objects of his satire dramatically in scenes which may or may not be based on actual incidents. Like the declaimer he imagines himself there, conveys the utmost immediacy in his description, and reports what is said. By his presentation or by direct analysis he attributes to his characters the motives which will provoke the most damning judgment. Furthermore, he does not confine himself to the description of vicious behavior but denounces his victims with the utmost vigor:

> What indignation boils within my veins,
> When perjured guardians, proud with impious gains,
> Choke up the streets, too narrow for their trains!
> Whose wards, by want betrayed, to crimes are led
> Too foul to name, too fulsome to be read!
> When he who pilled his province 'scapes the laws,
> And keeps his money, though he lost his cause;
> His fine begged off, contemns his infamy,
> Can rise at twelve, and get him drunk ere three;

---

6. *Medieval Rhetoric and Poetic* (New York, Macmillan, 1928), p. 20.
7. See Julius Dürr, *Das Leben Juvenals* (Ulm, 1888), pp. 22–3.

Enjoys his exile, and, condemned in vain,
Leaves thee, prevailing province, to complain.

I, 67–77

You think this feigned; the satire, in a rage,
Struts in the buskins of the tragic stage;
Forgets his business is to laugh and bite,
And will of deaths and dire revenges write.
Would it were all a fable that you read!
But Drymon's wife pleads guilty to the deed.
"I," she confesses, "in the fact was caught,
Two sons despatching at one deadly draught."
"What, two! two sons, thou viper, in one day!"
"Yes, seven," she cries, "if seven were in my way."
Medea's legend is no more a lie,
Our age adds credit to antiquity.

VI, 828–39[8]

In such passages as these Juvenal makes use of a most effective rhetoric, similar in many respects to the rhetoric of the orators, in order to persuade the reader of the viciousness of the times. His grievances are not imaginary, as are those of the rhetores, but his techniques are often so like theirs that his satires resemble the most successful declamations. Juvenal bequeathed to later generations above all a magnificent rhetoric of denunciation.

The role of the satirist as it was understood by Hall, Marston, and the others owes something to Renaissance theories of satire and more to the direct imitation of Juvenal, but it may have been affected also by the tradition of declamation, both through Juvenal and as it survived in the schools. For Hall and Marston, even more than their master Juvenal, seem to have been aware of playing a part, of exercising themselves in the depiction of the most lurid vices imaginable. Like Juvenal, but also like Seneca's rhetores, they make their major appeal in passages of oratorical eloquence:

ô stay, thou impious slave,
Teare not the lead from off thy Fathers grave,

The *Controversiae* and *Suasoriae* of Seneca the Elder were frequently printed in the Renaissance with the essays and epistles of the younger, more famous Seneca, to whom they had been attributed during the Middle Ages. These examples of the declamation were thus readily available to readers. Some indication of the popularity of the genre is given by a book called *Epitomes de cent histoires tragicques* (Paris,

---

8. I have quoted Dryden's translations of these passages from *The Works of John Dryden*, ed. Walter Scott, rev. George Saintsbury (Edinburgh, 1882–93), *13*, 128, 181–2.

1581), written by Alexandre van den Busche (called Le Sylvain), consisting in controversiae on the Senecan model. Forty-five of them are actually translations of the widely circulated *Excerpta* from Seneca the Elder, and the others present in identical form themes taken from Livy, the *Gesta Romanorum,* and other sources. Another edition appeared in 1588, and Lazarus Pyott (or Piot) translated it into English as *The Orator* in 1596.

The study of rhetoric, with which declamations were intimately allied, was one of the mainstays of education for centuries after the collapse of Rome. In the trivium of the sixteenth-century schools, which consisted of grammar, logic, and rhetoric, it was the most highly regarded subject and the one which was studied last.[9] The rhetorical training was divided into three kinds of composition: first epistles, then themes, and finally orations. Since declamations were practice orations they came at the culminating point of education in the upper grammar school or sometimes in the university.[1] That Seneca's collection still provided models for the students is clear from Bishop Pilkington's statutes for Rivington School (1566), in which, after recommending the study of the rules of rhetoric in the pseudo-Ciceronian *Ad Herennium,* he writes: "now he may use to declaim probably on any Questions propounded after the example of Aphthonius, Quintilian, or Seneca, and for example, follow and see the practice of these Rules."[2] Seneca is in distinguished company here, for Cicero and Quintilian were the great authorities on rhetoric and the *Progymnasmata* of Aphthonius (adapted for English students by Richard Rainolde as *The Foundacion of Rhetorike* in 1563) was one of the most widely used textbooks in rhetoric.

The Renaissance admired exorbitantly what was called "copiousness" of style, by which was meant the "enrichment" and "variation" seen to the best advantage in the prose of Cicero. The student was encouraged to master the figures of speech and to familiarize himself with the collections of commonplaces from which he could draw an apt allusion or comparison or perhaps a witty saying. He was prepared to elaborate on any theme. Now the declamation was an exercise of precisely this sort of skill and thus was ideally suited to follow the study of the rules of rhetoric. The declaiming was not done in the fashionable atmosphere of imperial Rome, but the procedure seems to

9. On the general subject of education in English schools in the sixteenth century see T. W. Baldwin, *William Shakspere's Small Latine & Lesse Greeke* (Urbana, Ill., University of Illinois Press, 1944).

1. John Brinsley believed that they should be reserved for the university or for specially qualified students, as he writes in his *Ludus literarius* (1612), ed. E. T. Campagnac (Liverpool, University Press of Liverpool, 1917), p. 185.

2. Margaret M. Kay, *The History of Rivington and Blackrod Grammar School* (Manchester, Manchester University Press, 1931), Appendix II, p. 187.

have been much the same. When the question had been posed, the pupil demonstrated his prowess by composing a declamation in favor of the father or the son, the husband or the tortured wife. Fortified by his native ingenuity and his repertoire of rhetorical devices, he did his best to be copious.

The declamation, to summarize briefly its pedagogical value in Elizabethan education, was one of several tests of the student's ability to improvise, and the supreme test of his oratorical powers. In his epistles he had written imaginary letters from Paris to Helen or from Alcibiades to Socrates, and in his themes he had dealt with such questions as whether or not it is good to marry, but the declamations of Seneca presented him with a different order of question. Or rather, the controversiae did so, for the suasoriae were little more than extensions of the exercises undertaken in the epistles. To produce a suitable declamation on one of the controversiae the student must project himself into the midst of an exciting fictitious narrative, fill in the outlines of the characters, imagine supplementary situations, give the story life and give it the meaning which would best serve the purposes of his "client." Above all, he must compose his declamation with an eye to effective oral delivery.

In the matter of delivery (what was called "pronuntiatio" or "actio" in the treatises on rhetoric) there was another noteworthy link between the stage and rhetorical training. B. L. Joseph has shown in his *Elizabethan Acting*[3] that there was an elaborate code of gestures corresponding to the gamut of emotions, and that the actor had only to cultivate for his special purpose what every schoolboy was taught to do in public speaking. In *The Arte of Rhetorique* (1585 edition) Thomas Wilson quotes from Cicero, "The gesture of man is the speech of his bodie . . ."[4] For the modern reader, therefore, one of the clearest insights into the tradition of Elizabethan acting is to be had by reading such books as John Bulwer's *Chirologia* (1644), discussed at length by Joseph, in which the proper gestures for rhetorical delivery are described and illustrated. From other sources we know that an important part of the training in pronuntiatio was accomplished by means of themes and declamations. Brinsley recommends, "Thus let them take speciall paines to pronounce Theames or Declamations, striving who shall do best: and in all their oppositions to dispute, as if *ex animo* in good earnest, with all contention and vehemencie."[5] In so doing the young orator was also learning the trade of the actor.

3. London, Geoffrey Cumberlege, Oxford University Press, 1951. See also Alfred Harbage, "Elizabethan Acting," *PMLA*, 54 (1939), 685–708.

4. *Wilson's Arte of Rhetorique*, ed. G. H. Mair (Oxford, Clarendon Press, 1909), p. 221. The quotation is presumably from *De oratore* iii. 222: "Est enim actio quasi sermo corporis . . ." There is also a similar statement in *Orator* 55.

5. *Ludus literarius*, p. 214.

The student who did well at these exercises had not only to be ingenious and eloquent but also to have a lively imagination and a gift for dramatizing. And if he had these gifts, the declamation might also be a dangerous exercise, as Tacitus saw, by providing a fascinatingly distorted view of human conduct. Henri Bornecque writes: "D'ailleurs l'imagination ne trouve nulle part de limites, car les déclamations nous transportent dans un monde de fantaisie, sans contact avec la réalité . . ." (*Controverses et suasoires, I,* xii.)

The Senecan declamations were surely a great potential influence on the drama, providing abundant material and prescribing a method of using it. Since they were still studied when Beaumont and Fletcher and Massinger went to school, it is most likely that these dramatists-to-be used the collection in their study of oratory, just as Juvenal and the authors of the Greek romances had done long before. Thus certain influential characteristics of satire and romance, derived originally from the declamations, may have been reinforced by familiarity with Seneca the Elder. It is certain that Fletcher and Massinger drew upon the *Controversiae* for the plots of at least three plays of the period 1616–20,[6] but the nature of the early plays suggests that even then their authors had felt the influence of their oratorical training. Both indirectly and directly the art of declamation may have influenced the pattern of tragicomedy.

The fantastic theme and the puzzling dilemma are as typical of the controversiae as of the romances. We noted the importance in declamation of the dramatic scene based on the central conflict of the given situation; the technique of scene structure in *The Faithful Shepherdess* and *The Maid's Tragedy* may owe something to Seneca as well as to Jonson. The temporary assumption of a role, so important in *The Malcontent* and in *The Maid's Tragedy,* is also part of the exercise of declaiming. The style of Fletcherian tragicomedy, which will be more fully discussed in the last chapter, is characterized by the very sort of rhetorical elaboration recorded by Seneca. Even Fletcher's conspicuous habit of repetition might have been learned from the ancient rhetores. Above all, the hypothetical quality of Fletcherian tragicomedy, present also in *The Malcontent,* is implicit in the Senecan declamations, where the student has to accept the most extravagant situations and then imagine what led the protagonists to their legal impasse. On the basis of these hypotheses he invents his copious declamation. This is the technique of those crises in *The Maid's Tragedy* or *A King and No King* in which one character confronts another to accuse him of disloyalty, ingratitude, or some other form of moral turpitude, in impassioned speech, gleaming with the "colors" of rhetoric. But when the conflict has been

---

6. *The Double Marriage, The Queen of Corinth,* and *The Laws of Candy.* See my "John Fletcher and the Art of Declamation," *PMLA, 66* (1951), 226–34.

fully exploited for its dramatic effect, the hypothesis is demolished. The contrivance of such improbable and insubstantial complications, similar in nature to the material of the Senecan *Controversiae,* is the essence of Fletcherian tragicomedy.[7]

These resemblances are striking. The following comment on the Senecan *Controversiae* by Henri Bornecque might almost be a description of the Beaumont and Fletcher plays:

> Quant aux sujets eux-mêmes, comme le montrera un coup d'oeil rapide jeté sur les matières proposées comme thèmes, ils sont généralement très compliqués et très subtils, présentent des cas d'une solution délicate ou douteuse, amènent en conflit des sentiments également forts et sacrés; ils mettent presque toujours en scène des personnages qui n'existaient plus à l'époque de Sénèque ou qui n'avaient jamais existé, tyrans, pirates, braves à toute épreuve, placés dans des situations invraisemblables ou tout au moins exceptionnelles, et ne cessant d'étaler des sentiments exactement contraires à ceux que l'on attendrait.
>
> *Controverses et suasoires, I,* xi

To the influence of satire and romance upon the pattern of tragicomedy we must add that of the declamation as it is seen in Seneca's collection. Its remoteness from actuality and emphasis upon rhetorical elaboration strengthened the forces that were pushing tragicomedy away from meaning and toward greater formalization.

7. There are, of course, other possible sources for the thorny problems and improbable hypotheses of the early plays. One might mention the medieval *jeu parti* with its descendants in those novelle which were arranged to illustrate the different sides of an argument, such as those in Boccaccio's *Filocolo* or the *Printemps* of Jacques Yver, or in certain dramatic interludes, such as Medwall's *Fulgens and Lucres.* The tradition of problems and debates cannot be cleanly separated from the special branch of rhetorical training represented by the controversiae, for Brinsley, *Ludus literarius,* p. 184, recommends declaiming on such questions as whether or not it is good to marry. However, the Senecan *Controversiae* present debates of a special sort, less governed by abstract principles than the medieval jeu parti, more intimately related to the details of an exciting narrative, and emphasizing oratory above everything else. They resemble Fletcherian drama more closely than the other forms of literary debate and they were readily available in the Elizabethan schoolbooks.

IV

The Pattern of Tragicomedy in Later Plays

ALL THE LATER plays manifest characteristics of the pattern we have observed in *A King and No King*. The tragicomedies, as we should expect, conform most rigidly to this pattern; in them every one of the characteristics is evident. In the comedies and tragedies some are absent or only faintly suggested, yet even here the pattern of tragicomedy is often so conspicuous that the conventional patterns of comedy and tragedy are almost obliterated. To study this large corpus of plays is to see how various they are and yet how remarkably similar.

For the purpose of this discussion I shall divide the plays into six groups: (1) the comedies of trickery, (2) the mixed comedies, (3) the romantic comedies, (4) *Henry VIII* and the more historical tragedies, (5) the less historical tragedies, and (6) the tragicomedies. For the large divisions of "comedy," "tragedy," and "tragicomedy" I rely chiefly upon the classification in the Second Folio. It would be easy to take issue with this classification at many points, but since I hope to demonstrate the fundamental similarity of these plays, it would be futile to attempt a reclassification which would make the distinctions between the genres more rigid.

Categories such as "comedies of trickery" and "romantic comedies" are useful only so long as they are not thought of as watertight compartments. An element of trickery will be found in some of the romantic comedies, as I shall show, and it is not the only important element in the group of comedies for which it provides the label. In these comedies, however, it predominates. Since it would be tedious to discuss even briefly every play in the canon, I shall pick from each group a small number, which the reader will have to accept as representative unless he is willing to assume the task of reading the others himself.

1. *Comedies of Trickery*

Wit at Several Weapons (1609—Middleton, Beaumont? Fletcher?),[1]

1. Dates are of no great importance in this chapter and in any case can rarely be given with certainty. But since the reader will naturally be curious to know approximately when each play was performed, I indicate here and throughout this chapter and the

The Scornful Lady (1613—Beaumont and Fletcher), *Wit without Money* (1614—Fletcher), *The Little French Lawyer* (1619—Fletcher and Massinger), *The Wild-Goose Chase* (1621—Fletcher), *Rule a Wife and Have a Wife* (1624—Fletcher), *The Elder Brother* (1625—Fletcher and Massinger), *The Noble Gentleman* (1626, but may have been written in 1613—Fletcher and Beaumont?).

The plays least affected by the pattern of tragicomedy are the comedies of trickery, in many of which the dominant gaiety is never disturbed by a more serious tone. We shall examine these plays first and then proceed to the plays more closely related to tragicomedy. The purest example of a comedy of trickery in the Beaumont and Fletcher canon is *Wit at Several Weapons,* which a number of critics place among the early plays and which, in any case, is probably the work of Middleton, with little if any assistance from Beaumont or Fletcher. It is a merry play, deriving its fun mainly from a succession of ingenious tricks. As in many of Middleton's comedies, the eccentric humor-characters are satirized rather gently, almost affectionately. The mainspring of the action is the whim of Sir Perfidious Oldcraft, "an old Knight, a great admirer of Wit," to make his son Witty-pate live by his wits. When Sir Perfidious discovers at the end of the play that he has been repeatedly cheated by Witty-pate, he is so delighted that he instantly makes his son a handsome allowance. The participation of Sir Ruinous Gentry, "a decaid Knight," in the trickery is similarly viewed with approval by cheaters and cheated alike, and in the sub-plot Sir Gregory Fop is well pleased to be tricked into marrying the niece of the "Guardianess" of the heiress whom he has been courting. Indeed no character is more than momentarily displeased in the entire course of this high-spirited romp.

The characters, many of them stock comic types, are made to speak and act like inhabitants of seventeenth-century London, where the scene is laid. The imitation of the manners of the familiar world, which is one characteristic of the Beaumont and Fletcher plays, is carried further here in the direction of what Renaissance critics expected of comedy. *Wit at Several Weapons* holds the mirror up to the lives of the

---

following one the dates given by Harbage, *Annals,* for the first performances. Though I occasionally mention the dates given by other scholars when there seems to be reason for departing radically from Harbage, I make no attempt to evaluate each of his suggestions. They are all reasonable but should not be understood as matters of fact.

A similar caution must be given with regard to my indication of authorship. One can be most nearly certain about the plays assigned to Fletcher alone, since his style is more easily distinguished than that of any of his collaborators. It is extremely doubtful whether we shall ever know for sure what parts of the other plays were written by what author, though more or less convincing divisions have been made in great detail by Oliphant and others. I give in each case what seem to me reasonable guesses, indicating with a question mark more than usual uncertainty.

people only slightly superior in rank to the citizen. The language (with
the exception of some Latin joking inspired by the scholar Priscian)
inclines toward the vernacular, as this speech of Witty-pate's shows:

> an honest man
> May eat of the same Pig some Parson dines with,
> A Lawyer and a fool feed of one Woodcock,
> Yet one ne'er the simpler, t'other ne'er the wiser;
> 'Tis not meat, drink, or smoak, dish, cup, or pipe,
> Co-operates to the making of a Knave,
> 'Tis the condition makes a slave, a slave,
> There's *London* Philosophy for you;
>
> IV, i; Cam., *9, 112*

The familiarity of the language here is an essential part of the effect,
for homespun humor is the staple of this play. The wit which Sir
Perfidious admires is not a verbal wit, and the dialogue is far less ingenious than the trickery. Though the ticket-names and the farcical
situations of *Wit at Several Weapons* are somewhat suggestive of
Restoration comedy, there is none of the keen edge of Congreve or
Wycherley in the humor or the language.

The Scornful Lady, the best comedy written by Beaumont and
Fletcher in collaboration, is another lighthearted play, but in characterization, in plot, and in the predominant tone it is remarkably different from *Wit at Several Weapons.* The characters are once more
types well known both on and off the stage—the two brothers, one wild
and the other sober, the crafty usurer, the rich widow, the Lady herself, who is beautiful and unapproachable. But in comparison to the
characters in *Wit at Several Weapons* they are more exactly balanced,
one against the other: the Elder Loveless, a devoted suitor, is opposed
to his prodigal brother and to the unreceptive Lady (she has no other
name), who in turn is contrasted with the amorous Abigal, her servant.
Here is, then, something of the artful arrangement of extreme characters which is part of the pattern of Fletcherian tragicomedy. This
characteristic alone makes *The Scornful Lady* seem a little more remote from actuality than *Wit at Several Weapons;* there is more distortion in the mirror. The plot, consisting mainly in the brilliant battle
of wits between the Elder Loveless and the Lady, serves to emphasize
the formal balance of the characters. The tone in some of their encounters
is considerably less gay, the humor more sharply satirical than anything
in *Wit at Several Weapons.*

In *Wit without Money* the balance of characters is even more conspicuous than in *The Scornful Lady.* Two brothers, Valentine and
Francisco, are courted and won by two sisters, the widow Lady Hartwell and Isabella. Valentine is a wild spendthrift, perversely deter-

mined to live by his wits, Francisco a prudent and serious scholar; Lady Hartwell is a stately, self-possessed, somewhat overbearing woman, Isabella unpretentious and retiring. These contrasts are heightened by the circumstances in which we first encounter the two pairs of characters: Valentine, by his debauchery, has deprived his brother of the means of pursuing his studies, and Lady Hartwell, by her flamboyance, has attracted to herself all the potential suitors of her sister. Yet Francisco, noble young man that he is, loyally defends Valentine's behavior, and Isabella, a model heroine, has nothing but praise for Lady Hartwell. Thus two romantically conceived characters, Francisco and Isabella, are paired with two who are familiar objects of satire, the wild gallant and the willful and wealthy widow.

The comedy is an interplay not only of contrasting temperaments but also of two opposed principles: Valentine's, that it behooves a man to dispose of his possessions and live by his wits, and his uncle's, that a man should seek material security by some conventional means, such as marrying a wealthy widow. The importance of these principles is in itself a Fletcherian characteristic which distinguishes the play from *Wit at Several Weapons,* where the subject matter is very similar. There one principle guides Sir Perfidious and Witty-pate and makes the action a contest of ingenuity in the choice and use of weapons. The conflict of principles in *Wit without Money* is in line with the schematic design of *The Faithful Shepherdess* or *Cupid's Revenge* or *The Woman's Prize.*

It is also characteristic of Fletcher's practice that the attitudes of the characters are pushed to extravagance. Valentine, defending his mode of life against his uncle, launches an attack on money getting with the ferocity of a formal satirist:

> are not these ways as honest as persecuting the starved inheritance, with musty Corn, the very rats were fain to run away from, or selling rotten wood by the pound, like spices, which Gentlemen do after burn by th' ounces? do not I know your way of feeding beasts with grains, and windy stuff, to blow up Butchers? your racking Pastures, that have eaten up as many singing Shepherds, and their issues, as *Andeluzia* breeds? these are authentique, I tell you Sir, I would not change ways with you, unless it were to sell your state that hour, and if it were possible to spend it then too, for all your Beans in *Rumnillo,* now you know me.[2]
>
> I, i; Cam., 2, 152

2. The objects of Valentine's attack were traditional with such satirists as Hall. In *Virgidemiae,* for instance, we read:
> They racke their rents unto a treble rate;
> IV, ii, 126
> But, *Nummius* eas'd the needy Gallants care,
> With a base bargaine of his blowen ware,

He has nothing but contempt for those that marry widows: "they that enjoy 'em, lie but with dead mens monuments, and beget only their own ill Epitaphs . . ." (II, i; Cam., *2*, 157); and, in fact, he is totally opposed to marriage: "why 'tis a monstrous thing to marry at all, especially as now 'tis made; me thinks a man, an understanding man, is more wise to me, and of a nobler tie, than all these trinkets; what do we get by women . . . ? What benefit can children be, but charges and disobedience?" (II, i; Cam., *2*, 157–8.) Lady Hartwell, for her part, cannot tolerate the idea of marrying a poor man. When she hears that Isabella has given a suit to the penniless Francisco she is scandalized: "Is she so hot, or such a want of lovers, that she must doat upon afflictions? why does she not go romage all the prisons, and there bestow her youth, bewray her wantonness, and flie her honour, common both to beggery . . . ?" (II, i; Cam., *2*, 156.) Both she and Valentine express themselves with an intemperance so extreme that it can only be taken as a pose or a *jeu d'esprit*.

The confrontation of Valentine and Lady Hartwell, carefully prepared during the first two acts, takes place in the third, in the very center of the play. The means of bringing them together is suggestive of dramatic satire, for Valentine, after lecturing his friends at length on the dangers of widows, finally agrees to call on Lady Hartwell in order to expose her faults. He comes to her like the most didactic of scourging satirists and accuses her of being "monstrous proud." He is surprised, however, when she both defends herself and attacks him with a verve equal to his own instead of retreating in shame, as he expected her to do. At this point occurs a reversal which might be compared to the dishumoring of the characters in *Every Man out of His Humor*: Valentine falls in love with the widow's brave spirit and she with his bluntness. Out of this new relationship between Valentine and Lady Hartwell arise the complications which occupy the rest of the play.

Wit without Money is a tissue of ironic reversals. The bashful Isabella sets her cap for Francisco and is married before her sister; her first present is given to Francisco just after Valentine has refused him money and urged him to live by his wits—to Valentine his brother's unexpected good fortune is welcome proof of his theories but also somewhat humiliating; the friends who urge Valentine to see the widow are furious when he is pleased by her; after Valentine's call Lady Hartwell, who has made her entire household miserable by insisting that they move to the country to get Isabella away from Francisco, suddenly countermands her orders and is subjected to the teasing of Isabella, who

---

Of fusted hoppes now lost for lacke of sayle,
Or mo'ld browne-paper that could nought availe:
IV, v, 115–8

urges her to go. So pervasive is the irony and so completely does each character go back on his principles or belie his established temperament that it is difficult to extract any clear meaning from the action. There is, perhaps, the shadow of a Jonsonian meaning, that the extreme attitudes of all the characters are equally foolish, or a romantic meaning, that love conquers all, but neither one is distinctly enunciated, and together they tend to destroy each other. When Valentine finally succumbs to Lady Hartwell his words reveal neither a fool reformed nor a romantic lover: "Come quickly gentle Ladie, the fit's upon me now . . . Take me quickly, while I am in this vein, away with me, for if I have but two hours to consider, all the widows in the world cannot recover me." (v, i; Cam., 2, 205.) His marriage is a wiser folly than the others, but undertaken in the same spirit of careless fun. The meaning of the event is negligible.

The critic in search of a meaning will also be troubled by the amount of pose in the play. The coy pretense of both women toward the end of the play that they are offended by their lovers' attentions might be dismissed as a conventional ruse. So might the strategy of Valentine's uncle in congratulating Lady Hartwell on her marriage when he knows that it has not yet taken place. But there are so many of these charades that the sincerity of all the characters becomes suspect. Does Valentine ever believe his preposterous theories? Is Lady Hartwell really so opposed to marrying a poor man? These are questions not to be asked, for the dramatic consequences of these diverse attitudes are all that matters. Whether these attitudes are sincerely held or affected, they make possible the constantly shifting oppositions of which the play is composed. Since the meaning of the details is doubtful and since the ironic reversals do not support any general structure of meaning, the play is essentially a series of theatrically effective moments arranged in a formal design.

The high points of the play are the tirades which mark the important reversals. At such moments the excitement of the situation is rendered in the exuberant invective of the principal characters. For example, when Valentine's friends turn against him they try to ruin him by obliging him to return their gifts of money and clothes, but thanks to Lady Hartwell he regains the upper hand and comes to her house outfitted more splendidly than ever, to put them to shame. As they start to retire in confusion he opens fire on them:

> You shall stay till I talk with you, and not dine neither, but fastingly my fury, you think you have undone me, think so still, and swallow that belief, till you be company for Court-hand Clarks, and starved Atturnies, till you break in at playes like Prentices for three a groat, and crack Nuts with the Scholars in peny Rooms again, and fight for Apples, till you return to what I found you, people betrai'd into

the hands of Fencers, Challengers, Tooth-drawers Bills, and tedious Proclamations in Meal-markets, with throngings to see Cutpurses:

IV, i; Cam., 2, 194

It is a tour de force of raillery, an exercise in the invention of mouthfilling curses. The vocabulary is familiar and the sentence structure is that of conversation, but though it is printed as prose, it falls readily into blank-verse rhythms, which are accentuated by frequent alliteration. However prosaic, it is a declamation to delight an actor.

In a general way the language of this comedy assumes a far greater importance than the language of *Wit at Several Weapons* or *The Scornful Lady*. As the situations and characters are more formalized, so the language is more self-conscious and the humor more verbal. To the fanciful speeches of Valentine and Lady Hartwell already quoted may be added Isabella's comparison of herself and her sister in reply to her maid's compliment, "You are as fair as she": "Who I? I thank you, I am as haste ordain'd me, a thing slubber'd, my sister is a goodly portly Lady, a woman of a presence, she spreads sattens, as the Kings ships do canvas every where, she may spare me her misen, and her bonnets, strike her main Petticoat, and yet outsail me, I am a Carvel to her." (1, i; Cam., *2*, 153.) The very contrasts between the characters, the sine qua non of the play, receive their ultimate form in this sort of verbal elaboration, which unmistakably points to Etherege and Congreve. The visible contrast between the actions of the two sisters is not so sharp as this figurative contrast, given in Isabella's speech. This is the ideal contrast. Its presentation as epigram is the final step in the process of formalization.

Richard Flecknoe gives "wit" as Fletcher's distinguishing quality:

> To compare our English Dramatick Poets together, without taxing them, *Shakespear* excelled in a natural Vein, *Fletcher* in Wit, and *Johnson* in Gravity and ponderousness of Style . . . Comparing him with *Shakespear*, you shall see the difference betwixt Nature and Art; and with *Fletcher,* the difference betwixt Wit and Judgement: Wit being an exuberant thing, like *Nilus,* never more commendable then when it overflowes; but Judgement, a stayed and reposed thing, always containing it self within its bounds and limits. . . . And here to speak a word or two of Wit, it is the spirit and quintessence of speech, extracted out of the substance of the thing we speak of, having nothing of the superfice, or dross of words, as clenches, quibbles, gingles, and such like trifles have: it is that, in pleasant and facetious discourse, as Eloquence is in grave and serious, not learnt by Art and Precept, but Nature and Company.[3]

3. "A Short Discourse of the English Stage," Spingarn, *2*, 93–4.

As Flecknoe uses it, wit is any exact appropriateness of words to the subject matter—what Dryden calls "a propriety of thoughts and words; or, in other terms, thoughts and words elegantly adapted to the subject."[4] It is not mere word play. Thus the language of *Wit without Money* is witty in its brilliant rendition of the essence of the characters and situations. But Flecknoe recognizes that wit consists in appropriateness to a special sort of subject, for it belongs above all "in pleasant and facetious discourse." It is calculated to provoke a laugh, or at least a smile, by its preposterous exaggerations, its extravagant comparisons. Flecknoe's analogy of wit and eloquence both makes the definition sharper and brings to light an important point about Fletcher. The exuberant wit of the speeches we have been considering corresponds to the passionate eloquence of the tragicomedies. A similar treatment of characters and situations, a similar blend of the familiar and the remote provide the context for the declamatory speeches which mark the high points of both comedies and tragicomedies. In one case we have the witty tirade of Valentine; in the other, the eloquent tirade of Spaconia in *A King and No King*. Without slighting the important differences in tone which make each appropriate to the play in which it occurs, we must note that Valentine's speech is not only witty but also eloquent, and that Spaconia's eloquence is marked by one or two witty comparisons:

> Thy faith is firm as raging over-flowes,
> That no bank can command; as lasting
> As boyes gay bubbles, blown i'th'Air and broken:
>
> IV; Cam., 1, 199

Wit and eloquence, derived from similar sources, are not mutually exclusive. By the same token Fletcherian comedy and tragicomedy not only are analogous in technique but share certain of their effects.

Though the comedies of trickery as a group do not seem at all like tragicomedy, several of the characteristics of the tragicomic pattern are present and produce important changes in the better known comic pattern. These comedies are more faithful imitations of the familiar world than the tragicomedies, and yet many of them are not the exact mirrors of life that comedy was expected to be. Often the formal intricacy of plot, the improbability of situation, and the changeability of character result in distortions as great as in the tragicomedies. In none of the comedies of trickery are the issues serious. Tragedy never threatens, and consequently the atmosphere of evil, that conspicuous characteristic of the tragicomedies, is never present, but neither is the warm, kindly gaiety of *Wit at Several Weapons* present in most of these comedies. Lastly, though the emotions of the characters are much less important

4. "The Author's Apology for Heroic Poetry," Dryden, *Essays, 1, 190.*

than in tragicomedy, a kind of emotional tension is generated in *The Scornful Lady* and the language of emotion has its equivalent in the elaborate wit which is best exemplified in *Wit without Money*. The least tragicomic of the Beaumont and Fletcher plays are seriously modified by the technique of tragicomedy.

2. Mixed Comedies

The Captain (1612—Fletcher and Beaumont?), *The Night-Walker* (1614—Fletcher and Shirley), *Monsieur Thomas* (1615—Fletcher), *The Nice Valor* (1625—Fletcher, Beaumont? Middleton?).[5]

The four comedies in this group are outstanding examples of plays in which the gaiety characteristic of the comedies of trickery is mixed with a more serious mood. Other Beaumont and Fletcher plays could be added to the group, but the mixture is nowhere more apparent than in these four. In *The Nice Valor* the conspicuous disparity between the elements of the play may be partly the result of ineffective collaboration or of the imperfect transmission of the text, for the authorship is doubtful and there are several inconsistencies. But here and in the three other plays the mixture of moods is partly due to the pattern of tragicomedy.

The Prologue to *The Captain* states: "This is nor *Comedy,* nor *Tragedy,* / Nor *History* . . ." (Cam., 5, 318.) The subplot of the play is a low farce, presenting the tricks played on Captain Jacomo, a woman-hater, by a group of his friends. Like a humor comedy, this part of the play ends with the vanquishing of the title character's unreasonable dislike of women. The mood of the main plot, while certainly not so lighthearted as that of the subplot, is not easy to determine. The story concerns Lelia, "a cunning, wanton widow," and her amatory adventures. The most bitter satirist could not contrive a more damning portrait of her than emerges from the scenes of this play. She is the subject of lewd conversations in the streets of Venice; she is heartless to her old father and hypocritical to Julio, a "noble gentleman" who is in love with her; in the most sensational scene of the play she tries to seduce an old man and does not desist even when he reveals himself as her father in disguise.[6] The ruthless exposure of

5. The dates of *The Night-Walker* and of *The Nice Valor* are particularly hard to determine. Maxwell, *Studies in Beaumont, Fletcher, and Massinger*, pp. 46–53, dates *The Night-Walker* 1611; other scholars, even earlier. There is little doubt that it was revised by Shirley in 1633. Maxwell, pp. 116–37, dates *The Nice Valor* convincingly 1615–16.

6. Gayley was so shocked by the depravity of the play that he believed Beaumont had little to do with it, for, as he explains, he found no vestige of Beaumont's "faith in sweet innocence," *Beaumont, the Dramatist*, p. 306. Certainly there is nothing of this kind in *The Captain*, and it is likely for other reasons, such as the versification, that Fletcher wrote most of the play.

Lelia to her lovers owes much to dramatic satire in both tone and technique.

It is startling, then, to hear the vicious heroine of *The Captain* express herself in such terms as these:

> what should I do here
> Like a decaying flower, still withering
> Under his bitter words, whose kindly heat
> Should give my poor heart life? No, curse me, *Julio,*
> Thou canst not do me such a benefit
> As that, and well done, that the Heav'ns may hear it.
>
> I, iii; Cam., 5, 245

And equally startling to hear her lover, though undeceived by her pose of virtue, reply in the same romantic vein:

> O fair tears! were you but as chast as subtil,
> Like Bones of Saints, you would work miracles;
>
> .   .   .
>
> For if she were as good as she is seeming,
> Or, like an Eagle, could renew her vertues,
> Nature had made another world of sweetness.
>
> .   .   .
>
> Pray wipe your eyes and kiss me; take these trifles,
> And wear them for me, which are only rich
> When you will put them on: indeed I love ye,
> Beshrew my sick heart, if I grieve not for ye.
>
> I, iii; Cam., 5, 245

A still more striking example is Julio's speech to his friend Angelo, where the imagery parallels a familiar song by Fletcher in *Henry VIII:*[7]

> And when she speaks, oh *Angelo,* then musick
> (Such as old *Orpheus* made, that gave a soul
> To aged mountains, and made rugged beasts
> Lay by their rages; and tall trees that knew
> No sound but tempests, to bow down their branches
> And hear, and wonder; and the Sea, whose surges
> Shook their white heads in Heaven, to be as mid-night
> Still, and attentive) steals into our souls
> So suddenly, and strangely, that we are
> From that time no more ours, but what she pleases.
>
> III, i; Cam., 5, 263

This sort of language blunts the satire of Lelia and presents the plight of her lovers as a romantic dilemma. At such moments she is not "a

---

7. It is probable that *Henry VIII* was written a year or so later.

cunning, wanton widow" but a temptress at once more dangerous and more appealing.

The main plot of *The Captain,* with its variations in tone between biting satire and moving romance, contains the raw material of Fletcherian tragicomedy, but the different elements, instead of being assimilated into one homogeneous entity as they are in *A King and No King,* remain separate; the play is too serious to be amusing, yet too farcical to take seriously. The effect of its fine passages is destroyed by crude workmanship. To the critic of Beaumont and Fletcher it is an instructive failure—an experiment in the combination of light comedy with tragicomedy.

In *Monsieur Thomas* the combination of serious and gay is managed differently. The subplot, a pure comedy of trickery, is composed of the pranks of Tom ("Monsieur Thomas" because he has just returned from travel abroad), a wild young fellow who is determined to win his Mary in spite of her disapproval of his behavior. Since she is equally determined never to give in to him until he reforms, the action is a battle of wits. Tom feigns illness in order to win her sympathy, pretends to have broken his leg or disguises himself as his sister Dorothy in order to gain access to Mary's house, and she not only sees through his stratagems but devises some of her own, such as putting her blackamoor maid in her bed. The subplot has a further complication, for while Tom is playing these unsuccessful pranks on Mary he perversely affects the sobriety of a reformed rake in the presence of his father, who wants him to be a madcap. In alternate scenes his behavior varies from a license which offends Mary to a dignified restraint which exasperates his father.

Tom's contradictory poses have serious parallels in the main plot, where the mood is wholly different. Valentine returns from abroad with a young friend, Francisco, whom he has met on his travels. He introduces Francisco to Cellide, a girl whom he has adopted and hopes to marry. When Francisco falls in love with Cellide a contest of nobility ensues, fought with no less zeal and ingenuity than the three-sided contest between Tom, his father, and Mary. For, since Francisco is bound by loyalty to Valentine, he says nothing to anyone about his consuming passion, but as he sinks into an apparently mortal illness, Valentine divines the cause and, making the supreme sacrifice, tells Cellide that only she can cure Francisco. She upbraids Valentine for being false to her but, out of pique, follows his suggestion by going to visit Francisco. In this interview the situation becomes complicated in the tradition of the most sophisticated romance. Francisco, at first delighted by Cellide's affectionate behavior, has a quick revulsion when he thinks of the wrong to his friend and speaks to Cellide as severely as Perigot to the disguised Amaryllis:

Ye have no share in goodness:
Ye are belyed; you are not *Cellide,*
The modest, immaculate: who are ye?
For I will know: what Devil, to do mischief
Unto my vertuous friend, hath shifted shapes
With that unblemished beauty?

III, i; Cam., *4,* 124

Francisco defends his friend with such ardor that Cellide is moved to
admit to him that although up to this point she has merely feigned affection, she is now truly in love with his virtue. Francisco, understand-
ably confused, hesitates whether or not to believe her new protestations:
"Is this serious? / Or dos she play still with me?" (III, i; Cam., *4,*
125.) The refinement of romantic sensibilities has indeed been carried
to the point where it is difficult to distinguish truth from pose. But
when Francisco is convinced of her sincerity, Cellide becomes for him
no longer a "devil" but an "excellent angel," the "honour of all thy
sex." The lovers now openly exchange their vows, but their loyalty to
Valentine imposes an unavoidable dilemma and they choose renunciation rather than dishonor: Francisco resumes his travels and Cellide
enters a convent.

The shifting tensions of this scene are those of Fletcherian tragicomedy. Even the absence of any intentional evil scarcely lessens the
atmosphere of threatened misfortune in which the lovers part, apparently forever. The characters are as changeable, the situation as improbable, and the language as emotional as those of tragicomedy, and
the denouement is altogether in keeping. Francisco is found to be the
long lost son of Valentine, is brought back and united to Cellide, who
agrees to leave her convent. The discovery of Francisco's identity has
mysteriously dissipated all the previous scruples of the lovers and
solved their dilemma.

The alteration of tragicomic and farcical scenes puts a severe strain
upon the artistic unity of the play even though the two plots are skill-
fully related and each good of its kind. However, there is no play in
the Beaumont and Fletcher corpus which better illustrates the extremes
of Fletcher's range and, at the same time, the analogies which relate
these extremes. Tom is as Protean a character as Cellide; his feigned
illness parallels Francisco's true love-melancholy; his disgust when he
finds himself in bed with a blackamoor instead of Mary is the comic
equivalent of Francisco's revulsion when Cellide plays the wanton.
The characters in both plots are from the same social milieu (Mary is
Valentine's niece) and all speak at times the language of polite conversation, but with frequent slips into broad vulgarity or into the
stylized speech of romance.

The many similarities between the main plot and *The Faithful Shepherdess* or *Philaster* are partially explained by the source of the story of Cellide, Valentine, and Francisco, which is the "Histoire de Celidée, Thamire et Calidon" in the second part of *L'Astrée,* a pastoral romance by Honoré d'Urfé. Although Fletcher has added complications to the story, such as the concealed relation of Valentine and Francisco, which provides him with the solution of his entanglement, it is not surprising that in working on the sort of material which inspired his first tragicomedies he should produce something very similar here.

3. Romantic Comedies

Love's Pilgrimage (1616—Beaumont, Fletcher, Jonson?), *The Pilgrim* (1621—Fletcher), *Beggars' Bush* (1622—Fletcher, Massinger, Beaumont?), *The Sea-Voyage* (1622—Fletcher and Massinger), *The Spanish Curate* (1622—Fletcher and Massinger), *The Maid in the Mill* (1623—Fletcher and Rowley), *The Chances* (1625—Fletcher), *Love's Cure* (1625—Massinger, Beaumont? Fletcher? Jonson?).[8]

The comedies of trickery are notably unlike tragicomedy in their gaiety, though many of the comedies in that group are analogous to tragicomedies in certain respects. In the mixed comedies the gaiety is much less apparent, sometimes confined to one plot. Tempering it and often dominating large sections of the plays is an emotional emphasis approaching that of the tragicomedies. Along with the "lively touches of passion" other characteristics of the pattern of tragicomedy are so clearly discernible that certain scenes of these plays could be transplanted without change into a tragicomedy. However, in spite of some remarkably vicious characters (in *The Captain,* for instance), the atmosphere of the mixed comedies is not evil.

In the romantic comedies the pattern of tragicomedy predominates. In these plays, as in several of the early ones, the conventions of pastoral are occasionally combined with those of romance. Less frequently the formality of the masque contributes to the removal of the play from the everyday world. Where romance, pastoral, and masque combine, these later plays follow in a direct line from those in which the pattern of tragicomedy begins to take shape—from *The Faithful Shepherdess* and *Cupid's Revenge.*

If the comedies of trickery take place in a world rather more familiar than that of *A King and No King,* the romantic comedies go to the

8. The date of the last play has been the subject of wide disagreement. Thorndike and Oliphant suggest 1605, though the later date is made more likely by the resemblance of this play to the others in the group, all of which can be ascribed with some certainty to the period 1616–25. They are all called comedies in the Second Folio, though some of them are almost indistinguishable from tragicomedy.

opposite extreme. The links with actuality are even less apparent than in the average tragicomedy. The world of these plays is a world of banished dukes, disguised princesses, mistaken identities, and adventurous peregrinations—a world more familiar to the seventeenth-century audience than to us, but at any time a storyteller's world. The most improbable of life's possibilities are the stock in trade of these stories. However, this world of romantic fantasy is more closely related to the world of tragicomedy than is the world of the comedies of trickery. Its remoteness is largely due to extravagant hypotheses and extreme situations such as are found in the Greek romances and, earlier still, in the Senecan declamations. Thus the tradition of Sophistic oratory, which is fundamental in the pattern of Fletcherian tragicomedy, is conspicuous in the plots and the characterization of the romantic comedies.

The differences between romantic comedy and tragicomedy are very slight in *The Maid in the Mill,* whose plot is derived from a Spanish romance. As in several of the romantic comedies, a family feud underlies the main complication and divides the characters into the adherents of the family of Julio or the family of Belides. The fatal love of a girl of one family and a man of another provides the ideal situation for tragicomedy—the danger and the chance of reconciliation. The plot of *Gerardo, the Unfortunate Spaniard,*[9] which Fletcher and Rowley used, is particularly well suited to the Fletcherian pattern, since, by giving the heroine a female cousin and the hero a male friend, it suggests a series of symmetrical contrasts. Ismenia and Antonio are the noble protagonists, while Aminta, who also falls in love with Antonio, and Martine, who also falls in love with Ismenia, are lustful intriguers. They are punished by a misunderstanding which results in their seducing each other instead of their intended victims. *Romeo and Juliet* and satirical comedy are equally implicit in the story.

Though romance and satire combine, romance is predominant—romance of the sort most characteristic of Beaumont and Fletcher. The tone of *The Maid in the Mill* is determined by the combination of pastoral romance and masque. When the four principal characters leave the city where they first meet for the country estate of Julio, their affairs are, so to speak, transposed into another key. Here, in the course of "country sports," Ismenia and Aminta appear as goddesses in a masque and Antonio and Martine, without recognizing them, are smitten again. The subplot, which may have been suggested by a story in Painter's *The Palace of Pleasure,* reinforces the pastoral atmosphere with the story of Count Otrante, who, in the midst of songs and disguisings, tries to seduce Florimell, the miller's daughter. When he is vanquished by her chastity and offers marriage, he discovers that she

9. The English translation (1622) by Leonard Digges of a romance by Gonzalo de Cespedes y Meneces.

is in reality no maid in the mill but the lost daughter of Julio. Everything that happens in the country, no matter how serious, takes on the festive atmosphere of a sheepshearing, and the most sinister plots dissolve in the presence of pastoral virtue. Even the family feud is ended on Julio's estate with a round of betrothals. The promise of a wedding feast is merely the culmination of the country sports which dominate the entire comedy.

Florimell's final defense of herself—a typically Fletcherian tour de force—is emblematic of *The Maid in the Mill*. When several stirring appeals to the honor and pity of the lustful count have failed, Florimell stuns him by the unexpected affectation of wantonness. But, not limiting herself to shocking conversation, she sings Otrante a series of five songs, as gay as they are erotic:

I

Now having leisure, and a happy wind,
Thou mayst at pleasure cause the stones to grind,
Sayls spread, and grist here ready to be ground,
Fie, stand not idlely, but let the Mill go round.

2

How long shall I pine for love?
   how long shall I sue in vain?
How long like the Turtle-Dove
   shall I heav[i]ly thus complain?
Shall the sayls of my love stand still?
   Shall the grists of my hopes be unground?
Oh fie, oh fie, oh fie,
Let the Mill, let the Mill go round.

3

On the bed Ile throw thee, throw thee down;
   Down being laid, shall we be afraid
To try the rights that belong to love?
   No, no, there I'll woe thee with a Crown,
   Crown our desires, kindle the fires,
When love requires we should wanton prove,
   We'll kiss, we'll sport, we'll laugh, we'll play,
     If thou com'st short, for thee I'll stay,
   If thou unskilful art [the] ground,
     I'll kindly teach, we'll have the Mill go round.

4

Think me still in my Fathers Mill,
   where I have oft been found-a
Thrown on my back, on a well-fill'd sack,
   while the Mill has still gone round-a:

Prethe sirrah try thy skill,
   and again let the Mill go round-a.

5

The young one, the old one, the fearful, the bold one,
   the lame one, though nere so unsound,
The Jew or the Turk, have leave for to work,
   the whilst that the Mill goes round.

v, ii; Cam., 7, 61–4

The situation, compounded of lust and love, reflects in a single image the contrasting affairs of the two other pairs of lovers. The language of the songs reflects both the sophistication of the well-bred characters and the coarseness of the rustics. The mill, which is part of the idyllic setting of the play, becomes also a symbol for sexual license and Florimell presents herself not as the paragon of chastity, which she is, but as the miller's daughter of ribald anecdote. But the distinctive character of *The Maid in the Mill* (and to a lesser extent of the other romantic comedies) lies in the circumstance that all these juxtapositions receive their ultimate expression in a song.

Since the romantic comedies show the fullest effect of one of the major influences on tragicomedy, they are excellent examples of what happens when that influence is supreme. In general the plots follow a narrative line more directly than does, for example, the plot of *A King and No King,* which is more influenced by the schematization of satire. The situations in which the characters are placed are not less serious than those of tragicomedy but they lack immediacy. Dominated by the remoteness of pastoral romance, the emotional content of the plays tends toward pathos and sentimentality rather than intense passion. Without the satirist's deliberate, sensational exaggeration of evil, the atmosphere of the romantic comedies is comparatively sunny.

One comedy of the group, *Beggars' Bush,* differs so much from the others that it must be considered apart from them. Signs of the romance tradition abound : the hero and heroine are a prince and princess in disguise, the villain is a tyrannical usurper, and the plot is a tale of improbable adventure. Again the pastoral element is important, but it appears in an unexpected form which constitutes one of the distinctive features of the play. The rag, tag, and bobtail of beggars, outlaws, and petty thieves are shown to be so superior to the corrupt officials in command of the state that, like Robin Hood and his men, they become the champions of the ideal. Their life in the woods is an escape from the evils of "civilized" existence to a community founded on the simple virtues. The beggars, it seems, have hearts as golden as those of shepherds, and their "king" is a persecuted nobleman who has disguised himself as a beggar, just as Musidorus disguises himself as a shepherd.

Their song on the occasion of the crowning of the "King of the Beggars" is a perfect expression of their jolly renunciation of the world:

Cast our Caps and cares away: this is Beggars Holy-day,
At the Crowning of our King, thus we ever dance and sing.
In the world look out and see: where's so happy a Prince as he?
Where the Nation live so free, and so merry as do we?
Be it peace, or be it war, here at liberty we are,
And enjoy our ease and rest; To the field we are not prest;
Nor are call'd into the Town, to be troubled with the Gown.
Hang all Officers we cry, and the Magistrate too, by;
When the Subsidie's encreast, we are not a penny Sest.
Nor will any go to Law, with the Beggar for a straw.
All which happiness he brags, he doth owe unto his rags.

                                    II, i; Cam., *2, 224*

The perversity of glorifying the beggars' life in this fashion is not overlooked. The note of irony may not be evident in this song, taken from its context, but it is heard distinctly in the oration of Higgen on the same occasion. Coming to the subject of the king's beard, he declaims:

This is the beard, the bush, or bushy-beard,
Under whose gold and silver raign 'twas said
So many ages since, we all should smile
On impositions, taxes, grievances,
Knots in a State, and whips unto a Subject,
Lye lurking in this beard, but all kemb'd out:
If now, the Beard be such, what is the Prince
That owes the Beard? a Father; no, a Grand-father;
Nay the great Grand-father of you his people.
He will not force away your hens, your bacon,
When you have ventur'd hard for't, nor take from you
The fattest of your puddings: under him
Each man shall eat his own stolen eggs, and butter,
In his own shade, or sun-shine, and enjoy
His own dear Dell, Doxy, or Mort, at night
In his own straw, with his own shirt, or sheet,
That he hath filch'd that day, I, and possess
What he can purchase, back, or belly-cheats
To his own prop: he will have no purveyers
For Pigs, and poultry.

                        II, i; Cam., *2, 223*

This obviously is an exercise of rhetorical ingenuity, the object being to contrive the highest praise of an unpromising subject. To the humor of this familiar device is added the humor of Higgen's lapses from the style he affects. His speech is a mock oration by a mock orator. However, this humor at the expense of the rustics and at the expense of rhetoric itself merely emphasizes the fact that in *Beggars' Bush* the pastoral ideal is sustained by a feat of rhetoric. Laughing at itself the whole time, the play almost persuades us against the dictates of common sense that the only happy life is the beggars'.

What differentiates this comedy still more from the other comedies is the emphasis on the evil of the world from which the beggars, real and pretended, are escaping. The play opens with an account of the wars in Flanders, followed immediately by an interview between Wolfort, the usurping earl, and Hubert, an honest and outspoken lord:

> *Hub.* I know my flight hath forfeited my head;
> And so I may make you first understand
> What a strange monster you have made your self,
> I welcome it.
> *Wol.* To me this is strange language.
> *Hub.* To you? why what are you?
> *Wol.* Your Prince and Master,
> The Earl of *Flanders*.
> *Hub.* By a proper title!
> Rais'd to it by cunning, circumvention, force.
> Blood, and proscriptions.
>
> . . .
>
> do not stop your ears,
> More are behind yet.
> *Wol.* O repeat them not,
> 'Tis Hell to hear them nam'd.
> *Hub.* You should have thought,
> That Hell would be your punishment when you did them,
> A Prince in nothing but your princely lusts,
> And boundless rapines.
>
> I, i; Cam., *2*, 211, 213

In Hubert's words there is the *saeva indignatio* of the virtuous satirist, confronted with rampant vice. It makes an initial impression which is not dispelled by the jokes and songs of the beggars in later scenes of the play. The immediacy of this evil world is reinforced by the use of names which actually occur in the history of the Netherlands and hence give an illusion of historical veracity. For instance, in J. F. Petit's *Generall Historie of All the Netherlands* (tr. E. Grimestone, 1608), in the account of thirteenth-century Holland (p. 66) there are Count Floris, Herman, Marguerite, Wolfard, and Gerard of Heemskerke, corresponding to Earl Florez, Herman, Margaret, Wolfort, Gerrard, and Hempskirke in the play. One or two incidents of history are vaguely suggestive of incidents in the play but do not constitute the source of the story, which is more likely to be a romance.

The situation in *Beggars' Bush* is not unlike that in *Philaster* except that Florez, the rightful heir to the throne, has been brought up unaware that he is the son of Gerrard, the consort of the late countess. The action of the play is based on the attempt of Wolfort and his henchman Hempskirke to find and kill Florez and his father Gerrard, who is disguised as the king of the beggars. Thanks largely to Hubert, this plot is foiled, Florez is put on the throne and is married to the girl he loves, whom he discovers to be the daughter of the duke of Brabant. The ending, like the beginning, is pure tragicomedy.

As the underlying situation of *Beggars' Bush* is more immediate than that of *The Maid in the Mill,* so the dilemmas of the characters are more compelling. When Gerrard in his disguise tells Florez to give up Gertrude, the hero's plight is projected in a more passionate speech than most of those found in the romantic comedies:

> Is she a thing then to be lost thus lightly?
> Her mind is ten times sweeter, ten times nobler,
> And but to hear her speak, a Paradise,
> And such a love she bears to me, a chaste love,
> A vertuous, fair, and fruitful love: 'tis now too
> I am ready to enjoy it; the Priest ready, *Clause,*
> To say the holy words shall make us happy,
> This is a cruelty beyond mans study,
> All these are ready, all our joyes are ready,
> And all the expectation of our friends,
> 'Twill be her death to do it.
> IV, v; Cam., 2, 267

As in the tragicomedies, the resources of Fletcher's rhetoric are put at the disposal of the actor, as a vehicle of impassioned declamation. There are fewer of these highly emotional scenes than in *Philaster* or *A King and No King,* but if this quantitative difference is overlooked, very little separates *Beggars' Bush* from tragicomedy.

4. Henry VIII and the More Historical Tragedies

Henry VIII (1613—Shakespeare and Fletcher), *Bonduca* (1613— Fletcher), *Thierry and Theodoret* (1617—Fletcher, Massinger, Beaumont?), *Sir John Van Olden Barnavelt* (1619—Fletcher and Massinger), *Rollo Duke of Normandy,* or *The Bloody Brother* (1619— Fletcher, Massinger, Jonson? Chapman?), *The False One* (1620—

Fletcher and Massinger), *The Prophetess* (1622—Fletcher and Massinger).[1]

On the fringe of the Beaumont and Fletcher plays are a few tragedies
which approach what a critic of the Renaissance expected of a tragedy,
just as there are a few comedies which approach what he expected of a
comedy. Not that all critics agreed on these matters, but it was generally accepted that comedy should amuse by its depiction of ordinary
people, while tragedy should arouse pity and terror by its depiction of
the suffering of princes and nobles. The plot of tragedy need not necessarily end in disaster, for even Aristotle had recognized a variety of
tragedy which ends happily (a point of which the defenders of tragicomedy made much). But the favored pattern for tragedy is indicated in
Puttenham's phrase, "the dolefull falles of infortunate & afflicted
Princes."[2] Many of the Italian critics insisted upon another difference
between comedy and tragedy, that, as Trissino put it, "while in tragedy
the actions and names are true, either all or the greater part, in comedy
the actions and names are all invented by the poet . . ."[3] In general
those plays in the Beaumont and Fletcher canon which present history
the most faithfully are in every way closest to the ideal of tragedy and
are the least affected by the pattern of tragicomedy. The sense of history is a strong link with actuality, corresponding to the careful imitation of the manners of everyday life which dominates some of the most
purely comic of the comedies. The less historical tragedies—those
founded on romantic tales—are the counterparts of the romantic
comedies. They come very near the tragicomic norm.

Henry VIII is the only chronicle history in which Fletcher collaborated. Since many history plays contain the elements of tragedy, it is
not surprising to find in the prologue:

> I come no more to make you laugh. Things now
> That bear a weighty and a serious brow,
> Sad, high, and working, full of state and woe,
> Such noble scenes as draw the eye to flow,
> We now present. Those that can pity, here
> May (if they think it well) let fall a tear:
> The subject will deserve it. Such as give

---

1. Fletcher's participation in *Henry VIII* is generally but not universally accepted.
See Kittredge, *The Complete Works of Shakespeare,* p. 837. Both authorship and date of
The Bloody Brother are debatable; J. D. Jump, the latest editor, agreeing with most
critics that Fletcher and Massinger wrote most of the play, assigns portions to Jonson
and Chapman. He presents convincing evidence for a date of 1624–25. See *Rollo Duke
of Normandy,* ed. J. D. Jump (London, University Press of Liverpool, Hodder &
Stoughton, 1948), pp. xxv–xxx.
2. "The Arte of English Poesie," G. G. Smith, *2,* 27.
3. "Poetica," in Gilbert, *Literary Criticism,* p. 225.

Their money out of hope they may believe,
May here find truth too.

    .   .   .

Be sad, as we would make ye. Think ye see
The very persons of our noble story
As they were living. Think you see them great,
And follow'd with the general throng, and sweat
Of thousand friends. Then, in a moment, see
How soon this mightiness meets misery.
        Prologue, ll. 1–9, 25–30[4]

Here are to be presented the *casus virorum illustrium,* both true and pitiful. In the treatment of this tragic material can be seen several of the characteristics which distinguish Fletcher as a tragedian.

Among Shakespeare's history plays *Henry VIII* is conspicuous for its disunity. As the crowd of notable historical personages parades before us, our attention is drawn first to Buckingham, then to Queen Katherine and Wolsey, and finally to Cranmer. No theme unites their successive stories except that most general of tragic themes: how are the mighty fallen! And even this unifying principle does not apply to Cranmer, who narrowly escapes the dismal fate of the other three and ends the play with the triumphant prophecy of the Elizabethan glories to come.

One substitute for continuity in this play is the impressive amount of pageantry. The King and his nobles enter and leave in state to the accompaniment of hautboys, trumpets, cornets, drums, and (to the destruction of the Globe) cannon. In the first act is Wolsey's banquet, to which the King and his company come "as Maskers, habited like shepherds"; in the second, the elaborately staged trial of Katherine; in the fourth, the coronation of Anne Bullen and Katherine's vision; and in the fifth, the christening of Elizabeth. The play is a series of magnificent shows, perfectly suited to the character of the titular hero but tending to make the chronicle even more like a masque than like a tragedy. Whether or not this preponderance of spectacular effect was due to Fletcher, it was a technique with which he was quite familiar, as we know from his other plays.

The high points of the play are generally conceded to Fletcher,[5] and though these scenes have not the extreme tension of his tragicomedies, they are marked by the sort of eloquent speeches on which he relies habitually for his biggest effects. Wolsey's farewell is the most memo-

---

4. All references to *Henry VIII,* which was not printed in the Second Folio, are to *The Complete Works of Shakespeare,* ed. Kittredge.

5. Kittredge, *The Complete Works of Shakespeare,* p. 837, assigns to Fletcher virtually all except I, i and ii; II, iii and iv; the first 203 lines of III, ii; and v, i.

rable thing in the play; Buckingham also has a moving farewell, the
Queen some spirited and some pathetic speeches, and Cranmer his re-
sounding prophecy. Since the narrative complications are relatively
slight, the play seems, even more than other Fletcherian plays, a vehicle
for declamation. Fluent rhetoric is its lifeblood.

The character of the play and of a good deal of Fletcherian tragedy
stands out in these speeches. Buckingham, who is portrayed as an innocent victim of Wolsey's scheming, has three long speeches of which
the following lines are typical:

> You few that lov'd me
> And dare be bold to weep for Buckingham,
> His noble friends and fellows, whom to leave
> Is only bitter to him, only dying,
> Go with me like good angels to my end;
> And, as the long divorce of steel falls on me,
> Make of your prayers one sweet sacrifice
> And lift my soul to heaven. Lead on, a God's name!
>
> .   .   .
>
> My vows and prayers
> Yet are the King's and, till my soul forsake me,
> Shall cry for blessings on him. May he live
> Longer than I have time to tell his years!
>
> .   .   .
>
> Henry the Eighth life, honour, name, and all
> That made me happy, at one stroke has taken
> For ever from the world.
>
> .   .   .
>
> The last hour
> Of my long weary life is come upon me.
> Farewell!
> And when you would say something that is sad,
> Speak how I fell. I have done; and God forgive me!
>
> II, i, 71–8, 88–91, 116–8, 132–6

Buckingham emphasizes his fall from high estate: whereas he was Lord
High Constable and Duke of Buckingham, he is now merely "poor
Edward Bohun." This theme is stated even more fully by Wolsey, the
archintriguer, when he, in his turn, is brought down:

> Nay then, farewell!
> I have touch'd the highest point of all my greatness,
> And from that full meridian of my glory
> I haste now to my setting. I shall fall

Like a bright exhalation in the evening,
And no man see me more.

. . .

Farewell, a long farewell, to all my greatness!
This is the state of man: to-day he puts forth
The tender leaves of hopes; to-morrow blossoms
And bears his blushing honours thick upon him;
The third day comes a frost, a killing frost,
And when he thinks, good easy man, full surely
His greatness is a-ripening, nips his root,
And then he falls, as I do.

. . .

I know myself now, and I feel within me
A peace above all earthly dignities,
A still and quiet conscience. The King has cur'd me—
I humbly thank his Grace—and from these shoulders,
These ruin'd pillars, out of pity taken
A load would sink a navy—too much honour.
O 'tis a burden, Cromwell, 'tis a burden
Too heavy for a man that hopes for heaven!

. . .

And when I am forgotten, as I shall be,
And sleep in dull cold marble, where no mention
Of me more must be heard of, say I taught thee—
Say Wolsey, that once trod the ways of glory
And sounded all the depths and shoals of honour,
Found thee a way (out of his wrack) to rise in—
A sure and safe one, though thy master miss'd it.
Mark but my fall and that that ruin'd me.
Cromwell, I charge thee, fling away ambition!

III, ii, 222–7, 351–8, 378–85, 432–40

Though Buckingham and Wolsey are presented as totally different sorts of men, their farewells are surprisingly similar. The likeness is not explained by the source of the play, Holinshed's *Chronicle,* which contains suggestions for Buckingham's speech but not for Wolsey's. Nor is the likeness made probable by the circumstance that Wolsey has repented of his evil ways at the end. The truth is that these two dissimilar men conform to a stereotype in their final moments. Each one appears as the pitiable victim of forces largely exterior to him. Wolsey, to be sure, confesses to his ambition, but his remarks on "the state of man" and especially his metaphor of the frost which "nips his root" generalize his plight to the vanishing point of personal responsibility and give his tragedy the inevitability of a seasonal phenomenon. Both speeches owe much of their feeling to the conventional concept of Fortune's wheel, which is at the center of medieval tragedy.

Brought face to face with the inevitable, Wolsey is every bit as noble as Buckingham in the acceptance of his fate and in undying loyalty to the King. Both men approach death like model Christians, with their eyes fixed firmly on transcendental values. This lofty nobility is the chief ingredient of Buckingham's heroism and the only ingredient of Wolsey's. The ultimate intention of these speeches, which have such a dying fall, is to persuade us of the pathetic discrepancy between the fate of the two men and their innate nobility and to elicit by a generalized presentation a general response to the waste of potential. The effect is well enough prepared in the case of Buckingham by early scenes in which Wolsey's plots against him are revealed. What is striking is the attempt to secure the same effect in the case of the man responsible for the misfortunes of Buckingham. The success of the venture rests entirely upon rhetoric.

It was recognized in the Renaissance that the heroes of epic and romance and tragedy should be lifted above the level of ordinary humanity, and in seventeenth-century drama we begin to meet heroes who seem to reflect this awareness by their determination to assume their heroic responsibilities. In other words, we meet certain characters who appear to be playing the role of hero. They are the characters who set the tone of heroic drama in the Restoration. But even Buckingham and Wolsey give something of this impression by their noble eloquence in the last dramatic moments of their lives. Wolsey in particular seems, like other Fletcherian characters, to be assuming a role, and an unexpected one. The part of the tragic hero, noble and pathetic victim, awaits Wolsey as it does Buckingham. It is fully prepared; they need only speak the lines. In the most tragic of Fletcher's tragedies we meet this same role and in those which verge on tragicomedy its outlines are still visible. Amintor's nobility is determined by a similar conception of the tragic hero.

The codification of literary criticism is partly responsible for the growth of this standard tragic hero, and both romance and pastoral with their powerful idealization influence the direction of the growth. But another considerable influence upon Fletcher's eloquent heroes is that of the classical declamation. Not only are the great speeches of such a play as *Henry VIII* examples of oratorical art but they tend to become dissociated from the speaker, as ends in themselves. Wolsey's farewell speech is less an expression of his individual character than of what a hero might be expected to feel at the moment of his downfall. As such, the speech closely resembles a rhetorical exercise. Its value to the play consists in rendering an intense theatrical moment.

History made Katherine of Aragon a dignified and pathetic figure, easily adaptable to the tragic pattern we have been considering. Shakespeare, in handling her moving defense of herself against the King and Wolsey, follows even the wording of Holinshed. Out of the arguments recorded by the chronicler he contrives her speeches in blank verse where rhythmical freedom is combined with a kind of toughness and density:

> Sir, call to mind
> That I have been your wife in this obedience
> Upward of twenty years and have been blest
> With many children by you. If in the course
> And process of this time you can report,
> And prove it too, against mine honour aught,
> My bond to wedlock, or my love and duty,
> Against your sacred person, in God's name
> Turn me away, and let the foul'st contempt
> Shut door upon me, and so give me up
> To the sharp'st kind of justice.
>
> II, iv, 34–44

In a scene usually ascribed to Fletcher, where Katherine's role in history is exploited more directly for its emotional effect, the verse is again more declamatory, impelled by more insistent rhythms, and decorated with conspicuous if unoriginal imagery:

> Would I had never trod this English earth
> Or felt the flatteries that grow upon it!
> Ye have angels' faces, but heaven knows your hearts.
> What will become of me now, wretched lady?
> I am the most unhappy woman living.
> Alas, poor wenches, where are now your fortunes?
> Shipwrack'd upon a kingdom where no pity,
> No friends, no hope, no kindred weep for me,
> Almost no grave allow'd me! Like the lily
> That once was mistress of the field and flourish'd,
> I'll hang my head and perish.
>
> III, i, 143–53

In her death scene (IV, ii) Fletcher emphasizes her noble forgiveness of her enemies and devises yet another farewell speech. Katherine assumes the discarded robes of Buckingham and Wolsey. If the division of labor between Fletcher and Shakespeare is that commonly accepted, with all the climatic scenes in Fletcher's portion, it is impossible to be entirely fair in comparing the treatment of any one character by the two men. The nature of the scenes necessarily influences the treatment. However, it is undeniably the scenes ascribed to Fletcher which present in the declamatory style the figure of the hero, larger than life, and clothed in a ready-made nobility.

It is also characteristic of Fletcher that the final reference to Wolsey's character takes the form of a debate. Katherine, though wishing that his faults may "lie gently on him," dwells upon his pride, materialism, and hypocrisy. Griffith, with her encouragement, replies with Wolsey's good points, his scholarship, eloquence, and generosity. Both views derive from Holinshed, but from passages separated by several pages. In the play they are juxtaposed so that the good and evil of the man are most dramatically contrasted. Here is a character who, like Arbaces of *A King and No King,* is compounded of extreme opposites and who may appear, as indeed Wolsey does appear on the stage, first in one role, then in the other, with scarcely a transition.

Of all the plays in which Fletcher had a hand, *The False One,* based on the history of Caesar and Cleopatra, comes closest to the tragic norm of his day. The plot has a logical development, not distorted by purely sensational scenes. Though the happy ending makes the tragedy the sort often cited as a precedent for tragicomedy, the evil of the play is convincingly solid, and the emphasis falls upon the temptations to which the protagonists are subjected. The illustrious hero and heroine are (unlike the hero of *Cupid's Revenge*) consistently and rather fully presented and their tragic situation is firmly related to the world in which they live. Septimius, "the false one" who betrays and murders Pompey, serves to focus attention on the theme of honor which unites the play. This is much more than a series of theatrically effective scenes.

And yet, considered as tragedy in relation to other tragedies of the period, *The False One* seems to pretend to more than it in fact possesses. Its great moments are hollow in spite of every merit. The treatment of the two protagonists explains much about this failure. Caesar is first presented at the moment of his meeting with Ptolemy, when Photinus, the evil counselor, offers the conqueror the head of Pompey. Caesar's reaction of horror, dramatically effective in being the exact opposite of the gratitude expected by the Egyptians, establishes the moral superiority of the hero. In his first long speech praise of his Roman enemy is matched by contempt of Egyptian perfidy:

> What poor fate follow'd thee, and pluckt thee on
> To trust thy sacred life to an *Egyptian;*
> The life and light of *Rome,* to a blind stranger,
> That honorable war ne'r taught a nobleness,
>
> II, i; Cam., 3, 319

Somewhat later he says to Ptolemy:

And study not with smooth shews to invade
My noble Mind as you have done my Conquest.

II, i; Cam., 3, 320

"Noble" and "honorable" are the key words. Caesar is as honorable as
the traitor Septimius, corrupted by Photinus, is dishonorable, and the
contrast is pointed up by the speeches of Septimius in the scene immediately following the first appearance of Caesar. For Septimius gold is "the
Lord I serve, the Power I worship," which makes him honorable no
matter what heinous crimes he commits. The irony is unmistakable.

The first suggestion of ambiguity in Caesar's character is given in the
soliloquy (II, iii; Cam., *3, 325*) where he regrets his civil wars. He
blames himself for his ambition, thinks sadly of Cato and other Romans
whom he has made his enemies, and ends by characterizing himself an
"honorable rebel." Here is a human failing—the hint of a tragic flaw—
but the impression it makes is counterbalanced by the patent nobility of
the hero's self-reproach. He remains honorable after all.

Caesar's reflections are interrupted by the arrival of Cleopatra in a
"packet," carried in by the bluff captain Scaeva. The presentation of the
heroine is an antiphon of coarse, soldierly observations from Scaeva and
enraptured comments from Caesar:

Caes. What heavenly Vision! do I wake or slumber?

.   .   .

Sce. A tempting Devil, o' my life;

.   .   .

A Spunge, a Spunge to wipe away your Victories:
And she would be cool'd, Sir, let the Souldiers trim her!

.   .   .

Caes. But that I see her here, and hope her mortal,
I should imagine some celestial sweetness,
The treasure of soft love.

II, iii; Cam., 3, 326–7

The contrast recalls *Antony and Cleopatra,* but instead of developing
gradually as in Shakespeare's tragedy, it is compressed into one scene
and, in the process, greatly sharpened and simplified. Here there is no
Enobarbus to weigh seductiveness and greatness or to suggest infinite
complexities; the loss is incalculable. Fletcher's contrast (for the scene
is probably his), brilliant and finite, presents us with a goddess and a
whore. And it soon becomes clear that Scaeva's opinion is merely a foil
for Caesar's intuitive perception of the nobility of Cleopatra, for, despite
her scheming, the heroine of *The False One* has nothing of the hoyden in

her. She has much more in common with the dignified enchantress of
All for Love, but even Dryden's Cleopatra is more wicked.

The characters of both Caesar and Cleopatra are developed by the
spectacular incident of Ptolemy's attempt to impress Caesar with the
wealth of Egypt. It is another scene of contrast, but now the contrast is
most insistently made between Cleopatra and Egyptian materialism.
Ptolemy has planned the show to distract Caesar from his sister, and as
the treasure is brought in, Cleopatra tries in vain to retain Caesar's attention. After a masque of Isis and Nilus celebrating the fertility of
Egypt, Caesar leaves with the words: "The wonder of this wealth so
troubles me, / I am not well: good night." (III, iv; Cam., *3*, 343.) In this
way another doubt is thrown upon the character of the hero, but the
heroine is put on the side of the angels. She is disappointed in Caesar not
only because he has neglected her but because:

> He is no man:
> The shadow of a Greatness hangs upon him,
> And not the vertue: he is no Conquerour,
> H'as suffer'd under the base dross of Nature:
> Poorly delivered up his power to wealth,
> (The god of bed-rid men) taught his eyes treason
> Against the truth of love:
> > IV, ii; Cam., *3,* 346

When Cleopatra confronts Caesar directly her nobility is made unmistakable, and also her ideal for Caesar:

> You flung me off, before the Court disgrac'd me,
>
> .   .   .
>
> Gave all your thoughts to gold, that men of glory,
> And minds adorn'd with noble love, would kick at:
> Souldiers of royal mark, scorn such base purchase:
> Beauty and honour are the marks they shoot at;
> > IV, ii; Cam., *3,* 349

But Caesar's defection is only temporary. The last act shows him once
more his noble self, defending Cleopatra against all calumny and finally
setting the crown of Egypt on her head. He is, in her words, "all honour."

Honor and nobility. Precisely what virtues are implied by these
terms, reiterated from the beginning to the end of the play? We seem to
be closest to a definition in the first act and again in the fifth (both of
which were probably written by Massinger). When Achoreus has ad-
vised Ptolemy to keep his faith with Pompey, Photinus makes a
Machiavellian distinction between honor and policy:

> *Achoreus* (great *Ptolomy*) hath counsell'd
> Like a Religious, and honest man,

Worthy the honour that he justly holds
In being Priest to *Isis:* But alas,
What in a man, sequester'd from the world,
Or in a private person, is prefer'd,
No policy allows of in a King,
To be or just, or thankfull, makes Kings guilty,
And faith (though prais'd) is punish'd that supports
Such as good Fate forsakes:

I, i; Cam., *3, 309*

A similar distinction is implied in Caesar's paradoxical term for himself, an "honorable rebel," and in his choice of Cleopatra rather than
gold, but honor remains, nevertheless, a most inclusive virtue. Cleopatra gives the essence of her conception of honor and nobility when
she defies fortune, asserting that she is still herself and that whatever
happens her mind will always be free. (v, iv; Cam., *3,* 365.) She
touches here upon the Stoical ideal of personal integrity valued by the
Duchess of Malfi or Shakespeare's Troilus and expressed in Polonius'
famous words: "This above all: to thine own self be true." But the
honor of Caesar and Cleopatra is so much more than personal integrity
—it is so stuffed with every virtue—that it becomes an equivalent for
goodness and loses any distinctive character. The hero and heroine
are like the ideal characters of romance, where honor is also a most
inclusive term. It is, so to speak, the moral qualification of a hero. To
say that Caesar and Cleopatra are honorable is to say little more than
that they are heroic.

Thus the meaning of honor in the play is extremely vague and yet
suggestive of all that is highest and best. It is closely associated with
nobility, that other indefinable quality constantly referred to. Once the
breadth and haziness of these key concepts are recognized, it is not difficult to see why the tragedy as a whole is disappointing. Caesar and
Cleopatra, paragons of honor and nobility, conform to a general notion
of what is heroic rather than being truly particularized. Because their
virtue is so comprehensive, the efforts of their enemies seem not only
despicable but puny. The defense of personal integrity is a theme which
may well evoke pity and terror, especially when the individual is obliged,
like Troilus or the Duchess, to defend his ideal against the superior force
of a materialistic and faithless world. But Caesar and Cleopatra are
much more than a match for Septimius, Photinus, and Ptolemy. Easy
victors over all forms of evil, the hero and heroine are almost super-
human. From the Fletcherian conception of the hero it is a short step
to the "heightened" figure of the Restoration heroic drama.

In Shakespearian and other Jacobean tragic heroes there is often a
contrast between human weakness, even carried to the point of evil-

doing, and an innate spiritual grandeur. Sympathy for the hero and acquiescence in his fall depend upon this duality. The Fletcherian concept is subtly and fatally different. The split has been widened to the point where the fault seems to bear no relation to the rest of the character, while the spiritual grandeur has been augmented and standardized. The fall is almost forgotten in the dazzle of the apotheosis. For this sort of effect a tragedy of prosperous ending, such as *The False One,* is almost as satisfactory a vehicle as the more familiar sort of tragedy. The situations seem calculated to evoke awe and admiration rather than pity and terror.

In practice the spiritual grandeur of the Fletcherian tragic hero is handed over to rhetoric. Here again a distinction must be made. The action of all Jacobean tragedies stops for the crucial declamations of the protagonists, but in Shakespeare the vital movement of the play occurs in these speeches. In Fletcherian tragedy each time the action stops there is a tableau with the protagonists frozen in striking postures. The speeches, like those of the controversiae, give rhetorical expression to firmly established conflicts. The exact content of the speeches becomes less important the more the general intention is taken for granted, until only intensity of feeling counts. In the declamations of Fletcherian tragedy the same general and vague sentiments are made as compelling as possible at every crisis by the persuasive power of rhetoric. In this way the cumulative power of Shakespearian tragedy is lost. In its place is the virtuosity of many dramatic moments in which the nobility of the hero is declaimed.

At their lofty eminence Caesar and Cleopatra assume the roles of hero and heroine like the noble figures of *Henry VIII.* Enough has already been said about the role of the Fletcherian tragic hero to indicate that some of the loss of meaning is due to the uniform pose which each adopts, regardless of his individuality. It is comparable to the official personality of a head of government—something deliberately put on for public appearance. In comedy and tragicomedy a variety of roles gives life to the constantly changing situation, and the discrepancy between character and role can be accepted as entertainment. The suspicion that heroism is a role is fatal to the effect of tragedy. The suffering individual is lost to sight and static contrasts take the place of tragic struggle.

Although the absence of meaning does not deprive tragicomedy of artistic value, tragedy, cut to a similar pattern, turns out to be either poor tragedy or tragicomedy plus death. *Cupid's Revenge* and *The Maid's Tragedy* are so closely related to tragicomedy that it seems a mistake to judge them entirely according to the requirements of tragedy, but *The False One* is close to the norm of tragedy and demands stricter consideration. Interesting as a link in the development of heroic drama, it is an artistic failure. When Fletcher's tragedies are compared to others of the period they are insipid; compared to his good tragi-comedies, they are dull.

The Prophetess, which is called a "tragical history," is considerably further from the tragic norm than *The False One.* An elegant and spectacular play, it contains little to arouse pity or terror. Not only is the ending happy but the force of evil is at no point a match for the beneficent magic of Delphia, the prophetess, whose supernatural powers enable her to play the part of a didactic providence. The remote yet historical setting, the improbable situations, the unsubstantial at-mosphere of evil are all elements in the tragicomic pattern. Together they produce an effect alien to tragedy.

Despite its kinship to tragicomedy, however, *The Prophetess,* like *The Maid in the Mill,* is so dominated by the conventions of pastoral and masque that it lacks the emotional intensity of the typical Fletch-erian tragicomedy. It is unabashedly remote and fantastic from begin-ning to end. In the two remaining historical tragedies the balance of remoteness and immediacy is more nearly what it is in the tragicomedies. *Thierry and Theodoret,* whose plot derives from French history, is in-tense and gripping as *The Prophetess* never is, though *Thierry and Theodoret* is even less true to historical fact. The tragedy is pervaded by factitious sensationalism, but no magic counteracts the persuasive presentation of familiar evils. In *The Bloody Brother* historical truth is again deformed. This tragedy is based upon the lives of Antoninus and Geta, the sons of the Roman emperor Severus, but the scene has been transferred to medieval France, as indicated by the alternate title *Rollo Duke of Normandy.* As the original story has been considerably altered and as Edith, one of the principal characters, is an addition, the connection with history is slight. Yet once again, as in *A King and No King,* there is an illusion of historical reality.

Even more important evidence of the influence of tragicomedy in these two tragedies is the treatment of character and situation. Many years ago A. H. Thorndike pointed out[6] that the prominent character types and many of the situations in *Thierry and Theodoret* have exact parallels in *Cupid's Revenge, Philaster, The Maid's Tragedy,* and *A King and No King*—in the plays in which the pattern of tragicomedy evolves. Two scenes in *Thierry and Theodoret* illustrate the adherence to this pattern. In one, Thierry, the childless king of France, who has been told that he may have children if he sacrifices the first woman he meets coming from the temple of Diana, waits outside the temple. Pres-ently a veiled woman appears to whom he explains why he must kill her. Without protest she agrees to her martyrdom, but as Thierry is about to strike her, she removes her veil, revealing herself to be Ordella,

6. *The Influence of Beaumont and Fletcher on Shakspere,* pp. 109–24.

his wife, whereupon he drops his sword, horrified. Lamb considered this "the finest scene in Fletcher." His comment is interesting in its entirety; after praising the character of Ordella, he continues:

> Yet noble as the whole scene is, it must be confessed that the manner of it, compared with Shakspeare's finest scenes, is slow and languid. Its motion is circular, not progressive. Each line revolves on itself in a sort of separate orbit. They do not join into one another like a running hand. Every step that we go we are stopped to admire some single object, like walking in beautiful scenery with a guide. This slowness I shall elsewhere have occasion to remark as characteristic of Fletcher. Another striking difference perceivable between Fletcher and Shakspeare, is the fondness of the former for unnatural and violent situations, like that in the scene before us. He seems to have thought that nothing great could be produced in an ordinary way. The chief incidents in the Wife for a Month, in Cupid's Revenge, in the Double Marriage, and in many more of his Tragedies, shew this. Shakspeare had nothing of this contortion in his mind, none of that craving after romantic incidents, and flights of strained and improbable virtue, which I think always betrays an imperfect moral sensibility.[7]

Fully aware of the effectiveness of this scene, Lamb points out the characteristic Fletcherian insistence on striking detail, and the extravagance of the situation, which he compares astutely with three other plays, including the tragicomedy *A Wife for a Month*. The resemblance consists in certain of the essential characteristics of the Fletcherian pattern: the situation is a dilemma; it is based upon the ingeniously contrived opposition of characters who in fact love each other; the contrivance is part of an intricate plot whose design dominates the play.

This scene is followed by another in which the manipulation of plot and character is even more remarkable. Martell, a faithful counselor, hopes to set a trap for Brunhalt, the mother of Thierry and Theodoret, and the source of most of the evil in the play. It is she who procures the murder of Theodoret, later assuring Thierry that his brother was a changeling, and it is she who arranges the scene at the temple, hoping that Ordella will be killed. Martell now announces falsely that Ordella has killed herself. In the midst of Thierry's grief for her, his niece Memberge comes to accuse him of the death of Theodoret. Although Thierry is innocent of the crime, he wishes to make some atonement to Memberge, and believing himself a widower and no blood relation to this girl, he offers to make her his queen. However, this runs so contrary to Brunhalt's plans that she confesses to her son that Theodoret was, after all, his own brother. Confronted by this abrupt change of

7. *Specimens of the English Dramatic Poets*, ed. I. Gollancz (London, 1893), *2*, 113.

his painful situation, Thierry refuses to believe his mother. His bitter comment to her emphasizes how dependent the plot is upon the disguise and the pretense of the chief characters:

> You deny'd it
> Upon your oath, nor will I now believe you,
> Your Protean turnings cannot change my purpose.
> <div align="right">IV, i; Cam., <i>10, 57</i></div>

The effect of the scene derives from these "turnings." Even Ordella with her veil and Martell with his well-intentioned lies are Protean characters.

Like *Thierry and Theodoret* and like the most characteristic Fletcherian tragicomedies, *The Bloody Brother* is a series of big scenes, each as surprising as it is appalling. One of these illustrates admirably the nature of the play. Rollo and his brother Otto, on the point of fighting each other for the dukedom, are interrupted by Sophia, their mother, who pleads so eloquently for reconciliation that Rollo offers to divide the country with his brother. Far from satisfied, Sophia pours forth another stream of eloquence:

> Divide me first, or tear me limb by limb,
> And let them find as many several Graves
> As there are villages in *Normandy:*
> And 'tis less sin, than thus to weaken it.
> To hear it mention'd doth already make me
> Envy my dead Lord, and almost Blaspheme
> Those powers that heard my prayer for fruitfulness,
> And did not with my first birth close my womb:
>
> .   .   .
>
> For as 'tis now, 'tis a fair Diamond,
> Which being preserv'd intire, exceeds all value,
> But cut in pieces (though these pieces are
> Set in fine gold by the best work-mans cunning)
> Parts with all estimation: So this Dukedom,
> As 'tis yet whole, the neighbouring Kings may covet,
> But cannot compass; which divided, will
> Become the spoil of every barbarous foe
> That will invade it.
> <div align="right">I, i; Cam., <i>4, 256–7</i></div>

Rymer, comparing this passage with the corresponding one in Herodian's history of Antoninus and Geta, says: "The former speech [in Herodian] seems to show a Woman of great spirit, labouring to contain her passion till she may utter her mind: But this latter seems to present a *well-breath'd* and *practis'd Scold,* who vents her passion and eases her

mind by talking, and can weep and talk everlastingly."[8] Once more the
observation is acute. Sophia, occupying the center of the stage, makes
her impression by weight and fluency of words. It has long been recognized that Massinger, who apparently wrote the scene, drew the inspiration for this speech and for some of the preceding ones from the
speeches of Jocasta in Seneca's *The Phoenician Women* where she
comes between Polynices and Eteocles. This is one of the more declamatory passages in Senecan tragedy and recalls vividly the oratorical
tradition about which the elder Seneca wrote. Thus the scene in *The
Bloody Brother* is like many other scenes in the Beaumont and Fletcher
plays: it grows out of the conflict between Rollo, the usurper, and
his good brother Otto and rises to its climax in the declamation of
Sophia, who is torn by the enmity of her sons. As Rymer was well aware,
there is no question of containing passion here but rather of venting
it artfully and fully. The scene is a powerful dramatization of Sophia's
dilemma.

5. The Less Historical Tragedies

Valentinian (1614—Fletcher), *The Double Marriage* (1620—
Fletcher and Massinger), *The Lovers' Progress* (1623—Fletcher and
Massinger).

The three tragedies in this group are based on largely fictitious nar-
ratives. The plot of *Valentinian,* the most historical of them, has a basis
in the accounts of the Roman emperor by Procopius and others, but
Fletcher seems to have leaned heavily upon the story as told in Honoré
d'Urfé's *L'Astrée,* from which he took the main plot of *Monsieur
Thomas.* History in this case is much colored by romance. Two Senecan
controversiae and a passage of history from Comines furnish the raw
material for *The Double Marriage,* and *The Lovers' Progress* is based
entirely on a romance by Vital d'Audiguier called, significantly, *Histoire
trage-comique de nostre temps, sous les noms de Lysandre & de Caliste*
(1620).

In *The Double Marriage* the pattern of tragicomedy determines all
but the outcome of the play. The historical background and the names
of many of the characters come from Thomas Danett's translation of
The Historie of Philip de Commines (1596). The seventh book contains the story of Ferrand of Naples (Ferrante 1), a tyrant against whom
the barons and princes of the realm rebelled. The description of the
evils of the reign (p. 294) is used by Massinger, sometimes verbatim,
for the speeches in the first act which establish the setting. Yet the plot
of the play is absolutely unhistorical. It is as romantic and improbable

8. *The Tragedies of the Last Age,* p. 52.

as the plot of any Beaumont and Fletcher play. The combination of such a story with the historical setting in the court of a wicked tyrant instantly recalls *Philaster* and *A King and No King*.

The hero is Virolet, described as "a noble gentleman, studious of his country's freedom." His equally noble wife Juliana, to whom he has confided his plan to murder the tyrant, is seized and tortured in an effort to extract information from her, but with heroic fortitude she tells nothing. In the meantime Virolet, who has been captured by a rebel duke, turned pirate, is freed by Martia, the duke's daughter, in return for his promise to marry her. This unusual combination of circumstances leads to as extraordinary a dilemma as any Fletcher ever devised—one which is made the core of the drama.

The nature of this tragedy is largely explained by the fact that its showy plot is derived from two Senecan *Controversiae*, referred to in Chapter III. One (ii. 5) provides the story of Juliana and the tyrant, while the other (i. 6) provides the story of Virolet and Martia. Both present characteristically romantic dilemmas to test the ingenuity of the student of oration, and Fletcher and Massinger, in combining the two, outdo the originals in the contrivance of a difficult and delicate problem and retain the emphasis on eloquence.

In the most effective scene of the play, the wife Juliana, just released from prison, meets Virolet, who, instead of welcoming her, presents her to Martia, whom he praises in the highest terms. After some moments of suspense he explains that he must marry Martia, and his lawyer makes Juliana's barrenness the pretext for a divorce. While Juliana makes a noble renunciation, Virolet's father defends her vehemently and Martia, with equal vehemence, defends Virolet and herself. No sooner have Martia and Virolet been left alone than Martia suggests that they go to bed. Virolet, who has just described her to Juliana as the epitome of goodness, bounty, and nobility, replies to her suggestion with unexpected fury:

> As soon to hell, to any thing I hate most;
> You must excuse me, I have kept my word.
> You are my Wife, you now enjoy my fortune.
> Which I have done to recompence your bounty:
> But to yield up those chast delights and pleasures,
> Which are not mine, but my first vowes
>
> .   .   .
>
> Good heaven forgive; no, no, the strict forbearance,
> Of all those joys, like a full sacrifice,
> I offer to the sufferings of my first love,
> Honor, and wealth, attendance, state, all duty,
> Shall wait upon your will, to make you happy,

> But my afflicted mind, you must give leave Lady,
> My weary Trunk must wander.
>
> III, i; Cam., *6*, 372–3

The occasion, though fantastic, is not beyond what Virolet can rise to oratorically.

Out of this intricate situation the remainder of the plot is evolved. Each of the notable scenes contains an unexpected turn and a sharp contrast between two characters. Martia, revealing the meanness of her true nature, goes to Juliana to propose revenge on Virolet and meets with a haughty rejection. Juliana warns Virolet, who is at first incredulous but is convinced when Martia arrives and insults him. Virolet makes love to Juliana but finds her virtuously determined to abide by the divorce in spite of her passionate love. Martia's father, leading the rebellion against the tyrant, hears of his daughter's conduct and renounces her. Virolet, shamed by the fact that he hasn't taken the initiative against Ferrand, disguises himself as Ronvere, the tyrant's henchman, but meets Juliana who, deceived by the disguise, kills him and immediately dies of grief. Finally Ferrand is killed by the duke, while Martia, who has become Ferrand's mistress, is killed by one of her father's men. By carnage alone the play aspires to tragedy.

The tragic end of Virolet and Juliana is as ironic and as accidental as the death of Aspatia in *The Maid's Tragedy*. It is merely one in the long series of startling incidents. Like Amintor, Virolet remains technically innocent throughout the action, so that his death is not a moral necessity, and he might be saved for Juliana by a turn no more surprising than several I have described. *The Double Marriage* might easily have ended with the repentance of Martia and the banishment of Ferrand. With no basic change in the characters, the tone, or the principles of construction, the play might have become a tragicomedy.

Of the nine tragedies among the later plays and the two among the early ones (*Cupid's Revenge* and *The Maid's Tragedy*)[9] the only three which come close to being straight tragedies, *The False One, Barnavelt,* and *Bonduca,* are so modified by the techniques of characterization and structure used in the tragicomedies that they constitute a new sort of tragedy. They are the precursors of the heroic drama. The rest are, to varying degrees, tragicomic tragedies. It is not a coincidence that the least tragic are also the least historical, for the weakening of the link with actuality is typical of Fletcherian tragicomedy.

Of the twenty comedies among the later plays and the four among the early ones (*The Woman-Hater, The Knight of the Burning Pestle, The Coxcomb,* and *The Woman's Prize*) the relatively large number of

---

9. All these plays are called tragedies in the Second Folio except for *The Prophetess,* which is called a "tragical history," and *Cupid's Revenge,* which is not classified.

ten may be called straight comedies (*The Knight of the Burning Pestle* and *The Woman's Prize* in addition to those later plays which I have listed as comedies of trickery). However, the wit and contrivance of five of these plays, closely resembling certain techniques of tragicomedy, place them in a special category of comedy. The fourteen remaining comedies merge almost imperceptibly into tragicomedy; one or two are comedies in name only.

Seventeen of the Beaumont and Fletcher plays—almost a third of them—are tragicomedies, without counting the one-act plays called *Four Plays, or Moral Representations, in One,* of which one is tragic and three are tragicomic.[1] When these seventeen are added to the tragedies and comedies which closely approach tragicomedy, the total is a very large percentage of all the plays. In the true tragicomedies the pattern that is perceived more or less distinctly in the other plays is unmistakable and is nowhere more conspicuous than in the tragicomedies Fletcher wrote alone. Reserving these for a separate chapter, I shall deal in the following section with the tragicomedies on which he collaborated with others.

6. *Tragicomedies Written in Collaboration*

The Two Noble Kinsmen (1613—Shakespeare and Fletcher), *The Honest Man's Fortune* (1613—Fletcher, Massinger, Field?), *The Queen of Corinth* (1617—Fletcher, Massinger, Field), *The Knight of Malta* (1618—Fletcher, Massinger, Field), *The Laws of Candy* (1619 —Fletcher, Massinger? Ford?), *The Custom of the Country* (1620— Fletcher and Massinger), *The Fair Maid of the Inn* (1626—Fletcher, Massinger, Webster? Ford?), *A Very Woman* (1634—Fletcher and Massinger).[2]

The factors in the comedies and tragedies most responsible for modifying the accepted comic and tragic patterns may be grouped under three

1. Three of the tragicomedies, *The Two Noble Kinsmen, The Knight of Malta,* and *The Custom of the Country,* were unclassified by their first publishers, but *The Two Noble Kinsmen* was entered in the Stationers' Register as a tragicomedy and the other two are obviously such. Although the *Four Plays in One* are interesting miniature examples of the Fletcherian technique, I have not listed them or discussed them with tragedy or tragicomedy, because in spite of the resemblances they are not altogether comparable to the full-length plays. They stand somewhere between masques and plays.

2. Shakespeare's collaboration on *The Two Noble Kinsmen* has been questioned but is now generally accepted. There is very little agreement about the authorship of *The Laws of Candy,* in which some critics even deny Fletcher's participation. The resemblance of the play to other Fletcherian tragicomedies, however, suggests that he had some hand in it, and the fact that the source of the plot is Seneca's *Controversiae,* from which *The Double Marriage* and *The Queen of Corinth* also derive, may strengthen the theory that *The Laws of Candy* is mainly the work of Fletcher and Massinger, who certainly collaborated on the other two. *A Very Woman* may have been written in the years 1619–22 by Fletcher; its final form is apparently due to Massinger, with whose plays it was published.

headings: (1) the weakening of the link with actuality to produce a theatrical imitation of life, neither quite familiar nor entirely remote; (2) the discontinuity of plot which results from sacrificing a single action to a series of situations; and (3) the poses which make many of the protagonists unconvincing or inconsistent, as the case may be. In the tragicomedies these factors operate the more powerfully because they do not conflict with any accepted pattern of the genre; they lead, in fact, to the triumphant assertion of all the characteristics which distinguish Fletcherian tragicomedy. The relation of these three factors to the Fletcherian pattern could be illustrated in any of the tragicomedies—it is already apparent in the early ones—but three of the collaborative plays provide notable examples.

The Queen of Corinth and *The Laws of Candy* rely primarily upon surprise for their effectiveness. The situations with which they deal are, to say the least, out of the ordinary, and they develop in the ways least expected. The most important of the many complications of *The Queen of Corinth* are due to the sensational wickedness of Theanor, the Queen's son, whom she forbids to marry Merione for reasons of state. To revenge himself upon his mother and upon the innocent woman of his choice he rapes Merione but, still not satisfied, attempts to throw the blame on Euphanes, the Queen's favorite, and also plans to rape Beliza, to whom Euphanes is engaged. The outcome of Theanor's grandiose schemes is the *pièce de résistance* of the plot. Merione is induced by friends to disguise herself as Beliza and is raped a second time. Then follows a trial scene in which Beliza and Merione both accuse Theanor of rape, Beliza demanding his death and Merione demanding that he marry her, for the law of the land allows either penalty. After a lively debate the Queen pronounces the sentence of death upon her son, but he is now overwhelmed by a sense of his guilt and determines to restore Merione's honor by marrying her before his execution. At this sign of repentance the ingenious trick is revealed, Theanor is happily united to Merione and Euphanes to Beliza. This sequence of scenes corresponds exactly to the pattern of tragicomedy, as can be seen at a glance, and it illustrates with remarkable clarity the importance to the pattern of a certain kind of plot. The central situation is the fantastic hypothesis that two women raped by the same man demand the incompatible penalties of death and marriage. In order to lead up to this dilemma and to provide a happy solution several other improbable situations are posited. In none of the Beaumont and Fletcher plays does plot dominate more completely and in none is it so clearly derived from improbable hypotheses.

The source of the plot is another of the hypothetical cases provided for the Roman students of oratory—the case described in Chapter III of the ravisher demanded in marriage by one of his victims while the other demands his death (*Controversiae* i. 5). In Seneca as in *The Queen of Corinth* the original hypothesis becomes the basis for many excursions of the imagination and ultimately for rhetorical display. Some of the speeches in the trial scene are modeled closely on the Senecan declamations.[3] To rhetoric and to the shock of a series of unexpected developments is sacrificed the continuity of plot.

The Laws of Candy has a plot whose developments are only slightly less startling. The initial situation, again taken from a Senecan controversia (x. 2),[4] is the conflict of a father and son for the reward offered to the man who has fought most nobly. When the son wins and demands as his reward certain public honors for his father, this generous behavior is countered by the father's furious renunciation of his son. The ensuing plot is intricate but the story of the relations of father and son shows in itself how one surprising turn is followed by another. The princess falls in love with the young man, who agrees to take pity on her if she will pay his father's debts. When she has done so the father comes before the senate to accuse his son of ingratitude (the penalty for ingratitude in Candy being death). The princess immediately accuses the father of ingratitude toward her, and the son completes the triangle by accusing the princess of ingratitude toward him in attacking his father. When the old man's daughter further accuses the entire senate of ingratitude toward her father in not recognizing his service, the old man sees the folly of the situation which he has precipitated and withdraws his charges against his son, whereupon all the other charges are also withdrawn. Once again, when the consequences of the central hypothesis have been pushed to the verge of tragedy, one of the basic assumptions is altered: the father is not after all irreconcilable, just as one of the two women in *The Queen of Corinth* was not after all raped. The hypothesis is dismissed and a happy ending follows the series of tense scenes in which misfortune is always imminent.

Character is surprisingly manipulated as well as plot in these two tragicomedies, but *The Knight of Malta* contains even better examples of the typical poses of the Beaumont and Fletcher protagonists. There are two scenes in which Miranda, the noble hero, acts quite out of character. In the first one (iii, iv) he makes passionate love to Lucinda while her lover Angelo looks on unobserved. Angelo's hopes fall as she seems to succumb to Miranda and then are resurrected by her eloquent defense of chastity which apparently makes him desist. Only when the little drama is finished does Miranda explain that he has been dissembling to try Lucinda's faith. In a similar fashion he later (v, i) tests Oriana, the wife of Gomera, leaving her in tears when he feigns anger at her steadfast refusal of him.

3. See Appendix.   4. See Appendix.

These scenes are from one point of view meretricious. They tease us with seeming indecency while assuring us that there is no overt immorality. The situation is to be relished without fear of any consequences. At the same time these scenes are legitimate parts of a play in which all the behavior is consistently artificial. Like many of the tragicomedies *The Knight of Malta* has a suggestion of historical truth and draws the names of most of its characters from history, but the plot is based on at least one novella and possibly on more that have not been identified. The atmosphere of the play is permeated by romance. Miranda is the perfect embodiment of the code of chivalry which the Knights of Malta represented in fact but even more in fiction. His pursuit of the ideal of honor and his fervent desire that Lucinda and Oriana should be no less than perfect—these, together with his unsurpassed courage on the field of battle, are the attributes of the hero of romance. They belong essentially to literary convention, and in a sense Miranda is always, though unconsciously, playing a part—a part similar to that played by some of the heroes in the Beaumont and Fletcher tragedies. The occasional changes in his role provide effective contrast without much altering the tone or seriously challenging the premises on which the tragicomedy rests. It is all seeming, all playing, though playing with serious ideas. Looked at from this point of view, the scenes I have described, however morally suspect they may be, represent the extension of one of the fundamental principles of tragicomedy, that appearances have an intrinsic importance for the moment but carry no implications for the future. Because *The Knight of Malta* adheres so faithfully to this principle it is one of the best of the tragicomedies.

V

Honor Triumphant: Fletcher's Mature Tragicomedies

THE BEST EXAMPLES of Fletcher's chosen form are the six tragicomedies which he wrote alone during the last ten years of his life: *The Mad Lover* (1617), *The Loyal Subject* (1618), *The Humorous Lieutenant* (1619), *Women Pleased* (1620), *The Island Princess* (1621), *A Wife for a Month* (1624). Although the eight characteristics of the pattern of tragicomedy are present in each of these plays, the mere demonstration of this fact would convey little of their individual quality. In spite of their formal similarity they are unlike in many respects, and it would be false to Fletcher's genius to suggest that his plays resulted from the mechanical application of a formula. In the analyses which follow I shall take the presence of the eight characteristics for granted except in the case of *A Wife for a Month,* the last tragicomedy, where their final manifestations will be briefly noted. The emphasis will fall upon the predominant traits of a particular play and upon its success or failure as an artistic whole. In this way the potentialities of the pattern will become more apparent, for each of the six tragicomedies displays to advantage at least one aspect of Fletcher's singular technique.

1. *The Mad Lover*

"Fooling's the thing, the thing worth all your fightings."

The first scenes of *The Mad Lover* are satirical comedy. Memnon, the "Generals General," the conqueror of untold enemies, returns from his victorious wars "through Storms and Tempests" at the bidding of his King. In his first speech he outstrips even his most ardent admirers in the praise of his achievements and expresses his soldierly contempt for the life at court:

> I have waded through
> Dangers would damp these soft souls, but to hear of.
> The maidenheads of thousand lives hang here Sir,
> Since which time Prince, I know no Court but Marshal,
> No oylie language, but the shock of Arms,
> No dalliance but with death; No lofty measures

> But weary and sad marches, cold and hunger,
> Larums at midnight Valours self would shake at,
> Yet I ne're shrunk:

> i, i; Cam., *3*, 3–4

In this overblown language Memnon reveals his humor, the vainglory of a soldier. And he does so before a highly critical audience, composed of the very courtiers and ladies he professes to despise. Only the King and Memnon's followers listen sympathetically. Calis, the King's sister, with manifest amusement exchanges satirical comments with the women on the great general's pretensions. The contrast is ideally suited to the comic exposition of character.

Scarcely has Memnon been made ridiculous in his capacity of battle-field general at court when he is transformed into another figure of fun, the blunt soldier in love. Seeing Calis, he kneels before her and, to the amusement of both soldiers and ladies, remains there in dumb admiration. During this action the contrast between soldier and courtier, soldier and lover, is heightened by a succession of martial and venereal metaphors from the ladies: "Sure his Lordship's viewing / Our Fortifications. . . . *Venus* grant his valour / Be not in love. . . . Now he begins to march: Madam the *Van*'s yours, / Keep your ground sure; 'tis for your spurrs." And as Memnon kneels he is able to exclaim only, "O *Venus*." (i, i; Cam., *3*, 5.)

This first seizure of Memnon's madness is followed by a conversation between Chilax, a blatantly normal soldier, and the Fool, who maintains the superiority of fooling to fighting. But Memnon's supreme gesture is still to come. Again approaching Calis, he offers her, like a second Tamburlaine, her choice of kingdoms and then, as a climax to all, offers his heart. This is not the empty protestation of the average lover, however. Memnon means to be taken literally. Rising to a height of heroic absurdity, he promises to send his heart to Calis in a golden goblet. At this point Memnon becomes not only a caricature of the soldier in love but a caricature of the romantic lover. The situation is farcical and only at some distance below the surface is there the hint of grotesque tragedy.

Memnon now indulges in splendid mock heroics. His soliloquy at the opening of the second act burlesques the noble contempt of the world expressed by tragic heroes. Memnon is planning the extraction of his heart:

> 'Tis but to dye, Dogs do it, Ducks with dabling,
> Birds sing away their Souls, & Babies sleep 'em,
> Why do I talk of that is treble vantage?
> For in the other World she is bound to have me;
>
> . . .

There love is everlasting, ever young,
Free from Diseases, ages, jealousies,
Bawds, Beldames, Painters, Purgers: dye? 'tis nothing,
Men drown themselves for joy to draw in Juleps
When they are hot with Wine: In dreams we do it.

II, i; Cam., 3, 17

The rhetorical flourish of the speech almost persuades us that it is truly heroic; the ludicrous situation and the occasional expression which is perfectly unsuitable—the dabbling ducks, the purgers, the juleps—provide the bathos necessary to the mock-heroic.

By means of two related devices Fletcher underlines his hero's folly. One is the imitation of Memnon which Chilax gives to the Fool. The other is a situation parallel to Memnon's in which Syphax, one of his soldiers, is also struck dumb by the sight of Calis. His manifestation of love is very different from Memnon's, however, for he decides to have the princess by fair means or foul. Memnon, mad as he is, never deviates from his code of honor.

The third act presents a third lover for Calis in Polydor, who comes to her on behalf of his brother Memnon. He attempts to frighten the princess by presenting her with a goblet containing, as he says, Memnon's heart. Unfortunately for the success of his scheme, the princess falls in love with him and he with her, but he loyally persists in rebuking her for her cruel treatment of his brother. His longest speech to her, though based on a nonexistent situation and though expressing a bitterness he is far from feeling, is the most serious yet given and materially alters the tone of the play:

Live then I say famous for civil slaughters,
Live and lay out your triumphs, gild your glories,
Live and be spoken this is she, this Ladie,
This goodly Ladie, yet most killing beautie;
This with the two edg'd eyes, the heart for hardness
Outdoing rocks; and coldness, rocks of Crystal.

III, i; Cam., 3, 42

This is a speech for the embittered hero of romance, and such is Polydor's role as he pursues his ideal of fraternal loyalty despite his own passions. But at the same time he plays another role similar to that of the satirist in comedy as he attempts by one trick to put Calis out of her humor of disdain and by another to cure his brother of his madness. His device for Memnon, particularly reminiscent of satirical comedy, is to have Cloe, a camp follower, disguise herself as the princess. The deception is so crudely carried out, however, that this trick is no more successful than the other. It is only as a romantic lover that Polydor makes good.

Once again Syphax is put in a situation parallel to Memnon's. He has plotted to have the Priestess of Venus trick the princess into marrying him, but Cloe is put to work again as a substitute for the princess, and Syphax, completely deceived, is married to her. His fate is a prime example of poetic justice, since he was Cloe's original seducer. The homely moral and the touches of farce in the story of Syphax oblige us to see Memnon in a different light, for the general's love is no ordinary love and his madness cannot be cured by any ordinary trick.

Syphax, the foolish soldier who falls in love with a princess, and Polydor, the noble hero with whom a princess falls in love, are the two points of reference in judging Memnon. It is Fletcher's extraordinary achievement to lift Memnon from a level not far above that of Syphax to the height of Polydor and in so doing to change the whole tone of the play from predominantly satiric to predominantly romantic. None of his characters is more brilliantly executed than his "mad lover." Memnon has the qualities of his defects: the logic of the madman, the sincerity of the simple-minded, the imagination of the dreamer. His madness is such that it inspires the utmost nobility in Polydor and even commands respect from Calis. At the end the utter selflessness of the ideal —the truly mad—lover is added to his other qualities.

The denouement is brought about by another trick, when Polydor has himself carried to the princess in a coffin along with a will in which he instructs her to marry Memnon. The situation is ironical, for not only is Memnon's joy at his success in love blotted out by his grief for his brother but also it is cruelly clear to Memnon that while he who longed for death is still alive, Polydor has succeeded in achieving death. Memnon's speech on this occasion, as extravagant as any he makes, is both grotesque and moving:

> O worthy young man!
> O love, love, love, love above recompence!
> Infinite love, infinite honesty!
>
> .   .   .
>
> Brave glorious griefs! was ever such a Brother?
>> v, i; Cam., *3, 71*

When he runs out of rhetoric and tells Calis to speak while he thinks, the situation becomes broadly comic, but it is still not the farce of the opening. Memnon prepares to kill himself in earnest and is only prevented by Polydor, who rises dramatically from the dead to carry on his effort to marry his brother to Calis. But Memnon is so nearly his equal in this contest of generosity that Calis can no longer choose between them. By the criteria of romance it is Memnon who finally wins, for he makes the decisive sacrifice of donning his armor and returning to the wars. He is still essentially a soldier and still, perhaps, a fool in love; yet at the end he seems what he did not seem at the opening, a hero. Through his half-comic, half-serious adventures Fletcher achieves a beautifully articulated piece of fooling with the material of romance and tragedy.

2. The Loyal Subject

"Honours Martyr"

Archas, the general in *The Loyal Subject,* is never for a moment made ridiculous. He is at all times the perfect embodiment of that all-inclusive virtue of honor which figures so largely in romance and in Fletcherian tragedy. Repeatedly attacked and disgraced by the Machiavellian Boroskie, "the enemie to honour, / The knave to worth" (v, vi; Cam., *3,* 168), Archas never flinches in his courage, honesty, humility, and loyalty to his master, the Great Duke of Moscovia. The basic contrast of the play is between the honor of Archas and the materialism of Boroskie. At first glance, then, the play seems much more serious than *The Mad Lover* and more concerned with an important ethical problem than the typical Fletcherian tragicomedy; materialistic corruption is, after all, the theme of some of the greatest Jacobean tragedies. But a closer scrutiny of *The Loyal Subject* reveals that Fletcher's treatment of his basic contrast is characteristic of him. Unlike *The Revenger's Tragedy,* in which the thoughts and emotions generated by a similar problem are given new life in a progression of superbly integrated actions and images, *The Loyal Subject* is a series of spectacular variations on the theme, executed with great ingenuity. The underlying idea is taken for granted and therefore never dealt with seriously. The novelty of the display is all that counts.

What Fletcher has done can better be understood by comparing his play with its sources. The story of *The Loyal Subject* derives from a novella by Bandello, which Painter translated.[1] Fletcher need never have read the story in this form, as he probably knew Thomas Heywood's play, called *The Royal King and the Loyal Subject.*[2] Here he would

1. William Painter, *The Palace of Pleasure* (2d ed., 1575), Tome II, Novel IV; ed. J. Jacobs (London, 1890), *2,* 176–208.

2. Heywood's play was not published until 1637, but most editors have conjectured that it was written about 1600. The "Epilogue to the Reader" seems to support this conclusion, and Fletcher's much wider departures from the Bandello story certainly suggest that his play was written later than Heywood's. Since a number of details in Fletcher's play bear more resemblance to Heywood than to Bandello, it is likely that Fletcher had at least seen a performance of *The Royal King and the Loyal Subject* or quite possibly had read it in manuscript. For discussions of this problem see *The Works of Francis Beaumont and John Fletcher* (Variorum ed.), *3,* 226–7; also E. Dietrich, *Th. Heywoods "The Royal King and the Loyal Subject" und J. Fletchers "The Loyal Subject"* (Königsberg, R. Lankeit, 1916), pp. 15–20, 73–6.

have found the outline and many of the details of the novella used as Heywood's main plot.

Bandello introduces the story by raising a delicate question in the ever delicate matter of Renaissance courtesy: "whether commendable deed, or courteous and gentle fact done by the gentleman or courtier towards his sovereign lord, ought to be called liberality and courtesy, or rather band and duty."[3] Precisely this problem troubles the relationship of Artaxerxes, King of Persia, and his amazingly generous seneschal Ariobarzanes. Bandello shows how in his very liberality Ariobarzanes departs from the "mean, wherein all virtue consisteth," and falls into the vice of prodigality, trying to excel his master. After a series of incidents which reveal this tendency, the king becomes displeased with Ariobarzanes and publicly humiliates him by depriving him of his office and banishing him from court. Another phase of the battle of courtesy is opened when the king requests Ariobarzanes to send to court the fairer of his two daughters. Ariobarzanes, now sly in his methods, sends the less fair of the two with instructions to reveal the deception as soon as she is with child by the king. When this happens and the king angrily sends the daughter home, Ariobarzanes is able to achieve a chef d'oeuvre of liberality by sending back, after a slight delay, both daughters and the infant heir of Artaxerxes. The contamination of Ariobarzanes' virtue becomes more apparent in this section of the story, and the new contention between sovereign and courtier ends even more spectacularly than the former one, when the king, backed by his council, sentences Ariobarzanes to death. The unexpected introduction of a new motif at this point makes possible a happy ending. It is suggested that envious courtiers are partially responsible for holding the king to his strict sentence when he might have weakened. When at the last moment the king offers to pardon Ariobarzanes if he will admit that he is overcome in liberality, Ariobarzanes makes his submission but saves his face by blaming the misunderstanding between his sovereign and himself upon the envious courtiers.

Heywood does not materially alter the outlines of this story, but he changes the scene to England and makes the contest between king and subject more credible to a middle-class audience by stressing the motivating force of the courtiers' envy. With Bandello's story Heywood combines the story of Captain Bonville, a noble young man supposed by the world to have lost his last penny in the wars. In reality he has acquired booty of enormous worth but deliberately (as he later admits) keeps this fact a secret "only to try the humour" of his friends. The theme of true worth as opposed to riches—of spiritual as opposed to material values—is thus introduced and receives an obvious and thorough treatment. The poor Captain is spurned by courtiers, insulted

3. Painter, *Palace of Pleasure*, ed. Jacobs, *2*, 176.

by the Host of a tavern, jeered at by bawds. Only Lady Mary Audley loves him for himself; against her father's wishes she unselfishly agrees to marry him. And not in actions only but in many words throughout the play she demonstrates her attitude. Heywood is not subtle and Lady Mary is as explicit as a character in a morality play:

> Should I despise my hand
> In a torn glove, or taste a poisonous draught,
> Because presented in a cup of gold?
> Virtue will last when wealth flies, and is gone:
> Let me drink nectar, though in earth or stone.
> II, ii[4]

By the time the "royal king" and "loyal subject" are reconciled, Captain Bonville has sufficiently convinced himself of the falseness of all his friends but one and has reappeared in fine clothes amidst general rejoicing. The denouement resolves the plot better than it demonstrates the triumph of virtue.

Fletcher transfers the scene to Russia, presumably making use of the study by his uncle Giles Fletcher, *Of the Russe Common Wealth* (1591). There are several significant departures from Bandello's story. Archas, "the loyal subject," is not a man whose virtue of liberality becomes the vice of prodigality but instead a great general, who is all honor. The word is constantly associated with him. He calls the eagle on his standard a "Bird of honour" (I, iii; Cam., *3*, 84) and praises his soldiers for defying danger "where honour is" (II, i; Cam., *3*, 102); he calls himself "honours Martyr" (IV, v; Cam., *3*, 151), and the Duke concludes the play with the pronouncement:

> he that can
> Most honour *Archas,* is the noblest man.
> v, vi; Cam., *3,* 169

Fletcher alters the initial situation of the story by showing the Duke already bent upon the humiliation of Archas. His antipathy derives from an occasion many years before, when Archas, acting under orders from the former duke, reproved the young man for his failure to draw up the troops properly for review. Fully aware of the Prince's resentment, Archas then vowed to resign his generalship, and the opening scenes of the play present the fulfillment of that vow.

The breach between ruler and subject is kept open by the continual efforts of the evil counselor Boroskie and over the protests of the good counselor Burris. Boroskie, the antithesis of Archas, is cowardly, dishonest, ambitious, and proud. The Duke is a man with a divided charac-

---

4. Thomas Heywood, *The Royal King, and Loyal Subject,* ed. J. Payne Collier (London, 1850), p. 25.

ter—with a "hot humour" which has been fostered since childhood by Boroskie but with a respect for honor which is entirely eclipsed in the early part of the play. Under Boroskie's influence he displays both the sensuality and the greed associated with materialism. At the end, owing to the ministrations of Archas' daughters, the Duke turns dramatically from Boroskie to Archas, and honor triumphs.

A noteworthy departure from Fletcher's sources is his treatment of the family of Archas. To the two daughters of Bandello's story are added two sons and a brother, and each member of the family is made to display Archas' leading characteristic, honor. One daughter, Honora, is militantly honorable; the other, Viola, is retiring as her name suggests but none the less firm in honor. Young Archas, a veritable projection of his father, demonstrates soldierly courage even under the handicap of the feminine disguise which he wears through most of the play. The character of Theodore, the other son, is well summed up in the Dramatis Personae of the Second Folio as "valorous but impatient." Briskie (disguised as Putskie) is Archas' "noble brother" but is not above scheming, for it is he who devises the crafty plan of sending Young Archas to court as a girl, with the twin hopes of protecting the lad from the Duke's wrath and of influencing the Duke in favor of Archas by means of a strategically placed apologist. In Fletcher's play Archas himself does none of the scheming suggested by Bandello or Heywood.

To the main plot, consisting of the humiliations imposed upon Archas (public insult, exile, imprisonment, and torture), each followed by a national crisis in which he loyally exerts himself to save his country, Fletcher adds a secondary plot dealing with the love of Young Archas for Olympia, the Duke's sister. The affair is complicated by the young man's disguise and by a misunderstanding on the part of Olympia which results in an unjust accusation of dishonorable conduct and a temporary break in the relationship, parallel to the exile of Archas. Thus both plots are based on the play's fundamental contrast between abused honor and gold-plated dishonor. This is closely akin to the ethical contrast used by Heywood in his subplot, and it may be that the juxtaposition of this theme and the story of the loyal subject in one play suggested to Fletcher the idea of reconstructing the main plot as he did.

These changes make for greater simplicity and greater unity. The character of Archas does not change from virtue to vice; it remains virtuous throughout. The actions of the Duke are clearly separated into two categories: the bad, which emanate from his "hot humour" and the influence of Boroskie; the good, which emanate from inborn honor and the influence of Archas and his family. The quarrel of the sovereign with his subject does not develop gradually but appears, fully developed, at the opening and continues unchanged throughout the play until, at the end, it is suddenly replaced by reconciliation. Since it is depicted as the inevitable conflict between good and evil, the basis of the play is not a subtle question of etiquette but a clear-cut ethical contrast. Finally, the invention of situations presenting additional members of the family of Archas produces secondary action much more closely allied to the main action than Heywood's story of Captain Bonville.

Fletcher's debt to satirical comedy is seen in the curing of the Duke's "hot humour" and in his presentation of the family of Archas as a group of highly simplified characters related to each other by the ethical concept which they all represent. Out of the material of the novella with hints from Heywood's play Fletcher creates a tragicomedy of humors.

In spite of Fletcher's anatomy of honor and his insistence upon the conflict of honor with materialism, *The Loyal Subject* has neither the homely didacticism of Heywood's play nor the solid morality of a Jonsonian comedy. As I have already suggested, it is a set of variations on a theme. The theme is moral; the variations exploit this moral content for the sake of the emotional tensions implicit in it. None of the tragicomedies shows the operation of this technique more clearly.

The moral conflict is most apparent in the scenes where Archas and his son Theodore confront Boroskie, the evil counselor. The first of these opens with Archas' "farewell to the military profession," in which Fletcher's rhetoric is lavished upon the recollection of noble exploits. The Duke then summarily dismisses his "loyal subject" from court and bestows his office upon Boroskie, but even in the face of this insulting treatment Archas remains loyal, thanking the Duke for past favors and for the opportunity to retire from active life. Boroskie explains these words as a "smooth humble Cloak he has cas'd his pride in," an accusation which reveals Boroskie's envy and ambition. (1, iii; Cam., *3, 87.*) Since the pride of the two worshipers of Mammon is as clear as the humility of the noble Archas, Fletcher's first presentation of the contrast is characterized by a note of irony.

The fullest presentation of the difference between the characters of Boroskie and Archas occurs when Archas returns with his soldiers from a successful campaign. Boroskie has been too cowardly to conduct the campaign himself, but now that the danger is past he warns the Duke that Archas' ambition must not be fostered by undue praise and that it will be advisable for the Duke not to receive Archas and his men. In the ensuing dialogue between Boroskie, Archas, and other officers Theodore comments angrily on Boroskie's great wealth, now secured to him by the victory, and when Boroskie criticizes his manner he defends soldierly bluntness against Boroskie's love of flattery. Like white on black, Archas' virtues stand out as we see him remain impervious to insult, solicitous only on behalf of his honorable soldiers. The contrast is finally summed up by Putskie, Archas' brother, when Boroskie, still refusing to grant Archas a triumph, attempts to satisfy the army by a cash payment:

you should have us'd us nobly,

.   .   .

Then ye had paid us bravely; then we had shin'd Sir,
Not in this gilded stuff but in our glory:
You may take back your mony.

II, i; Cam., 3, 104

Here the main theme is explicitly stated.

If Fletcher seems to be illustrating the Pardoner's text, *Radix malorum est cupiditas,* he by no means slights the concomitant sin of lechery, which, held up against the purest chastity, provides one of the many variations on his theme. An important part of the plot concerns the attempt of the Duke to corrupt Young Archas, disguised as a girl. Her refusal to accept a jewel as a substitute for her honor relates the incident closely to the one I have just described. And the same sort of contrast is made in a different way when the Duke's sister Olympia questions her new "lady in waiting" about the Duke's attentions to her. Young Archas' answers are all innocence, but each one is willfully misconstrued in an obscene sense by a jealous attendant, Petesca. Again chastity and lechery are juxtaposed, and this variation parallels the false interpretation given by Boroskie to the words of Archas.

In all the scenes described thus far a character representing honor in at least one of its aspects is faced by an exponent of the corrupt philosophy of materialism. The usefulness of the many members of Archas' family is apparent in these scenes; for, in the first place, it is part of the role of "the loyal subject" to accept passively every attack made upon him, and the aggressive defense of his position must be left to Theodore and Putskie; in the second place, the presence at court of other representatives of Archas' ideals makes it possible to maintain the contrast in the absence of Archas. But by scenes in which only the good characters appear Fletcher avoids the monotony of an uninterrupted sequence of scenes in which the eager defenders of the cause of the spirit are subjected to the fiendish machinations of the Duke and Boroskie. Furthermore, even these scenes in which honor confronts honor are so handled by Fletcher that they, too, become variations on the main theme.

The simplest example of such scenes is the misunderstanding between Olympia, who is an emblem of purity, and her pure and loyal "gentlewoman," the disguised Young Archas. Because Olympia has been led to suspect the honor of her attendant, she dismisses her in the tones of a pure woman confronted by a courtesan. (IV, i; Cam., *3,* 134–6.) Another example is the scene in which Archas instructs his daughters Honora and Viola to go to court. Here the effect of contrast is maintained by a lengthy discussion of the evils of court. The difference in temperament between Honora and Viola suggests another reflection of the contrast, for Honora's description of the corrupt life is so lively and bold that, in comparison to the modest phraseology of Viola, it seems almost the speech of a hoyden. Sheer verbalization and the different humors of these two girls maintain the contrast between material and spiritual values in a scene where the stage is loaded with honor.

Honora's immodest talk is one of a series of variations dependent upon speech which is out of character. When Theodore brings Honora and Viola to court he assumes for the moment the cynicism of the most profligate courtier and introduces them as accomplished courtesans. So appallingly direct is his recommendation that two lecherous Gentlemen are frightened away. (III, iv; Cam., 3, 126-8.) Two scenes later Young Archas, still in his disguise, also affects the wantonness of court in instructing the two girls how to behave themselves with men. (III, vi; Cam., 3, 130-4.) And when the Duke attempts a simultaneous seduction of the two, Honora so dazzles him by a sudden shift from militant chastity to equally militant lovemaking, shouting encouragement to Viola between kisses, that he is shocked into repentance. In this instance, the climax to the series of dissimulations, Honora assumes something very like the role of the satirist.

Finally we come to a series of scenes presenting the conflict between two thoroughly honorable characters, Archas and his son Theodore. There is no misunderstanding here and no disparity between the behavior and the true character of the persons involved. But Theodore's humor of impatience provides one more type of variation of the theme. Again and again Theodore's outspoken censure of the dishonorable conduct of the Duke and Boroskie forces Archas to rebuke his son in the noble-Roman manner, for although Theodore's devotion to honor is beyond cavil, his expression of it disregards loyalty, which is an all-important part of the ideal conception of honor represented by Archas. Thus the old patriarch is placed in a typically Fletcherian dilemma. In the climactic last scene Archas is about to kill Theodore for being a "villain," a "rebel," a "fatal firebrand," and by implication a traitor. Theodore's only plea is that Archas, though killing him, should not disown him. Thus we are presented with the fascinating spectacle of honor branding honor as dishonorable, while the accused continues to insist that to life he prefers his inheritance of honor: "Strike me a thousand blows, but let me dye yours." (v, vi; Cam., 3, 166.) The situation is made just twice as spectacular when, to prevent the disaster, Putskie enters with Young Archas, threatening to kill him the moment Archas kills Theodore. The intricacy of this presentation of conflicting loyalties is only exceeded in the denouements of *The Queen of Corinth* and *The Laws of Candy*, and, as in those plays, the steadily increasing tension is suddenly resolved by a general reconciliation. Preposterous as the whole situation is, it has an undeniable effectiveness for one who has been following the series of variations from the first simple ones, through others of greater complexity, to this, the showpiece of the lot.

The Loyal Subject is marked by an extravagance unusual even among the Beaumont and Fletcher plays. Its situations become progressively more bizarre; its characters react in the least expected ways. One is reminded of Bornecque's comment on the characters in the Senecan declamations, "placés dans des situations invraisemblables ou tout au moins exceptionnelles, et ne cessant d'étaler des sentiments exactement contraires à ceux que l'on attendrait."[5] Certainly this is one of the tragicomedies in which the influence of the tradition of the declamations is felt most strongly, for the development of the given situation by means of ingenious hypotheses not taken from the source is parallel to the imaginary situations of the orators. And the legalistic refinement of some of the points of honor is exactly in the spirit of certain of the *Controversiae*.

There may have been a direct influence of the declamations upon the play, though the evidence is not conclusive. When Archas returns from one of his victorious campaigns Boroskie orders that he be condemned to death for sacrilegiously taking from the temple the arms which he left there at his retirement. The fourth controversia in the fourth book deals with a hero who is prosecuted by his ungrateful country for having taken from the tomb of a famous warrior the arms in which he won the battle.[6] This situation, unlike anything in Heywood or Bandello, is at least remarkably similar to that in *The Loyal Subject*. The final situation of the play, in which Archas threatens to disown and kill his son, is like that of several of the declamations in Seneca's collection. It is fair to conclude that at the time of writing this play (the period in which the plays certainly based on Senecan declamations were written) the *Controversiae* were close to the surface of Fletcher's mind.

The extraordinary situations and the extreme attitudes of the characters provide the ideal setting for the almost continuous flow of declamatory rhetoric in *The Loyal Subject*. Some of it has a satirical flavor as in Honora's disquisition on the evils of court:

> Would ye have your Children learn to forget their father,
> And when he dies dance on his Monument?
> Shall we seek Vertue in a Sattin Gown;
> Embroider'd Vertue? Faith in a well-curl'd Feather?
> And set our Credits to the tune of green sleeves?
> This may be done; and if you like, it shall be.
> You should have sent us thither when we were younger,
> Our maiden-heads at a higher rate; our Innocence
> Able to make a Mart indeed:
>   III, ii; Cam., *3,* 118

5. *Controverses et suasoires,* I, xi.   6. See Appendix.

The speeches of Archas, if tinged occasionally with satire, are chiefly notable for their passionate eloquence. A characteristic example is his defense of himself for having taken his arms from the temple:

> O base ungrateful people,
> Have ye no other Swords to cut my throat with
> But mine own nobleness? I confess, I took 'em,
> The vow not yet absolv'd I hung 'em up with:
> Wore 'em, fought in 'em, gilded 'em again
> In the fierce *Tartars* blouds; for you I took 'em,
> For your peculiar safety, Lord, for all,
> I wore 'em for my Countries health, that groan'd then:
> Took from the Temple, to preserve the Temple;
> That holy place, and all the sacred monuments,
> The reverent shrines of Saints, ador'd and honour'd,
> Had been consum'd to ashes, their own sacrifice;
> Had I been slack, or staid that absolution,
> No Priest had liv'd to give it; my own honour,
> Cure of my Country murder me?
>
> IV, vi; Cam., 3, 151

Archas plays the role of the noble hero to perfection. The fact that it is patently a role does no damage to the play as tragicomedy, though, as we have seen, a similar treatment of character in the tragedies seriously weakens the tragic effect. The pattern of tragicomedy demands that every role be played to the hilt.

3. *The Humorous Lieutenant*

"Instead of Arts and Arms, a Womans kisses."

The antithesis of lover and warrior which generates the humor of *The Mad Lover* is again prominent in *The Humorous Lieutenant*. The hero of the play is the Macedonian general and king Demetrius, shown as a young man during the lifetime of his father Antigonus. Many of the incidents in the play are drawn from Plutarch's life of Demetrius and give the suggestion of historical veracity characteristic of the tragicomedies. But the main tension comes from the passionate attachment of Demetrius to Celia, his prisoner, and, though he does not know it, the daughter of King Seleucus. Of this love affair history says nothing, though Demetrius was famed for his lust.[7] Fletcher's depiction of him

---

7. Plutarch relates two incidents in the life of Demetrius which may be vaguely related to Fletcher's story of Celia. One is the infatuation of Demetrius for Lamia, one of his many mistresses. The other is a famous anecdote about Stratonice, the daughter of Demetrius, married to Seleucus and then surrendered by Seleucus to become the wife of his son, who was dying of love for her. A situation similar to that of the second anecdote is the subject of the seventh controversia in the sixth book.

is much romanticized. Demetrius, the most courageous and noble of soldiers, is torn between his love and the demands of valor—a much simplified Antony[8] and the precursor of many a love-and-honor hero.

The subplot presents a coarse burlesque of this conflict in the career of the "humorous" Lieutenant, who has served "under Captain *Cupid*" and has contracted a venereal disease so painful that it prompts him to reckless bravery on the battlefield. When he is well he becomes a coward and tries to sneak away to pursue his venery. To make him fight again his companions have to persuade him that his old trouble has returned. A similar incident is told of one of Antigonus' soldiers in Plutarch's life of Pelopidas, but it is Fletcher who specifies the nature of the disease and thus fits the farce to the romance of Demetrius.

Antigonus, described as "an old man with young desires," complicates the lives of the young lovers by attempting to seduce Celia while Demetrius is away fighting. Antigonus has her approached by a procuress and lodged at court where he has access to her, but her chastity is proof against every assault and in the end it is Antigonus who capitulates by a sudden repentance.

As in *The Mad Lover,* romance and satire are side by side, though *The Humorous Lieutenant,* despite its lighter moments, is more emotionally taut and hence predominantly more romantic. The combination of the two elements is differently managed, for there is no character in *The Humorous Lieutenant* who shifts, like Memnon, from buffoon to hero. Instead there are two characters in whom the satiric and the romantic are oddly mixed. Antigonus as the lecherous king is a figure common to romance and satire, and Celia is both innocent victim and satirical reformer. Antigonus appears as a sinister villain in his deception of Demetrius and in his plotting with bawds and panders to corrupt Celia. But when he tricks himself out like a young lover, he appears, like old Leontius in *Cupid's Revenge,* as a ridiculous object of satire. Celia comments :

> Curl'd and perfum'd? I smell him ;
> He looks on's legs too, sure he will cut a caper ;
> God-a-mercy, dear *December.*
> IV, V; Cam., 2, 350

Celia's purely romantic moments are infrequent. When Antigonus at his most villainous is trying to buy her with jewels, she makes a moving appeal whose tone is that of the damsel in distress :

> Then can these, Sir,
> These precious things, the price of youth and beauty ;
> This shop here of sin-offerings set me off again?

8. Plutarch compares the lives of Antony and Demetrius.

Can it restore me chaste, young, innocent?
Purge me to what I was? add to my memory
An honest and a noble fame? The Kings device;
The sin's as universal as the Sun is,
And lights an everlasting Torch to shame me.

IV, i; Cam., *2*, 335

However, her defense of herself often merges into a reforming zeal:

O wretched man, below the state of pity!
Canst thou forget thou wert begot in honour?

.   .   .

Canst thou forget this, and decline so wretchedly,
To eat the Bread of Bawdry, of base Bawdry?

IV, i; Cam., *2*, 336

Here and in her comment on the King's appearance she is clearly the
agent for satire.

The quality of Celia's nature most commented on by the other characters is her rare spirit. Not often so solemn as in the last two quotations,
she takes a particular delight in exercising her wit. Her reaction to the
discovery of one plot against her is characteristic: "Since I am fool'd, /
I'le make my self some sport, though I pay dear for't." She is, in fact,
much too clever for her own good, for her tricks imperil her romance
more seriously than does Antigonus. Demetrius has been told by his
father that Celia is dead and that, in any case, she was unfaithful. At
first unwilling to believe this slander, Demetrius is sufficiently touched
by it to ask Celia a number of leading questions when he discovers that
she is alive. Perversely, she encourages him to suppose the worst and
brings on herself a vituperative denunciation:

Out thou impudence,
Thou ulcer of thy Sex; when I first saw thee,
I drew into mine eyes mine own destruction,
I pull'd into my heart that sudden poyson,
That now consumes my dear content to cinders:
I am not now *Demetrius*, thou hast chang'd me;
Thou, woman, with thy thousand wiles hast chang'd me;
Thou Serpent with thy angel-eyes hast slain me;
And where, before I touch'd on this fair ruine,
I was a man, and reason made, and mov'd me,
Now one great lump of grief, I grow and wander.

Her reply is a denunciation equally passionate and equally rhetorical:

I will go from ye, never more to see ye:
I will flie from ye, as a plague hangs o're me;

And through the progress of my life hereafter;
Where ever I shall find a fool, a false man,
One that ne're knew the worth of polish'd vertue;
A base suspecter of a virgins honour,
A child that flings away the wealth he cri'd for,
Him will I call *Demetrius:* that fool *Demetrius,*
That mad man a *Demetrius;* and that false man,
The Prince of broken faiths, even Prince *Demetrius.*

IV, viii; Cam., 2, 358

This is the high point of the action—an intensely emotional and seem-ingly tragic moment—after which the misunderstanding is quickly dis-posed of and the lovers are reconciled. The climax is achieved, then, because Celia is as fond of tricks as Jonson's Brainworm or Macilente, though she is at the same time a heroine as pure and adorable as Jonson's Celia or as Amoret in *The Faithful Shepherdess.* Shakespeare creates witty romantic heroines, such as Rosalind in *As You Like It* or Helena in *All's Well That Ends Well,* but in them the dichotomy is not made so glaringly apparent. Rosalind never rises to the emotional pitch of Celia in this scene with Demetrius; Helena does not play her famous trick for fun but ultimately for her honor. In Celia the two sides of her nature are developed independently and each to an ex-treme which makes the character, if not impossible, highly improbable and, in the last analysis, without significance. Her role of satirical trick-ster almost cancels out her role of romantic heroine.

Celia is emblematic of the play. Her versatility corresponds to the wit and the eloquence of *The Humorous Lieutenant.* Her engaging personality corresponds to its technical excellence. And Celia, like the entire play, is stunningly, unashamedly factitious.

4. *Women Pleased*

"Give 'em their sovraign Wills, and pleas'd they are."

As Celia gives the clue to the special character of *The Humorous Lieutenant,* to its virtues and its limitations and to the diverse elements of which it is composed, so Claudio gives the clue to the failure of *Women Pleased,* the least good of Fletcher's tragicomedies. Because it is a fail-ure and yet has many of the characteristics of the successful tragi-comedies, this play is one of the most valuable for the understanding of Fletcher's art.

Claudio first appears as the friend and rival of Silvio, the hero, with whom he quarrels over the princess Belvidere. As Claudio is about to scale the wall of the citadel where Belvidere is kept by her mother to avoid the importunity of suitors, Silvio stops him by offering to defend the lady's honor in a duel. Claudio next sends his man Soto to scale the wall, dressed in Claudio's clothes. Again Silvio appears, fires a pistol at him, and though he misses, scares Soto into falling off the ladder. Silvio now believes that he has killed his friend, and Claudio is so chastened by the narrow escape of Soto that he renounces his love for Belvidere and determines to keep out of Silvio's way. He disguises himself as a merchant in order, as he says, to observe "how my incensed friend carries my murther," but in fact Claudio's connection with the main plot of the love of Silvio and Belvidere now ends, and the disguise serves quite another purpose. Claudio obtains access to the house of the miserly and jealous Lopez, who has a beautiful wife named Isabella. The subplot of the play presents the intrigues of Claudio and Isabella to outwit Lopez and Bartello, another lover. Through a series of farcical situations probably suggested by stories in the *Decameron,* Claudio and Isabella seem always on the verge of success until the last act, when a most surprising change occurs. Lopez now gives Isabella control of her own fortune, and she offers, as proof that she has never been unfaithful, to let him overhear her next interview with Claudio. In the scene which follows it becomes increasingly difficult to understand the motives of any of the characters involved. Claudio enters and tells Isabella sadly that she really should have held out longer against him, to which she replies that she now realizes her behavior was inexcusable. Claudio protests that he was only teasing; she insists on taking him at his word. At this he becomes angry and accuses her of not rewarding his faithful devotion to her. Now Isabella protests that she doesn't mean what she has just said, and Claudio replies that in that case he will put Lopez out of the way and marry her. Lopez breaks in at these words; Claudio accuses Isabella of betraying him and she accuses Claudio of trying to seduce her. But Claudio has the last word. With the aside, "I must use a Players shift," he removes his disguise and reveals himself as Isabella's brother. All his intrigue with her has been an elaborate trial of her virtue. (v, ii; Cam., *7,* 302–6.)

The final revelation of the motives of Claudio and Isabella, coming after the succession of twists and turns of this scene, seems to deflate the entire subplot—to reduce it in retrospect to a disappointing tameness. But before exploring the reasons for this failure we must glance at the main plot from which Claudio withdraws after the first act. It, too, is somewhat disappointing. Silvio's uncle Bartello is the captain of the citadel where Belvidere is kept. After killing Claudio (as he thinks) to preserve Belvidere's honor Silvio persuades his aunt to let him see Belvidere and is promptly caught by Bartello. He is then tried before the Duchess, Belvidere's mother. The trial becomes a contest of nobility when Belvidere insists upon taking all the blame upon herself while Silvio argues eloquently that she is innocent and he alone guilty. This much of the situation is taken from some version of the Spanish romance *La historia de Grisel y Mirabella* by Juan de Flores, but the remainder of the main plot is an adaptation of the *Wife of Bath's Tale*. The Duchess condemns Silvio to banishment for a year, at the end of which time he must die unless he can answer the question of what women most desire. While he is away Belvidere comes to him, disguised as an ugly hag, and promises to answer the question for him. When he returns she does so, demands him in marriage, gives him his choice of having her old and faithful or young and fickle, and, when he leaves it up to her, reveals herself as Belvidere.

Every characteristic of Fletcherian tragicomedy is present; the play is outstanding for its intricacy of plot, its improbable hypotheses, and its Protean characters. The trial of faith, so prominent in *The Knight of Malta* and *The Humorous Lieutenant,* is carried to extraordinary lengths in the plot of Claudio and Isabella. But the familiar Fletcherian characteristics do not add up to the usual total effect. *Women Pleased,* by comparison with the other plays discussed in this chapter, is weak and unconvincing. It would be easy to attribute this failure to the diversity of the material or to the prominence of artifice were it not that some of the most effective tragicomedies, such as *The Loyal Subject,* are derived from a great variety of sources and are equally contrived. The faults with *Women Pleased* are not so readily analyzed.

Claudio, as I have already suggested, is a useful indication of what is wrong. His temptation of his sister, extended through four acts of the play, not only puts an unusual strain on credulity even by Fletcherian standards but, considered as a dramatic device, is remarkably ineffectual. For one thing, the audience is unable to sense the contrast between his role and his true self, since the first scenes do not establish his character firmly (he appears as a disloyal friend and then seems to repent) and the succeeding ones seem to mark him unmistakably as a would-be seducer. The revelation of the truth comes too late to create the tension felt in other comparable situations. When Miranda tempts Lucinda and Oriana, when Honora or Clorin plays the wanton, or when Panthea unexpectedly encourages the incestuous advances of Arbaces, there is an exciting contrast between character and behavior, though the explanation of the behavior is different in each of these instances. Whether or not the surprising behavior can be realistically explained, it constitutes a hypothesis whose very strangeness can be relished. Such manipulations of character are sins against the canon of probability and tend to destroy any coherent meaning, but when they are made momentarily acceptable within the framework of the play, their daring becomes a virtue—the trick is recognized as such and still enjoyed. Fletcher's is a baroque art in which distortion is a legitimate part of the elaborate design.

Claudio's role is ineffectual, then, because it cannot be appreciated as such while it is played; it cannot be seen as a distortion. On the contrary, the truth, when it comes in the last moments, appears to be the distortion. Claudio refers to his unmasking as a "player's shift," and so it seems. The situation is the opposite of what it should be.

There is another reason why the last-minute revelation is an artistic failure: its relation to the plot is flimsy. In this respect also *Women Pleased* differs from the successful tragicomedies. The revelation of the true identity of Arbaces at the end of *A King and No King* requires a complete reassessment of his previous behavior, but it is prepared for on the basic level of plot construction by numerous hints, and it explains his unbrotherly and unkingly passions. The revelation of Claudio's identity is unprepared for and makes his previous behavior less easy to understand. The revelation in *A King and No King* solves an old problem; that in *Women Pleased* raises a new one. I am not suggesting that the denouement of *A King and No King* or of any of the tragicomedies is inevitable, as is clearly not the case, but that it is in perfect keeping with the rest of the play and therefore seems to be an integral part of the plot. The denouement of Claudio's story fits imperfectly and therefore seems like an afterthought.

When we re-examine Claudio's behavior we discover that the idea of his temptation is as weakly related to the theme of the play as the revelation itself is to the plot. The main theme of the play is that women should have the "maistrye," or as Fletcher says, "their soveraign Wills." When Isabella has teased Lopez into giving her her way, she becomes a model of wifely deportment. In this subplot there is the further point that the jealous miser is cozened out of his humor by his wife's tricks. Isabella's affectation of wanton behavior and her use of Claudio are obviously germane to the demonstration of feminine superiority and to the special problem of curing one foolish male, but Claudio's simultaneous test of Isabella's chastity is an irrelevance. Miranda's tests of Lucinda and Oriana are directly related to the chivalric ideals upon which *The Knight of Malta* is based; Honora's wantonness is part of her defense of the honor of the entire family of Archas, "the loyal subject"; and Clorin's is similarly a means of guarding the chastity of "the faithful shepherdess." Panthea's sudden warmth is clearly related to the theme of overmastering passion which is central to *A King and No King*. Not every trick, not every hypothesis will do. The situation, however implausible, must have some immediate relevance to the design of the play. It is this relevance which makes the most daring of Fletcher's hypotheses acceptable in the better tragicomedies. Although the integrity of the character may be sacrificed and the coherence of the plot impaired, there remains the sort of consistency demonstrated by *The Loyal Subject,* where every scene is a variation on the central theme.

Such interrelations as these are conspicuously missing in *Women Pleased*.

5. *The Island Princess*

"Nay, I will out of vengeance search your Temples.
And with those hearts that serve my God, demolish
Your shambles of wild worships."

Armusia, the Christian hero of the play, flings this brave challenge at Quisara, "the Island Princess," who has made acceptance of the pagan religion a condition to his marriage with her. (IV, i; Cam., *8,* 156.) Through several scenes of the fourth and fifth acts the religious controversy rages until by the end of the play Quisara has been converted to Christianity, and her brother, the King of Tidore, half converted. Unlike the other tragicomedies *The Island Princess* appears to have a religious theme, yet the treatment of religion does not support this interpretation. The theme, as a close inspection reveals, is less specific— wider in its general implications, narrower in its significance. Of all the tragicomedies, *The Island Princess* is the best example of how the theme may be dilated to the point where it gives a hazy impression of seriousness.

The religious problem is first raised when a "Moor-Priest" approaches the King of Tidore (at the opening of the fourth act) to warn him that the Portuguese Armusia is a dangerous alien in spite of the heroic deeds he has performed. Armusia has rescued the King from the prison of his great enemy, the Governor of Ternata, and now seeks marriage with Quisara. The first major scene in which the religious issue predominates is an interview between Armusia and Quisara, observed by the King and the priest. Armusia comes to declare his love and demand a task that may make him worthy of his fair lady. Quisara, prompted by the priest, tells him that he may win her by changing his religion and worshiping the gods of the islands. The effect of her words upon Armusia is electric:

Now I contemn ye, and I hate my self
For looking on that face lasciviously,
And it looks ugly now me thinks. . . .
It looks like death ìt self, to which 'twou'd lead me;
Your eyes resemble pale dispair, they fright me,
And in their rounds, a thousand horrid ruins,
Methinks I see; and in your tongue hear fearfully
The hideous murmurs of weak souls have suffer'd;
Get from me, I despise ye; and know woman,
That for all this trap you have laid to catch my life in,
To catch my immortal life, I hate and curse ye,

Contemn your Deities, spurn at their powers,
And where I meet your *Mahumet* gods, I'll swing 'em
Thus o'r my head, and kick 'em into puddles,
Nay, I will out of vengeance search your Temples.
And with those hearts that serve my God, demolish
Your shambles of wild worships.

IV, i; Cam., 8, 155–6

The King immediately orders him bound and thrown into prison, but
Quisara is noticeably affected by Armusia's defiance. In the next important scene her women bring her bound before the King, explaining that she has become delirious. After she has cursed both her brother
and the priest, Armusia is brought in and threatened with torture, and
as the instruments are being prepared, Quisara, to the dismay of the
King, takes her place beside Armusia with a speech as fervid as any of
his:

Stand fast, Sir,

And fear 'em not, you that have stept so nobly
Into this pious Trial, start not now,
Keep on your way, a Virgin will assist ye,
A Virgin won by your fair constancy,
And glorying that she is won so, will dye by ye:

v, i; Cam., 8, 163

The two lovers are rescued from martyrdom by Armusia's Portuguese friends, led by Captain Ruy Dias. In the melee the priest is captured and shown to be no priest but the Governor of Ternata. At this
discovery the King is instantly reconciled to Armusia and his sister
and "half perswaded" to be a Christian, although the perfidy of his old
enemy is scarcely a serious indictment of the heathen religion. One
cannot avoid the uneasy feeling that this denouement is no solution to
the religious problems that have been raised. But it is a speech of Ruy
Dias which gives the show away:

Why what a wretch
Art thou to work this mischief?
To assume this holy shape to ruine honor,
Honor and chastity?

v, i; Cam., 8, 169

The whole pagan attack upon Christianity has masked the fundamental
attack upon honor and chastity.

Armusia is a hero essentially like Miranda of *The Knight of Malta*
or Demetrius of *The Humorous Lieutenant,* dedicated to the ideal of
honor. The preservation of the faith is part of that ideal when the hero
is a Christian, as Armusia and Miranda are, but it is a nonessential.

The pagan Demetrius speaks and acts very much like Armusia, for the chivalric ideal in the seventeenth century has become a matter of personal integrity. Armusia's noble defiance of heathendom is merely the culminating proof of his heroic individuality.

The vindication of honor is the true theme of the play. It is presented satirically in the story of Ruy Dias, one of the many suitors of the princess. When she announces that she will give herself to whoever rescues her brother by force from the Governor of Ternata, Ruy Dias hangs back from the attempt and is thus contrasted with Armusia, who tries and succeeds. To the cowardice of Ruy Dias is now added a base craving for revenge, which leads him to ask his nephew Piniero to arrange Armusia's murder. Piniero, who has already acted as a satirical commentator on the various suitors in the opening scenes, sums up the degradation of his uncle's character in the following words, vowing to make him honest if he can:

> What a malicious soul does this man carry!
> And to what scurvy things this love converts us!
>
> .　　.　　.
>
> Murther's a moral virtue with these Lovers,
>
> .　　.　　.
>
> Love and Ambition draw the devils Coach.
> > > > III, i; Cam., *8,* 127

By pretending to agree to this plan and failing to execute it, Piniero proceeds with his scheme of reformation. As he hopes, Ruy Dias eventually perceives his own cowardice and challenges Armusia to open combat. Piniero, still the commentator, observes:

> I am glad to see this mans conversion,
> I was afraid fair honor had been bed-rid,
> > > IV, i; Cam., *8,* 145

When Armusia defeats Ruy Dias but spares his life at the request of the princess, the conversion is complete, as Ruy Dias shows in his words to Piniero:

> You teach well Nephew,
> Now to be honourabl[e] even with this Gentleman,
> Shall be my business, and my ends his.
> > > IV, i; Cam., *8,* 152

Thanks to Piniero, who has assumed a satyr's depravity in order to accomplish his moral purpose, Ruy Dias has been purged of his evil humors and won for the cause of honor.[9]

---

9. The character of Piniero is greatly enlarged from the original in Fletcher's source, *Conquista de las Islas Malucas* (1609) by Bartolome Leonardo de Argensola, which

Even Quisara acquires honor slowly, for she at first gives her approval to the underhanded schemes of Ruy Dias but begins to realize her mistake when she sees the true nobility of Armusia. In a similar way, it will be recalled, she at first agrees to help the Moor-Priest in his more serious plot against the hero but is converted for good by Armusia's courage.

Finally, honor has another champion and exemplar in the King of Tidore, who prefers death by starvation to seeing his daughter married to the wicked Governor. Only temporarily and by an insidious appeal to his religion is his adherence to honor weakened. It is he who first urges Quisara to marry Armusia, "so excellent in nature! / In honor so abundant!" (II, i; Cam., *8, 123.*)

In spite of its satirical touches *The Island Princess* is one of the most expansively romantic of the tragicomedies. Its setting is one of the most exotic; its emotional intensity, greatest in the scenes of religious conflict, is unsurpassed. And it is also one of the most successful of the tragicomedies because of its varied but well-unified design. The theme is the familiar triumph of honor over all comers. What distinguishes *The Island Princess* from the other tragicomedies is the rather grandiose treatment of the theme, appropriate to the play's uninhibited romanticism.

The Loyal Subject demonstrates more clearly than do the other plays that the structure of Fletcherian tragicomedy is a series of variations on a theme. But the comparative study of the tragicomedies leads to the further realization that, as the theme is always the same, each tragicomedy can also be regarded as one of a series of variations. In this series are ranged not only the tragicomedies but also most of the tragedies and many of the romantic comedies—a large proportion of all the Beaumont and Fletcher plays.

The vagueness of theme which makes possible this great number of variations is characteristic of Fletcher and his collaborators. The honor which includes every virtue, in the tragicomedies as in *The False One,* lies in a hazy borderland between ethics and etiquette—a land inhabited, no doubt, by many of the cavaliers in Beaumont and Fletcher's audiences. This imprecision reduces the meaning of the often-fought conflict to a negligible quantity. The meaning of the best tragedies of this period is achieved by a particularity lacking in Beaumont and Fletcher. In discussing *The Loyal Subject* I have already briefly compared Fletcher's theme with Tourneur's in *The Revenger's Tragedy.* A very inclusive materialism is the evil force in this tragedy as it is throughout Fletcherian tragicomedy, and Vindice's opposing honor is not unlike

---

Fletcher may have read in the French translation of De Bellan, *Histoire mémorable de Dias espagnol, et de Quixaire princesse des Moluques* (1614). Piniero's function as a satirical reformer is largely Fletcher's invention.

the honor of the Fletcherian hero, but the painted skull of Vindice's dead mistress is a central symbol which informs *The Revenger's Tragedy* with a particular meaning. The powerful emotions of the play are concentrated and directed by an individual way of looking at a familiar topic. Tourneur's treatment of the theme does not show original thought but his particularity shows a fresh application of thought. In *The Duchess of Malfi* Webster presents the attack of corrupt materialism upon innocence, but the character of his victim is realized with such clarity that the ancient conflict of the individual against an evil world is perceived anew. And in both *The Revenger's Tragedy* and *The Duchess of Malfi* particularity extends the significance through the action of the concrete symbol. The implications of Vindice's struggle reach out to the roots of Christian thought on death and revenge, while the implications of the heroism of the Duchess lead to the fundamental problem of the nature of man.

To reconsider *The Island Princess* after these two tragedies is to see that Fletcher's treatment of his theme is neither so particular nor so far-reaching in its implications. The concept of personal honor presented in the person of Armusia differs in no important respect from the concept as presented in Polydor, Archas, Demetrius, or Silvio. And although at first one might think otherwise, Armusia's honor does not become a fresh instance of Christian virtue; rather, a stereotyped Christian virtue is bundled into the concept of honor along with many other things.

The feelings aroused by Fletcherian tragicomedy are not focused on a point but diffused over a large area. They derive from stock responses to the familiar, indefinite theme and hence partake of sentimentality. But for the very reason that the theme is so indefinite that it is always the same, the presentation must be varied to provide a new stimulus, and therefore the emotional effect of the plays is directly related to the important principle of variation. Instead of renewing the life of the theme by embodying it each time in a fresh symbol and thus giving each play its own meaning, Beaumont and Fletcher concentrate upon the novel situation, the surprising change of character, the rhetorical tour de force. In this sort of invention they display, like the ancient orators, an unwithering ingenuity which is one of their most remarkable qualities. The limitations and the virtues of their technique are inseparable.

6. *A Wife for a Month*

"Honour and everlasting love."

It is appropriate to conclude a study of the Beaumont and Fletcher plays with *A Wife for a Month,* the last play which Fletcher wrote alone,[1] for this tragicomedy shows more fully than any of the others the characteristics of the pattern first glimpsed in *The Faithful Shepherdess*. The combination of the familiar with the remote is made according to the formula worked out in *Philaster* and followed in most of the later tragicomedies. The setting is Naples under the "unnatural and libidinous" ruler Frederick, younger brother to the good Alphonso, whose melancholia confines him to a monastery. This situation is somewhat reminiscent of Alphonso II of Naples, who abdicated the throne to his son and retired to a monastery to be succeeded, after the death of his son, by his brother Frederick. The character of Fletcher's Frederick, however, is more like that of Ferrante I, who is also the model of Ferrand in *The Double Marriage*. The more carefully one examines the situation in the play, the more one realizes how different it is from any actual situation in Neapolitan history; Fletcher was probably influenced by the story of Sancho II of Castile, who put his brother Alphonso in a monastery and usurped his throne. *A Wife for a Month* is not fictionalized history but pseudo-history, and the main action is unadulterated romance.

The plot is an intricate arrangement of the most surprising situations, resting upon the improbable hypothesis that a lover is forced to live up to one of his extravagant protestations in a love poem. Frederick and his "wicked instrument" Sorano, who devise the persecution of the hero, provide the atmosphere of evil which all but engulfs the noble lovers. Their plight is so continuously harrowing that the play abounds in "lively touches of passion," which are projected, as we should expect, in some of Fletcher's most eloquent rhetoric. Of all the characteristics of the pattern *A Wife for a Month* demonstrates most clearly the Protean character. The theme is once more the triumph of honor—or "honor and chastity," as Ruy Dias says in *The Island Princess,* giving special mention to female honor—but the characters who represent the abstract poles of Fletcher's opposition do not remain constant. They shift even more strikingly than the characters of *The Loyal Subject,* playing first one part and then another. Richard Flecknoe wrote in 1664: "*Beaumont* and *Fletcher* were excellent in their kinde, but they often err'd against *Decorum,* seldom representing a valiant man without somewhat of the *Braggadoccio,* nor an honourable woman without somewhat of *Dol·Common* in her . . ."[2] Some of the shifts in *A Wife for a Month* are sins against decorum; some are poses, deliberately assumed. Only the contrast between honor and dishonor remains the same.

The opening scene reveals Sorano offering to procure his sister, the chaste Evanthe, for Frederick. Sorano, like Boroskie in *The Loyal Sub-*

---

1. It was licensed in May, 1624, and Fletcher died in August, 1625.
2. "A Short Discourse of the English Stage," Spingarn, *2,* 94.

ject, is a cynical materialist, motivated entirely by concern for his own
advancement, while Frederick is a villain of much darker hue than
Boroskie's Duke. Frederick and Sorano together are the ideal antagonists. When Evanthe is brought on, the King, encouraged by Sorano,
loses no time in making advances, but in the presence of Lust and Ambition, Chastity stands forth boldly, impregnable to the assaults of either.
Evanthe reminds the King of his duty to the Queen, whom she serves.
She discourses passionately on honesty, piety, loyalty, and love, ending with the assertion:

> I had rather be a Leper, and be shun'd,
> And dye by pieces, rot into my grave,
> Leaving no memory behind to know me,
> Than be a high Whore to eternity.
>
> I, i; Cam., *5, 7*

Frederick and Sorano conclude from her speeches that she must have
a lover; otherwise, argues Lust, why would she turn down so princely
an offer?

The balance of characters in this scene gives place to a different sort
of balance when the Queen enters, looking for the King. The moment
she sees Evanthe she suspects that the King is about to have a new mistress, and Evanthe for some time cruelly encourages her suspicion.
When the Queen begins to weep, however, Evanthe drops her pose and,
on her knees, protests her loyal devotion. The Queen then addresses
her as "true friend" and "virtuous bud of beauty," and the two chaste
ladies leave together in perfect accord. Here is the first shift. Evanthe's
gratuitous cruelty is best understood as part of the design of the scene,
a foil to bring out the pathetic plight of the Queen.

A group of courtiers, familiar Jacobean gentlemen like the courtiers
in every Beaumont and Fletcher play, now comment somewhat satirically on the corruption of the times, which might have been checked if Alphonso had reigned. When they mention "the good Brandino," father
of Frederick and Alphonso, we realize how thoroughly the authentic
names of Neapolitan history have been scrambled with the fictitious.

When Frederick and Sorano seize the private belongings of Evanthe,
they find a verse letter from the noble Valerio, containing the fatal lines:

> To be your own but one poor Month, I'd give
> My Youth, my Fortune, and then leave to live.
>
> I, i; Cam., *5,* 11

Frederick vows instant vengeance, and the attack on honor and chastity
is on.

As Valerio is sent for, Evanthe enters, cursing her servant Cassandra for surrendering her papers. Cassandra replies impudently, and

her mistress is stimulated to such an outburst of vituperation that Frederick intervenes with the appropriate question, "Has your young sanctity done railing, Madam . . . ?" (ı, i; Cam., 5, 13.) Railing it is, and not merely the rebuke of a betrayed heroine; Evanthe speaks like any citizen-housewife cursing at the proverbially stupid and impudent servant. This second shift is again part of the design of the scene: the opposition of Chastity to Impudence is brilliantly expressed at the expense of the decorum which would ordinarily on the stage distinguish the behavior of the courtly heroine from that of the housewife.

The act ends with the posing of the improbable hypothesis on which all the rest of the action depends. The King rules that Valerio shall be held to the extravagant promise made in his love poem—that he shall marry Evanthe, live with her one month, and then be executed. If by that time she cannot find another man to marry her on the same terms, she is also to die. Valerio unhesitatingly announces that fortune could not have pointed out to him a straighter and nobler path to honor, that Evanthe's love is all that he lives for, and that her love is a paradise which no man could deserve to enjoy for long.

In the second act Evanthe is shown receiving encouragement from the Queen, who tells her that if she appears to welcome her fate the King may relent, and that in any case death with honor is a blessing to be hoped for. Immediately following this scene is one in which Frederick is goaded to further lust by Sorano, who promises to procure Evanthe after all, if the King will grant him sufficient power. The two scenes are almost exact parallels. The contrast between the characters is not within the scene but is carried from one scene to another: Evanthe, fortified by virtuous counsel, is balanced against Frederick, fortified by wicked counsel.

Toward the end of the act Valerio appears, talking in the same manner as before. He is assuring the courtiers that the King has honored him, and once again he speaks of the infinite pleasure he anticipates in Evanthe's embraces, as a prelude to which he invites his friends to have a "rouse before we go to bed . . . a lusty one, 'twill make my blood dance . . ." (ıı, i; Cam., 5, 24.) Valerio's sensuality, like Amintor's in *The Maid's Tragedy,* is an important ingredient of his character, providing for behavior quite different from his strictly "noble" behavior, though not absolutely inconsistent with it. Fletcher makes the most of the combination. In the scene which I am describing the impression of Valerio as a sensualist is balanced, if not outweighed, by the impression of his nobility, for he declares that death is far better than old age, when both the body and the mind disintegrate and precious honor is lost. To reinforce this impression the courtiers are shown as somewhat hesitant to renounce the joy of life. Against a background of genteel timidity Valerio's bravery stands out in his alliterative reply to one of them: "I would not live to learn to lye *Cleanthes*." (II, i; Cam., *5*, 24.)

In the third act Alphonso, the rightful king, is reported to be in a deathlike coma, and Sorano plots to make away with him. However, the act is chiefly concerned with the new complications of the wicked plot against Valerio and Evanthe. As Valerio is gloating over his prospects, "hot with wine" by his own admission and "lustily warm," Sorano enters. His appearance immediately brings to the surface Valerio's nobility, which manifests itself in a virtuous condemnation:

> Go glory in thy mischiefs thou proud man,
> And cry it to the world thou hast ruin'd vertue;
> How I contemn thee and thy petty malice!
>
> III, i; Cam., *5*, 28

Thus the good Christian addresses the devil.

After this speech, however, comes a powerful reaffirmation of Valerio's sensuality, and now for the first time the dramatic usefulness of this trait becomes clear. Sorano informs Valerio that by order of the King, if he more than kisses Evanthe during their month of marriage, she will instantly be killed, and that if he gives the true reason for his abstention, they will both be killed. From the peak of joy Valerio is hurled to the depths of anguish, asserting that the marriage with these conditions is the worst punishment that could possibly have been devised. The horror of the story's central situation is greatly augmented by Valerio's anticipation of the joys of the marriage bed; the pure Perigot would not be affected by the restriction to the extent that Valerio is.

Soon after his interview with Sorano, Valerio encounters the King, who taunts him by wishing him a good night. Valerio momentarily rebels, threatening to disobey the orders, but the King, reminding him of the penalty, again wishes him a good night and leaves. Valerio says bitterly:

> But for respect to her and to my duty,
> That reverent duty that I owe my Sovera[ig]n,
> Which anger has no power to snatch me from,
> The good night should be thine; good night for ever.
>
> III, i; Cam., *5*, 33

Like Amintor he is caught between passion and loyalty, and it is typical of Fletcher to present both in an extreme form. In this scene, however, honor is clearly in the ascendant as Valerio confronts the dishonorable King.

In the scenes at the end of the third act Fletcher presents the situation for which he has so carefully prepared—the wedding night of Valerio and Evanthe. The treatment of Evanthe in these scenes is reminiscent of the earlier treatment of Valerio. When she is brought to her bed by the Queen and other ladies, with Valerio looking on, she speaks incessantly of "the lawful sweets" of the marriage bed, the thought of which so transports her that she no longer thinks of the tragic shortness of her marriage. It is hardly necessary to point out that such speeches are nicely calculated to increase Valerio's agony. After the others leave the stage the chaste Evanthe manifests even greater eagerness in her behavior toward Valerio. She immediately urges him to come to bed and offers to undress him. When he makes evasive replies, suggesting that he is ill, she promises to make him well; when he says that he loves her "above the base bent of desire," she replies that lawful love is no sin and again offers to help him undress. When he continues to talk about the sin of passion, she grows angry and tells him that, unless he is impotent, he obviously must have a mistress. At this he tells her, amidst tears, that he is indeed impotent. Evanthe, after lamenting her fate, resigns herself nobly with the words:

All fond desire dye here, and welcom chastity,
Honour and chastity, do what you please Sir.

III, i; Cam., 5, 39

The irony in this enunciation of the theme is conspicuous.

I have described the scene at length in order to show how far Fletcher goes from the conventional portrayal of the chaste heroine. The depiction on the stage of such immodesty is much more suggestive of Temptation than of Chastity, for one must keep in mind that however possible Evanthe's behavior might be if she were an actual person, it does not fit the expectations one has of her as a stage heroine. Her modesty is emphasized in earlier scenes, where the Queen and Sorano refer to it (I, i; Cam., 5, 6, 8) ; yet here it is nonexistent. It is this sort of shock that Flecknoe expressed when he said that even an honorable woman in Fletcher's plays has "somewhat of *Dol Common* in her."

The effectiveness of the scene is undoubtedly increased by treating Evanthe as Fletcher does. Her eagerness is the exact counterpart of Valerio's forced inaction; his emotional torment could not be fully depicted if Evanthe were as passive as St. Cecilia's husband when he received the news of his wife's determined virginity. Once again the inconsistency in behavior is brought about by designing the scene as a contrast between the two characters involved.

The opening scene of the fourth act reveals Sorano's attempt to poison Alphonso, but before we see the effects of the fatal draught we are returned once more to the main plot. In this act the contrast between the virtue of Valerio and Evanthe and the villainy of Frederick and Sorano is made sharper than ever before. The King calls in Valerio to gloat over him and receives a noble rebuke. When the King attempts to bribe Valerio to surrender Evanthe temporarily upon reprieve of the death sentence, Valerio's honor is emphasized by his pretense of acceding to the King's demands. Just as Frederick imagines that the deal is arranged, Valerio emerges in his true color and again rebukes the King. Immediately after this scene is a parallel one in which Evanthe's maid, sent by the King, tempts her to become Frederick's mistress. Like Valerio she pretends to listen to the arguments only to turn suddenly on Cassandra with a virtuous rebuke. As in a previous scene Evanthe's castigation of her servant resembles the railing of a virago:

> If e'r I see thee more,
> Or anything that's like thee, to affright me,
> By this fair light I'll spoil thy Bawdery,
> I'll leave thee neither Eyes nor Nose to grace thee.
>
> iv, i; Cam., 5, 50

Frederick now tempts Evanthe further by telling her a half-truth—that he ordered Valerio to abstain from her or be killed. The King cunningly suggests that Valerio has probably pretended to be impotent, and for a moment Evanthe's faith is shaken. As the King continues to heap infamy upon her lover, however, she recovers herself and delivers to Frederick the third virtuous reproof that he has received in succession within the act. He retires, muttering. It is significant that Evanthe's language here is quite free of the undignified railing she addresses to her servant, though the intensity of feeling is greater. Chastity rebukes Lust with a certain dignity, but when Impudence extols the rewards of an unchaste life, Chastity expresses scorn as well as anger. In Evanthe's scenes with Cassandra, therefore, a variation of the heroine's speech and behavior indicates this special relationship and breaks the monotony of a series of similar scenes in which Virtue reproves Vice. The fact that Cassandra is Evanthe's servant suggests the tone for the scenes in which they are together, and the result is that in Cassandra's presence Evanthe is more the angry mistress than the insulted heroine.

The last scene of the act shows the two lovers again as Evanthe tells Valerio of the King's accusation. When Valerio answers her truly that it was to save her that he lied about himself, it appears that a complete understanding is imminent. A new development gives the scene a dramatic turn, however. Evanthe, instead of praising Valerio for his nobility, reproves him bitterly for not having realized that she would prefer death to a life without his love. She wishes she had married a veritable eunuch rather than a cowardly liar. Thus Fletcher contrives a new antithetical relationship between the lovers, though patterned upon the previous one. In each case Evanthe displays a quality which contrasts with Valerio's forced reticence: in the earlier scene she is eager almost to the point of shamelessness; in this scene she is so aggressively noble that she excells Valerio in bravery. Valerio is again reduced to tears and urges her to continue chiding him, that he may learn true nobility of her. At this Evanthe melts, begging his forgiveness. The tempestuous misunderstanding between the lovers is finally ended by a reconciliation. They have just vowed to consummate their love despite the King when soldiers enter to seize them both, informing them that by a new command their sentence is to be executed the following day. The lovers receive the news with noble fortitude.

The fifth act deals mainly with the counterplot which results in the surprise ending of the play. The poison given to Alphonso has resulted in a miraculous cure, and, with the aid of the monks and certain army officers, he plots to seize the throne from his younger brother. In the meantime Evanthe is made to ask for another man to marry her for a month, and Valerio, released by the guards, disguises himself as a suitor. The final showdown between the forces of honor and dishonor is a sort of charade, comparable with the masque in *The Malcontent* or the rigged trial in *The Queen of Corinth*. Frederick and Sorano are unaware that their evil power is now without substance, but the truth is dramatically revealed by the last scene. When the strange knight agrees to take Evanthe as his wife, Frederick is so angry that he orders him to be taken into custody, but at this moment the bells of the castle are rung and Alphonso enters with the guard to take Frederick and Sorano prisoners. At a stroke the evil atmosphere is dispelled. Frederick repents of his sins, and he and Sorano are sentenced to live in the monastery. Only Sorano remains unrepentant and he alone is barred from the celebration of the reunion of Valerio and Evanthe, the preparations for which close the play.

VI

The Rhetoric of Tragicomedy: The Poet as Orator

THE PATTERN OF tragicomedy which dominates the Beaumont and Fletcher plays imposes upon them a special language whose effect, as we have already seen, is above all emotional. There are, of course, speeches whose sole purpose is to convey information, and others which define a character or present an idea, but the most memorable and distinctive speeches are the tirades, the laments, the defenses of honor, which contain the very life of Fletcherian tragicomedy. Therefore, a study of the genre culminates logically in an examination of this emotional language. Since the comedies provide the least suitable material for such an examination, I shall not add to the comments already made on the language of Fletcher's comedy. Much of the language of the tragedies, however, is indistinguishable from the language of the tragicomedies. The examples to be considered come from these two sources.

The language of the poet was commonly described in the Renaissance in the terms of rhetorical analysis, for Aristotle's clear distinction between poetic and rhetoric had been lost. In Aristotle's scheme the function of the poet is to imitate an action, the function of the orator to persuade men of the truth; the poet's enterprise is imaginative, while the orator's is practical. Hence, as C. S. Baldwin makes clear,[1] the play, presenting action, is the emblem of poetic, and the public address, exhorting to action, is the emblem of rhetoric. In Rome, in the last years of the republic and the beginning of the empire, rhetoric was so much in the ascendant that it largely took over the province of poetic. Horace's unsystematic art of poetry ascribes to the poet the didactic function of the orator and thus blurs the basic Aristotelian distinction. The most detailed studies of language are made by the rhetoricians Cicero and Quintilian, who also tend to confuse the functions of orator and poet. And in the declamation, popular and influential in spite of the disapproval of the best rhetoricians, poetic is incorporated in rhetoric, for the imaginative presentation of a scene is one of the chief devices for scoring a point in a *controversia*. In the Renaissance Cicero and Quintilian were the great authorities on style, Horace was widely ad-

1. *Ancient Rhetoric and Poetic*, p. 134.

mired, and the declamation was a school exercise. It is not surprising that rhetoric dominated poetic.

To discuss poetic style from the point of view of rhetoric is to regard the poem as a means to elicit a certain response rather than to regard it, as we are more apt to do, as almost an end in itself—a living entity whose form gives unique expression to certain thoughts and feelings. Each method has its advantages. The Renaissance method is well suited to the study of dramatic poetry, especially when it is poetry of primarily emotional appeal, for this sort of poetry is good just to the extent that it creates its effect. Rhetorical analysis is singularly appropriate, as I hope to show, in examining the language of Fletcherian tragicomedy.

George Puttenham makes the connection between poet and orator explicit in his *Arte of English Poesie* when he says that "the Poets were also from the beginning the best perswaders, and their eloquence the first Rethoricke of the world . . ."[2] He develops the comparison at greater length in a passage where he is discussing the use of rhetorical figures:

> Now if our presupposall be true, that the Poet is of all other the most auncient Orator, as he that by good & pleasant perswasions first reduced the wilde and beastly people into publicke societies and civilitie of life, insinuating unto them, under fictions with sweete and coloured speeches, many wholesome lessons and doctrines, then no doubt there is nothing so fitte for him, as to be furnished with all the figures that be *Rhetoricall,* and such as do most beautifie language with eloquence & sententiousnes. . . . So as if we should intreate our maker to play also the Orator, and whether it be to pleade, or to praise, or to advise, that in all three cases he may utter, and also perswade both copiously and vehemently.[3]

This conception, shared by Puttenham with most of his contemporaries, that the office of the poet is to persuade men of the truth derives most directly from Roman rhetoric and underlies the familiar Renaissance doctrine of the dual function of poetry. In Sidney's words, which owe much to Horace:

> Poesie therefore is an arte of imitation, for so *Aristotle* termeth it in his word *Mimesis,* that is to say, a representing, counterfetting, or figuring foorth: to speake metaphorically, a speaking picture: with this end, to teach and delight.

.   .   .

2. G. G. Smith, *2, 9.*
3. *The Arte of English Poesie,* ed. G. D. Willcock and A. Walker (Cambridge, University Press, 1936), p. 196. This passage is not included by G. G. Smith in his selections.

> And that mooving is of a higher degree then teaching, it may
> by this appeare, that it is wel nigh the cause and the effect of
> teaching. For who will be taught if hee bee not mooved with de-
> sire to be taught?[4]

The importance of "moving" in relation to teaching is recognized by
Aristotle not in the *Poetics* but in the *Rhetoric* (ii. 1), where he shows
that the orator cannot depend on argument alone but through his knowledge of human nature must make his point emotionally convincing. The
Greek word for persuasion, the accepted aim of rhetoric, was *psycha-
gogia,* sometimes translated as "enchantment of the soul," a word
which was used first of the conjuring of the souls of the dead and then
applied metaphorically to the magic of words by which the mind may be
directed. To effect this enchantment the mind must be transported, not
merely reasoned with. Thus the poet as a persuader, confronted with the
same problems as the orator, finds his task divided like the orator's into
two parts, one of which is an appeal to man's rational faculties, the
other to his emotions.

In order to achieve these distinct objectives both poet and orator must
master certain appropriate variations of style, for Renaissance rhetoric
(following in the steps of Cicero) taught that a given style is necessary
to produce a given effect upon an audience. As G. L. Hendrickson has
pointed out,[5] Aristotle's division of rhetoric soon gave rise to a distinction between a pragmatic style appropriate for argumentation and
a more elaborate style appropriate for an emotional appeal. Furthermore, since the nature of Aristotle's division is such that one style
corresponds to proofs drawn from the subject matter itself, while the
other style corresponds to proofs extraneous to the subject matter, it is
easy to regard the elaborate style as consisting in unessential ornament
and to make a distinction between content and form.

It is possible to interpret Aristotle's division as threefold by emphasizing his subdivision of the orator's second function into *ethos* (making his character look right) and *pathos* (putting his hearers in the right
frame of mind).[6] Following this lead, Cicero in *De oratore* (ii. 115)
and *Orator* (69 ff.) assigns to the orator the functions of teaching,
pleasing, and moving (*docere, conciliare* or *delectare,* and *movere*) and
equates with these functions the plain style, the middle style, and the
grand style—the first clear, precise, and conversational in tone, the second
highly ornamented to please the ear, the third even more exuberantly
figurative to sway the passions by its vehemence. All the figures of
rhetoric are suitable for the middle and grand styles, and Cicero es-

4. "An Apologie for Poetrie," G. G. Smith, *1,* 158, 171.
5. "The Origin and Meaning of the Ancient Characters of Style," *American Journal
of Philology, 26* (1905), 248–90.
6. *Ibid.,* p. 260.

pecially recommends to his orator the practice of amplifying his theme. Thomas Wilson expresses his understanding of Cicero as follows:

> Exornation is a gorgious beautifying of the tongue with borowed wordes, and change of sentence or speech with much varietie. First therefore (as *Tullie* saith) an oration is made to seme right excellent by the kind selfe, by the colour and juice of speech. There are three maner of stiles or inditings, the great or mightie kinde, when we use great wordes, or vehement figures.
>
> The small kinde, when wee moderate our heate by meaner wordes, and use not the most stirring sentences.
>
> The lowe ["lawe," 1585 edition] kinde, when we use no *Metaphores* nor translated words, nor yet use any amplifications, but goe plainly to worke, and speake altogether in common wordes.[7]

The conviction that "moving is of a higher degree than teaching" and the association of an elaborate style with the power to move partly explain the emphasis which the Renaissance placed upon "copiousness" and upon the figures of rhetoric with which the style can be embellished. All rhetoricians were convinced that the object of eloquence was to inculcate wisdom, but, as it were in spite of themselves, they allowed the weight of their criticism to fall upon the means of achieving this end. While believing that the ideal orator must be not a specialist but a man of almost universal learning, Cicero makes such a point of the superiority of the grand style that he gives ammunition to those who would make eloquence an end in itself. His treatment of the Sophists, who are ordinarily accused of this perversion of rhetoric, indicates his own position. In the *Orator,* far from condemning them wholly, he merely points out their limitations—that they seek to delight more than to persuade, that their style is more charming than vigorous. The Sophists are the orators of the middle style, which is "fuller and somewhat more robust than the simple style . . . but plainer than the grandest style. . . . It is, as a matter of fact, a brilliant and florid, highly coloured and polished style in which all the charms of language and thought are intertwined."[8] The grand style of oratory excels the Sophistic in being yet more "copious" and more vehement. Thus Cicero and his followers consciously or unconsciously separate content from form, isolate style, or *elocutio,* which Wilson calls "that part of *Rhetorique,* the which above all other is most beautifull,"[9] and encourage elaborateness as a means to persuasion.

Since poet and orator were so closely associated, rhetorical theory

7. *Wilson's Arte of Rhetorique,* ed. Mair, p. 169.
8. *Orator,* ed. and tr. H. M. Hubbell, Loeb Classical Library (Cambridge, Mass., Harvard University Press, 1942), 91, 96.
9. *Wilson's Arte of Rhetorique,* p. 160.

inevitably had a powerful effect on poetic style. Moody Prior has shown[1] the fondness of the early writers of Elizabethan tragedy for a highly ornamented style in which patterns of sound play an important part. The imitation of Seneca, which encouraged this tendency, may itself have been partly due to the cultivation of a Ciceronian taste in rhetoric. In Seneca's plays, in any case, the Elizabethan dramatists found a declamatory style closely related to the Sophistic tradition recorded by the Elder Seneca for the benefit of his sons. The flowers of rhetoric bloom luxuriantly in Senecan tragedy. As Elizabethan tragedy developed, the formal and florid style of the early plays was superseded by a style less self-conscious and, as Moody Prior observes,[2] more closely bound to the dramatic action. Although the style of Fletcherian tragicomedy is affected by this movement in that it often borrows the vocabulary of conversation, as Dryden noticed, and makes use of flexible and varied rhythms, it is characteristically elaborate and related more loosely to the poetic action than is the style of Shakespeare, Webster, Tourneur, or Jonson. The Beaumont and Fletcher plays provide more examples of Sophistic rhetoric than the plays of any of their contemporaries. In the poetry of these plays eloquence is more important than wisdom; virtuosity is cultivated at the expense of relevance. It may be that this style is the result of the reinforcement of current rhetorical theory by the influence of the declamatory style in satire and romance and, more directly, of the declamations of Seneca the Elder. But all questions of influence aside, it is apparent that such a style is peculiarly oratorical and that it is by Renaissance standards the proper choice for a sort of drama which seeks mainly to delight and to move, or, as we should say, in which there is a marked decrease in meaning and a proportionate increase in the relative importance of emotion.

Although the style of Fletcherian tragicomedy is typically elaborate, there are two reasons why it is not uniformly so. One is that the three styles distinguished by Cicero were thought not only to be conducive to three different effects but to be appropriate to three categories of speakers and of topics—the grand style for gods and princes and what concerns them (and hence for hymns, epics, and tragedies), the middle style for the "civiller and better sort" of citizens and their affairs (and hence for comedy), and the plain style for laborers of all kinds, including shepherds, and for "base and low matters" (and hence for pastoral and satire, although the Juvenalians, as we have seen, often soared above this level).[3] The decorum of tragicomedy, which is the inheritor of tragedy, epic (via romance), comedy, pastoral, and satire, properly makes room for every style. The second reason for stylistic variation in the Beau-

---

1. *The Language of Tragedy* (New York, Columbia University Press, 1947), pp. 24–6.
2. *Ibid.*, pp. 31, 59.
3. Puttenham, "Arte of English Poesie," G. G. Smith, *2*, 158–9.

mont and Fletcher tragicomedies is, of course, their multiple authorship. Much has been written about the styles of the three chief collaborators, Fletcher, Massinger, and Beaumont, which the verse tests have helped to distinguish.[4] It is not of the first importance which dramatist was responsible for a given style, and in what I have to say I shall not be primarily concerned to prove that certain characteristics were Fletcher's and his only, or Massinger's or Beaumont's. Accepting in the main the distinctions already made, I shall illustrate what seem to me valid differences between the styles of the three chief authors, but I shall discuss them as variations of one style, as they would doubtless appear to be if nothing were known of the authorship of the plays. The differences I shall mention may properly be thought of as gradations of the tragicomic style.

The range of the style between the obviously elaborate and the seemingly plain can be seen by comparing the lament of Demetrius in *The Humorous Lieutenant* upon the supposed death of Celia with the speech which Arbaces makes in *A King and No King* when he first realizes that he is in love with his sister.[5] Demetrius speaks as follows:

> O matchless sweetness, whither art thou vanished?
> O thou fair soul of all thy Sex, what Paradise
> Hast thou inrich'd and blest?
>
>   .   .   .
>
>   art thou dead *Celia,*
> Dead my poor wench? my joy, pluckt green with violence:
> O fair sweet flower, farewel; Come, thou destroyer
> Sorrow, thou melter of the soul, dwell with me;
> Dwell with me solitary thoughts, tears, cryings,
> Nothing that loves the day, love me, or seek me,
> Nothing that loves his own life haunt about me:
> And Love, I charge thee, never charm mine eyes more,
> Nor ne're betray a beauty to my curses:
> For I shall curse all now, hate all, forswear all,
> And all the brood of fruitful nature vex at,
> For she is gone that was all, and I nothing—
>
>   IV, ii; Cam., *2*, 339

This is what we should call "rhetorical" language today, meaning that the style is showy and calls attention to itself by its wealth of ornament.

---

4. See, for example, Gayley, *Beaumont, the Dramatist*, pp. 243–99, and Oliphant, *The Plays of Beaumont and Fletcher*, pp. 31–94.

5. Here, as elsewhere in this chapter, the examples are taken from the high points of dramatic action. Such a principle of selection seems to me justified by the fact that all the other distinctive characteristics of the pattern of tragicomedy appear most clearly at these high points. It is reasonable to look in the same places for characteristic use of language.

With its balance and antithesis, its repetition and alliteration, it is "brilliant and florid" like the style which Cicero associates with the Sophists. The sound of the lines is vastly important.

Superficially very different is Arbaces' speech:

> Why should there be such musick in a voyce,
> And sin for me to hear it? All the world
> May take delight in this, and 'tis damnation
> For me to do so: You are fair and wise
> And vertuous I think, and he is blest
> That is so near you as your[6] brother is;
> But you are nought to me but a disease;
> Continual torment without hope of ease;
> Such an ungodly sickness I have got,
> That he that undertakes my cure, must first
> O'rethrow Divinity, all moral Laws,
> And leave mankind as unconfin'd as beasts,
> Allowing 'em to do all actions
> As freely as they drink when they desire.
>
> III; Cam., 1, 181–2

In this passage patterns of sound are much less obvious than in Demetrius' lament: there is none of the repetition and very little of the alliteration which are so abundant in the other passage. The one conspicuous aural effect which is used here and not in the passage from *The Humorous Lieutenant* is rhyme, and that is used sparingly. Although the rhythm is a more regular iambic pentameter, relatively free of the extra syllables found in every line of Demetrius' lament, the pattern of five accents is less insistent on account of the greater number of run-on lines. The passage from *The Humorous Lieutenant* is typical of Fletcher's versification and the passage from *A King and No King* of Beaumont's. With regard to the relative importance of patterns of sound the two original partners represent opposite ends of the scale.

In vocabulary both passages are as simple as they are extravagant in sentiment, but Beaumont's passage begins, at least, on a conversational tone, while Fletcher's launches immediately into the formality of a set piece. In spite of the hyperbole in which Arbaces indulges, his speech conveys some impression of naturalness, while that of Demetrius appears to be flamboyant artifice from beginning to end. The difference, though it is one of degree, has a marked effect on the appeal which each passage makes.

The less formal rhetoric tends to produce a sharper delineation of character. For the emotional effect at which it aims, Fletcher's passage

6. I have preferred the reading of the first two quartos here to the "my brother" of the Second Folio.

relies heavily upon its compelling rhythm, its verbal elaboration, and the formal tone which serves notice immediately that what follows is pitched in a high emotional key. Beaumont's passage, with its quieter tone and simpler diction, relies much more upon the depiction of an individual in a tragic plight. The definition of character is one of the means by which Arbaces' speech evokes pity; his lines are characteristic of him in this situation, whereas the lines of Demetrius might have been spoken by many others. They express the situation but not the man. The rhetorical means chosen to make this situation emotionally persuasive might equally well be applied to other situations as well as to other characters. Beaumont's more careful suiting of language to a particular character in a particular situation is comparable to the use of description as a rhetorical device in the Senecan declamations and elsewhere. The emotional effect is heightened by the clarity and immediacy of the representation. In this respect Beaumont's rhetoric is a good example of rhetoric in poetic—of rhetorical means closely related to poetic action.

The projection of the complex character of Arbaces can be seen in two other speeches which are also distinctly and painfully personal:

> *Arb.* Nay, you shall hear the case in short *Panthea,*
> And when thou hear'st it, thou wilt blush for me,
> And hang thy head down like a Violet
> Full of the mornings dew: There is a way
> To gain thy freedome, but 'tis such a one
> As puts thee in worse bondage, and I know,
> Thou wouldst encounter fire, and make a proof
> Whether the gods have care of innocence,
> Rather than follow it: Know that I have lost,
> The only difference betwixt man and beast,
> My reason.
>   *Pan.* Heaven forbid.
>   *Arb.* Nay 'tis gone;
> And I am left as far without a bound,
> As the wild Ocean, that obeys the winds;
> Each sodain passion throwes me where it lists,
> And overwhelms all that oppose my will:
> I have beheld thee with a lustfull eye;
> My heart is set on wickedness to act
> Such sins with thee, as I have been afraid
> To think of, if thou dar'st consent to this,
> Which I beseech thee do not, thou maist gain
> Thy liberty, and yield me a content;
> If not, thy dwelling must be dark and close,

Where I may never see thee; For heaven knows
That laid this punishment upon my pride,
Thy sight at some time will enforce my madness
To make a start e'ne to thy ravishing;
Now spit upon me, and call all reproaches
Thou canst devise together, and at once
Hurle 'em against me: for I am a sickness
As killing as the plague, ready to seize thee.

IV; Cam., *1, 210–11*

But certain factors in these speeches tend to counteract the emphasis
on the particular. For instance, the hyperbole by which the horror of
Arbaces' situation is exaggerated has the simultaneous effect of general-
izing his passion. His incestuous desire is described vaguely and
ominously as the loss of distinction between man and beast, the triumph
of lawless passion, a fatal sickness. And this impression of generality
is strengthened by the use of conventional similes—the modest violet,
the sea of passion. These speeches of Arbaces are not wholly lacking
in the general rhetorical effectiveness found in Demetrius' lament.

One of the best speeches in *The Maid's Tragedy* again shows Beaumont's style to advantage, while revealing a little more about its operation. Evadne has just come to Amintor holding the knife with which
she has killed the King and proclaiming, "Joy to *Amintor!*" He replies:

Those have most power to hurt us that we love,
We lay our sleeping lives within their arms.
Why, thou hast rais'd up mischief to his[7] height,
And found out one to out-name thy other faults;
Thou hast no intermission of thy sins,
But all thy life is a continual ill;
Black is thy colour now, disease thy nature.
Joy to *Amintor!* thou hast toucht a life,
The very name of which had power to chain
Up all my rage, and calm my wildest wrongs.

v; Cam., *1, 70*

The quiet, reflective tone of the first two lines is extraordinarily effective in the circumstances and makes a brilliant contrast to the bitter
denunciation which follows. As in the speeches of Arbaces the diction
is free of the more conspicuous patterns of sound. Here, however, the
relative simplicity does not accompany a concentration upon the individual character. Although Amintor's nature is reflected in the speech,

7. I have preferred the reading "his height" of the early quartos to "this height" in
the Second Folio.

the pathos of his situation is rendered by other means—first by a generalization and then by a hyperbolic denunciation which makes Evadne the epitome of evil. In spite of the explicit statement of Amintor's characteristic respect for royalty, the speech is less personal than the speeches of Arbaces which I have quoted above. This moment in the drama is given the maximum of effectiveness by the familiar rhetorical means of amplification—by the sententious generalization and hyperbole—but the lines could be applied with only the slightest changes to other situations in other plays.

Since the sententious utterance recommended by the experts in rhetoric is used by many dramatists who are quite unlike Beaumont or Fletcher, a brief comparison may be useful here. When Ferdinand is killed in the last scene of *The Duchess of Malfi* his dying breath is spent on a sententious couplet:

> Whether we fall by ambition, blood, or lust,
> Like Diamonds, we are cut with our owne dust.

This speech is effective not because of its aphoristic expression of a moral truth but because it applies so exactly to the principal characters of the play. Even the Duchess, though only slightly tainted by the encompassing evil, has destroyed herself by stooping to a deception of which she disapproves. At the same time her tragedy illustrates the superlative value of human nature and its resistance to all but its own corruption. The power of Ferdinand's aphorism, then, is seen in its sudden illumination of the compound tragedies in this play. Amintor's touching observation,

> Those have most power to hurt us that we love,
> We lay our sleeping lives within their arms.

has no such effect. It applies primarily to the relationship of the King and Evadne and hence seems to evoke pity for the murdered tyrant. The generalization has no direct bearing upon the denunciation which follows or upon Amintor's situation. The effectiveness of the lines depends upon generality rather than particularity. Vagueness is all.

The process of amplification, associated with the more elaborate styles, is better illustrated by a longer quotation from the scene in which Amintor discovers on his wedding night the truth about Evadne:

> Is flesh so earthly to endure all this?
> Are these the joyes of Marriage? *Hymen* keep
> This story (that will make succeeding youth
> Neglect thy Ceremonies) from all ears.
> Let it not rise up for thy shame and mine
> To after ages; we will scorn thy Laws,

If thou no better bless them; touch the heart
Of her that thou hast sent me, or the world
Shall know there's not an Altar that will smoak
In praise of thee; we will adopt us Sons;
Then vertue shall inherit, and not blood:
If we do lust, we'l take the next we meet,
Serving our selves as other Creatures do,
And never take note of the Female more,
Nor of her issue. I do rage in vain,

. . .

I know too much, would I had doubted still;
Was ever such a marriage night as this!
You powers above, if you did ever mean
Man should be us'd thus, you have thought a way
How he may bear himself, and save his honour:
Instruct me in it; for to my dull eyes
There is no mean, no moderate course to run,
I must live scorn'd, or be a murderer:
Is there a third? Why is this night so calm?
Why does not Heaven speak in Thunder to us,
And drown her voice?

II; Cam., I, 20–1

The unexpected shift at the end is the one device which conveys (by a stroke of psychological verisimilitude) the impression of a particular individual in a particular situation. In the rest of the speech apostrophe, hyperbole, and the commonplace contrast between man and beast, equally useful in the speeches of Arbaces, amplify Amintor's rage. Repetition and alliteration, though nowhere near so frequent as in Demetrius' lament, heighten the emotional effect.

Philaster's tirade when he comes upon Arethusa and Euphrasia (disguised as Bellario) shows that Beaumont's style can be yet more oratorical and that when it is so it relies more heavily, like Fletcher's style, upon stock rhetorical devices and especially upon patterns of sound:

Let me love lightning, let me be embrac'd
And Kist by Scorpions, or adore the eyes
Of Basilisks, rather than trust to tongues,
And shrink these veins up; stick me here a stone
Lasting to ages in the memory
Of this damn'd act.

IV, i; Cam., I, 123

The scorpions and basilisks (and the asps which he mentions a few lines later) are part of the standard equipment of Elizabethan amplifiers, though such similes are most frequently associated with Lyly. Wilson recommends similitudes using "brute Beastes, and things that have no life" as a means of amplifying.[8] The amount of alliteration in the passage is striking.

Although Beaumont's versification is usually easy to distinguish from Fletcher's, the styles of the two men are not so different with regard to rhetorical devices as they might seem from the first two examples I have quoted. Beaumont's poetry is usually less ornamented but far from plain. In tone it tends to be more conversational. Sometimes, but not often, it operates through a vivid realization of an individual in a unique situation. Most often some of the familiar rhetorical devices for amplification are used to make the character's plight moving, and the more indiscriminately these devices are used the less precisely the emotion evoked fits the given situation. There comes a point beyond which rhetoric is not simply a means of making the action of the play persuasive but rather the means of exciting emotions for which the action of the play provides an occasion. Where this is the case the emotion is more vague and the rhetoric more ornamental. The change could be illustrated by many more passages which extend all the way from the plainest style of Beaumont to the most elaborate style of Fletcher. The point I have described would be passed long before leaving Beaumont for Fletcher.

One more quotation from *Philaster* will show how the styles of the two men blend on occasion. Here the repetition and alliteration of Fletcher are combined in such a way with versification more characteristic of Beaumont that the passage has been attributed to both authors. It is an antifeminist tirade so general that it is unnecessary to give the occasion on which it is spoken by Philaster:

> Now you may take that little right I have
> To this poor Kingdom; give it to your Joy,
> For I have no joy in it. Some far place,
> Where never womankind durst set her foot,
> For bursting with her poisons, must I seek,
> And live to curse you;
> There dig a Cave, and preach to birds and beasts,
> What woman is, and help to save them from you.
> How heaven is in your eyes, but in your hearts,
> More hell than hell has; how your tongues like Scorpions,
> Both heal and poyson; how your thoughts are woven
> With thousand changes in one subtle webb,
> And worn so by you. How that foolish man,
> That reads the story of a womans face,

8. *Wilson's Arte of Rhetorique*, p. 188.

And dies believing it, is lost for ever.
How all the good you have, is but a shadow,
I'th' morning with you, and at night behind you,
Past and forgotten. How your vows are frosts,
Fast for a night, and with the next sun gone.
How you are, being taken all together,
A meer confusion, and so dead a *Chaos,*
That love cannot distinguish. These sad Texts
Till my last hour, I am bound to utter of you.
So farewel all my wo, all my delight.

III, i; Cam., I, 115

Again a comparison may help to show what is distinctive in Beaumont and Fletcher's use of common rhetorical devices. Shakespeare contrives for Troilus a speech in which individual disillusionment is amplified and generalized:

This she? No, this is Diomed's Cressida!
If beauty have a soul, this is not she;
If souls guide vows, if vows be sanctimonies,
If sanctimony be the gods' delight,
If there be rule in unity itself—
This is not she. O madness of discourse,
That cause sets up with and against itself!
Bifold authority! where reason can revolt
Without perdition, and loss assume all reason
Without revolt: this is, and is not, Cressid!
Within my soul there doth conduce a fight
Of this strange nature, that a thing inseparate
Divides more wider than the sky and earth;
And yet the spacious breadth of this division
Admits no orifex for a point as subtle
As Ariachne's broken woof to enter.

Troilus and Cressida, v, ii, 137–52

It is clearly a trick of rhetoric to develop to the point of logical absurdity the impossibility of Cressida's betrayal, yet all the rhetorical energy here is harnessed to accelerate the main movement of the play. The story of Troilus' fatal infatuation is seen against a background of ideal order described in the famous speech on "degree" given by Ulysses in one of the opening scenes. Inversions of moral values are directly related there to disturbances of the entire cosmic hierarchy:

Frights, changes, horrors

Divert and crack, rend and deracinate
The unity and married calm of states

Quite from their fixure!

I, iii, 98–101

The statement "If there be rule in unity itself— / This is not she" makes explicit the connection of the hero's dilemma with the philosophical scheme of the play. It is a generalization which not only enhances the dramatic moment but reveals its place in the larger structure. The speech is furthermore perfectly suited to the character of Troilus, for the duplicity which it cries out against is the very fault to dismay one who is "as true as truth's simplicity / And simpler than the infancy of truth." Here, as in no play by Beaumont and Fletcher, the rhetorical elaboration is thoroughly integrated with the other elements of the drama.

Before discussing further the relation between elaborate style and emotional effect, we must consider another use of language in the Beaumont and Fletcher plays which at first appears to aim at an intellectual rather than an emotional effect. One of the best examples is the reply of Cleopatra in *The False One,* when her sister Arsino asks her whether she can "stand unmov'd" in the face of the present danger:

> Yes, *Arsino,*
> And with a Masculine Constancy deride
> Fortunes worst malice, as a Servant to
> My Vertues, not a Mistress; then we forsake
> The strong Fort of our selves, when we once yield,
> Or shrink at her assaults; I am still my self,
> And though disrob'd of Soveraignty, and ravish'd
> Of ceremonious duty, that attends it,
> Nay, grant they had slav'd my Body, my free mind
> Like to the Palm-tree walling fruitful *Nile,*
> Shall grow up straighter and enlarge it self
> 'Spight of the envious weight that loads it with:
> Think of thy Birth (Arsino) common burdens
> Fit common Shoulders; teach the multitude
> By suffering nobly what they fear to touch at;
> The greatness of thy mind does soar a pitch,
> Their dim eyes (darkened by their narrow souls)
> Cannot arrive at.

v, iv; Cam., *3,* 365

This passage resembles others I have quoted in its somewhat conversational tone and its freedom from conspicuous patterns of sound such as adorn Demetrius' lament and Philaster's denunciation of women. With regard to other forms of rhetorical ornament, Cleopatra's speech, without being flamboyant, contains many metaphors and one simile of epic formality ("Like to the Palm-tree . . ."). The rhetoricians usually referred to such figures as "tropes," since the words are "turned" from their ordinary, literal meaning; Puttenham, who makes a different sort of classification, considers metaphor and simile as "sensable figures," appealing chiefly to the mind, in contrast to the "auricular figures," which appeal chiefly to the ear. On the basis of this classification of figures Cleopatra's speech would seem to appeal more to the mind than those speeches which depend heavily on "auricular figures" such as alliteration.

This kind of distinction seems to be supported by another difference between Cleopatra's speech and those we have been considering. Not only are there many run-on lines, as in Beaumont's verse, but several lines are grouped together in a tightly cohesive unit. A more solid logical structure unites the passage "I am still my self . . . that loads it with" than unites any six-and-a-half lines previously quoted. It is necessary here to follow the logical connections: "Though disrob'd . . . and ravish'd . . . [and though] they have slav'd my Body, my free mind . . . shall grow up . . . 'Spite of the envious weight that [i.e., fortune's malice] loads it with." Though flexible, this blank verse does not flow freely. It has a distinctive toughness and density derived from its argumentative structure.

The kind of blank verse just described is typical of Massinger. As Maurice Chelli says, "ses personnages pensent et raisonnent beaucoup. Ils s'efforcent constamment de prouver, de convaincre, par des arguments bons ou mauvais, sincères ou sophistiques . . ."[9] Swinburne's criticism is also to the point: "The style of Massinger . . . is radically and essentially unlike the style of his rivals: it is more serviceable, more businesslike, more eloquently practical, and more rhetorically effusive —but never effusive beyond the bounds of effective rhetoric—than the style of any Shakespearean or of any Jonsonian dramatist."[1] "Serviceable, businesslike, eloquently practical" well describe a style whose great virtue, as seen in Cleopatra's defense of personal integrity, is the persuasive definition of an idea—in this case an ideal of conduct. For the emphasis of the speech is not so much on the character of the speaker as on what is said.

It might be concluded from this line of analysis that while the poetry of Beaumont and of Fletcher aims to please and to move, Massinger's poetry aims to teach, but this distinction is not valid. One flaw in such an argument is suggested by Cicero's comment that the plain style, which aims to teach, should be very sparingly embellished with metaphor (Wilson countenances no metaphors in the "lowe kind" of style).[2] Massinger's style, though "businesslike," is metaphorical and not truly

9. *Le Drame de Massinger* (Lyon, M. Audin, 1923), p. 119.

1. A. C. Swinburne, "Philip Massinger," *Contemporaries of Shakespeare,* ed. E. Gosse and T. J. Wise (London, Heinemann, 1919), p. 175.

2. Cicero *Orator* 79–82; *Wilson's Arte of Rhetorique,* p. 169.

plain. Swinburne also characterizes it as "rhetorically effusive." And when the effect of Cleopatra's speech is carefully studied, the arousing of emotion is seen to be an important factor. Within the framework of the play the speech is designed to bolster the courage of Arsinoe, who responds to Cleopatra with the assurance, "I am new created." In the audience the speech is clearly intended to arouse admiration for Cleopatra by setting forth the nobility of her ideal. Intellectual and emotional appeals are combined here as Cicero believed they should be. The prominence of reasoning (when the speech is compared with Fletcher's poetry or Beaumont's) should not obscure the characteristics which make Cleopatra's words moving.

Most of Massinger's speeches in the Beaumont and Fletcher plays do not have this combination of wisdom and eloquence. More typical is the following speech of Sophia in *The Bloody Brother:*

> Divide me first, or tear me limb by limb,
> And let them find as many several Graves
> As there are villages in *Normandy:*
> And 'tis less sin, than thus to weaken it.
> To hear it mention'd doth already make me
> Envy my dead Lord, and almost Blaspheme
> Those powers that heard my prayer for fruitfulness,
> And did not with my first birth close my womb:
> To me alone my second blessing proves
> My first of misery, for if that Heaven
> Which gave me *Rollo,* there had staid his bounty,
> And *Otto,* my dear *Otto,* ne're had been,
> Or being, had not been so worth my love,
> The stream of my affection had run constant
> In one fair current, all my hopes had been
> Laid up in one; and fruitful *Normandy*
> In this division had not lost her glories:
> For as 'tis now, 'tis a fair Diamond,
> Which being preserv'd intire, exceeds all value,
> But cut in pieces (though these pieces are
> Set in fine gold by the best work-mans cunning)
> Parts with all estimation: So this Dukedom,
> As 'tis yet whole, the neighbouring Kings may covet,
> But cannot compass; which divided, will
> Become the spoil of every barbarous foe
> That will invade it.
>
> I, i; Cam., 4, 256–7

Again groups of lines are held together by the logical structure of the sentences, and the process of reasoning is conspicuously used, as in the careful analogy of the dukedom with a diamond. But the substance of what is said is very slight when compared to what Cleopatra says. The whole paraphernalia of logical argument is used to elaborate Sophia's appeal for unity. Her speech is an example of amplification and, as such, is primarily addressed to the emotions, though making use of the process of reasoning. Rymer shows his awareness of the copious elaboration by his comment, already quoted, that the speech "seems to present a *well-breath'd* and *practis'd Scold,* who vents her passion and eases her mind by talking, and can weep and talk ever-lastingly."[3] Like many of Massinger's speeches, this one is, within the framework of the play, an oration, designed to move other characters on the stage while it also appeals to the emotions of the audience. Sophia's advice is made persuasive by devices which are conspicuous in the Senecan declamations—by an appeal for pity and by an ingenious analogy. Ingenuity is, in fact, the most notable characteristic of the speech. The means of persuasion, so cleverly chosen, make their own separate appeal, in the hope that the audience may be as much pleased by the performance as moved with pity for Sophia. This is rhetoric in the Sophistic tradition.

Chapman, who was powerfully influenced by classical rhetoric, uses reasoned argument and elaborate simile to very different effect in the opening speech of *Bussy d'Ambois:*

> Man is a torch borne in the wind; a dream
> But of a shadow, summ'd with all his substance;
> And as great seamen, using all their wealth
> And skills in Neptune's deep invisible paths,
> In tall ships richly built and ribb'd with brass,
> To put a girdle round about the world,
> When they have done it, coming near their haven,
> Are fain to give a warning-piece, and call
> A poor, staid fisherman, that never pass'd
> His country's sight, to waft and guide them in:
> So when we wander furthest through the waves
> Of glassy Glory, and the gulfs of State,
> Topt with all titles, spreading all our reaches,
> As if each private arm would sphere the earth,
> We must to Virtue for her guide resort,
> Or we shall shipwrack in our safest port.
>
> I, i, 18–33[4]

At first sight this passage, with its descriptive detail and its marked alliteration, may seem more ornamental than the speech from *The Bloody*

3. *The Tragedies of the Last Age,* p. 52.
4. Reference is to *The Tragedies of George Chapman,* ed. T. M. Parrott (New York, E. P. Dutton, 1910).

Brother, but when the terms of Chapman's comparisons are studied, they prove to be rigorously functional in revealing the mind of Bussy. The shifting imagery ("a torch," "a dream," "great seamen"), unlike Sophia's neat comparison of a diamond or Cleopatra's palm tree, conveys something of the hero's intellectual turmoil in the mental effort it imposes upon the listener. The pictorial development of the voyaging ships is important for the understanding of Bussy's complex attitude toward the nature of man, one of the chief concerns of the tragedy. Thus the reasoning, based upon much more elaborate similes than Massinger's, cannot ultimately be summed up as ingenious. It is in reality even more intellectually solid than it appears, whereas the reasoning in *The Bloody Brother* is only speciously intellectual. Chapman's rhetoric, different as it is from Webster's or Shakespeare's in the examples I have cited, nevertheless functions like theirs in contributing to a closely integrated design of plot, character, and theme. It constantly makes manifest a central core of meaning.

It remains to see how Massinger's rhetoric is related to that of Beaumont and Fletcher. Though it may not often be so intensely emotional as theirs, the main distinction to be made is that Massinger relies upon the structure of argument even when the emphasis of the speech is clearly emotional. Two roughly comparable speeches from *The Double Marriage* illustrate the difference. The first, by Fletcher, is Pandulpho's lament for his son and reproach to his daughter-in-law who is the unwitting murderess. The second, by Massinger, is the tirade in which Sesse expresses grief and rage at the behavior of his daughter Martia.

> O my Son,
> Nature turns to my heart again, my dear Son,
> Son of my age, would'st thou go out so quickly?
> So poorly take thy leave, and never see me?
> Was this a kind stroak daughter? could you love him?
> Honour his Father, and so deadly strike him?
> O wither'd timeless youth, are all thy promises,
> Thy goodly growth of Honors come to this?
> Do I halt still ith'world, and trouble nature,
> When her main pieces founder, and fail dayly?
> v, i; Cam., *6,* 399

> Thou, I want a name,
> By which to stile thee: All articulate sounds
> That do express the mischief of vile woman,
> That are, or have been, or shall be, are weak
> To speak thee to the height. Witch, Parricide,
> For thou, in taking leave of modesty,
> Hast kild thy father, and his honor lost;

He's but a walking shadow to torment thee.
To leave, and rob thy father; then set free
His foes, whose slavery he did prefer
Above all treasure, was a strong defeazance
To cut off, even the surest bonds of mercy.
After all this, having given up thy self,
Like to a sensual beast, a slave to lust,
To play the whore, and then (high Heaven it racks me)
To find out none to quench thy appetite,
But the most cruel King, whom next to Hell,
Thy father hated; and whose black imbraces
Thou shouldst have fled from, as the whips of furies;
What canst thou look for?

v, i; Cam., 6, 405–06

Pandulpho's emotion is projected in the repetition of "son" and "so" and in such combinations as "founder and fail dayly." It is the patterns of sound which make the pathos compelling in spite of a phraseology which is otherwise undistinguished. The feelings of Sesse are given a logical formulation: no names are adequate for Martia, but metaphorically speaking she is a parricide, since she has utterly disgraced her father; to have left and robbed him and freed his enemies is enough to deprive her of any claim to mercy, but having, in addition to all this, made herself the mistress of her father's worst enemy, what treatment can she expect? Sesse presents the legal case against his daughter, appealing to the judgment of an imaginary arbiter and in effect appealing to the sympathy of the audience.

Massinger's rendering of a typically tragicomic dilemma can be seen in *The Custom of the Country,* where Guiomar addresses Rutilio after discovering that he has killed her son. Since she has previously promised him protection from the police, her situation is painfully delicate:

What ere thou art
To whom I have given means of life, to witness
With what Religion I have kept my promise,
Come fearless forth, but let thy face be cover'd,
That I hereafter be not forc't to know thee,
For motherly affection may return
My vow once paid to heaven. Thou hast taken from me
The respiration of my heart, the light
Of my swoln eyes, in his life that sustain'd me:
Yet my word given to save you, I make good,
Because what you did, was not done with malice,

II, i; Cam., 1, 332

The restrained and lucid statement of Guiomar's position makes her speech quietly affecting, though it has not the intensity that one often finds at such moments in Fletcherian tragicomedy. The potentialities of Massinger's style for presenting complex and tightly articulated thought are largely wasted on the bold contrasts of this sort of situation, while at the same time the style lacks the more direct emotional appeal which the situation seems to call for. Here and also in Sesse's speech the progression is too gradual and methodical to be exciting.

There is a special sort of brilliance, however, in which Massinger excels and which has a direct bearing upon the problem of appraising the style of Fletcherian tragicomedy. In *The Queen of Corinth* occurs a sort of *débat* between the lovers Euphanes and Beliza on the question of whether Euphanes should feel indebted to Beliza for the financial assistance she has given him. She offers to prove

> That whereas you profess your self my debtor,
> That I am yours.
>   *Euph.* Your Ladyship then must use
> Some Sophistry I ne'r heard of.
>   *Bel.* By plain reasons,
> For look you, had you never sunk beneath
> Your wants, or if those wants had found supply
> From *Crates,* your unkind and covetous brother,
> Or any other man, I then had miss'd
> A subject upon which I worthily
> Might exercise my bounty: whereas now
> By having happy opportunity
> To furnish you before, and in your travels,
> With all conveniencies that you thought useful,
> That Gold which would have rusted in my Coffers
> Being thus imploy'd, has rendred me a partner
> In all your glorious actions. And whereas
> Had you not been, I should have dy'd a thing
> Scarce known, or soon forgotten: there's no Trophy
> In which *Euphanes* for his worth is mentioned,
> But there you have been careful to remember,
> That all the good you did came from *Beliza.*
>
>   I, ii; Cam., *6, 9*

Ingenuity of reasoning, which plays some part in Sophia's speech, is here the whole show. There is no question of evoking powerful feeling but simply of delighting the audience with the cleverness of the debater's points. The same effect is even more apparent in the preposterous denouement of this play, when Beliza pleads for the death of Theanor

on the grounds that he has raped her, though she knows that in fact he
has not done so but has twice raped Merione, supposing her, on the second occasion, to be Beliza. Merione has just demanded Theanor in marriage when Beliza declaims:

> Is that justice?
> Shall one that is to suffer for a Rape
> Be by a Rape defended? Look upon
> The publick enemy of chastity,
> This lustful Satyr, whose enrag'd desires
> The ruine of one wretched Virgins honor
> Would not suffice; and shall the wrack of two
> Be his protection? May be I was ravish'd
> For his lust only, thou for his defence;
> O fine evasion! shall with such a slight
> Your Justice be deluded? your Laws cheated?
> And he that for one fact deserv'd to die,
> For sinning often, find impunity?
> But that I know thee I would swear thou wert
> A false Impostor, and suborn'd to this;
> And it may be thou art *Merione*:
> For hadst thou suffer'd truly what I have done,
> Thou wouldst like me complain, and call for vengeance,
> And our wrongs being equal, I alone
> Should not desire revenge: But be it so,
> If thou prevail, even he will punish it,
> And foolish mercy shew'd to him undo thee,
> Consider, fool, before it be too late,
> What joys thou canst expect from such a Husband,
> To whom thy first, and what's more, forc'd embraces,
> Which men say heighten pleasure, were distastful.
>
> v, iv; Cam., 6, 73–4

In estimating the effect of this speech, it must be remembered that the
audience and several characters on the stage, including notably Merione,
are well aware that the situation presupposed by Beliza is entirely
hypothetical. Persuasion is out of the question. The pleasure an audience derives from the speech may come in part from the perpetration
of a trick upon the villain Theanor but much more from the display
of forensic ability. Beliza's farfetched reasoning is calculated to amaze
and entertain. Several of her arguments are taken directly from the
amazing and entertaining sallies of the declaimers whom Seneca the
Elder heard on the case of the two maidens raped in one night (*Controversiae* i. 5). In the play as in the school of declamation the real object is not to convince anyone of anything and not to move the pas-

sions violently but to provide a certain emotional thrill and to delight by means of virtuosity.

In Fletcherian tragicomedy the "reasoning" style associated with Massinger is effective in realizing a typical scene of conflict as a sharply pointed debate. If the scene is to be realized in terms of intense passions Fletcher's verbal gymnastics or Beaumont's less obvious devices of amplification are more suitable. But these alternative methods, while distinct, are also similar in one respect, that they are all on the same side of the main dividing line between the various sorts of style. For Cicero and other classical rhetoricians, the low style, whose aim is to teach, is in a category by itself. Both the middle and grand styles make an emotional appeal, though they are assigned the respective aims of pleasing and moving. These aims cannot be kept wholly distinct and the means by which they are to be achieved admittedly overlap. The styles of Beaumont, Fletcher, and Massinger are similar, then, in that they all concentrate upon an emotional effect.

The implications of the analogy I have drawn between Massinger's style and Sophistic oratory point to a still closer similarity between his style and those of Beaumont and Fletcher. I have suggested that Beaumont and Fletcher are more intensely "moving," Massinger more "pleasing," but if we reconsider the emotional effects of Beaumont and Fletcher with the precedent of the Sophistic declaimers in mind, we realize that even the most stirring speeches of Arbaces, Amintor, Philaster, and Demetrius do not thoroughly engage the emotions. The response to this sort of rhetoric is double: the hearer is moved and aware of being moved. He admires the verbal technique at the same time that he responds to it. Such a response, though I have described it in a most un-Ciceronian fashion, seems to be what Cicero means by being "pleased" as opposed to being "moved" and "swayed." His description of Sophistic oratory, the origin of the middle style, applies to the styles of all three collaborators on the Beaumont and Fletcher plays and thus underlines their essential similarity. In the following passage Cicero arbitrarily reserves the word "oratorical" for the style of the practicing orator as opposed to the declaimer of the schools:

> More care must be taken to distinguish the oratorical style from the similar style of the Sophists mentioned above, who desire to use all the ornaments which the orator uses in forensic practice. But there is this difference, that, whereas their object is not to arouse the audience but to soothe it, not so much to persuade as to delight, they do it more openly than we and more frequently; they are on the look-out for ideas that are neatly put rather than reasonable; they frequently wander from the subject, they introduce mythology, they use far-fetched metaphors and

arrange them as painters do colour combinations; they make their
clauses balanced and of equal length, frequently ending with similar
sounds.[5]

In this description are compounded elements of the styles of Beaumont,
Fletcher, and Massinger. It might well serve as a description of the
style of Fletcherian tragicomedy.

From the comparisons already made it may be apparent that Fletcher's
style represents a greater specialization than the styles of his collaborators. He concentrates narrowly upon certain devices of which repetition is the most conspicuous. Puttenham puts repetition first in his
third category of figures, the "sententious" or "rhetorical" figures, which
appeal both to the ear and to the mind: "And first of all others your
figure that worketh by iteration or repetition of one word or clause
doth much alter and affect the eare and also the mynde of the hearer,
and therefore is counted a very brave figure both with the Poets and
rhetoriciens . . ."[6] In Demetrius' lament the bravery of this figure is
emphatically courted with the repetition of "dead," "dwell with me,"
"nothing that loves," "all," and less important words and phrases. The
repetition of "all" in the last three lines not only is the most insistent
repetition in the passage but illustrates a habit of Fletcher's of placing
the repeated word first in an accented then in an unaccented position in
the line:

> For I shall curse all now, hate all, forswear all,
> And all the brood of fruitful nature vex at,
> For she is gone that was all, and I nothing—

In this way the emphasis resulting from repetition is counterpointed
against the regular pattern of emphasis and produces the effect of synco-
pation. The excitement of this sort of repetition is brilliantly exploited in
Evadne's words as she stabs the King to death. In reply to his plea for
pity she says:

> Hell take me then; this for my Lord *Amintor;*
> This for my noble brother: and this stroke
> For the most wrong'd of women.
>
> v; Cam., *1, 63*

Both the first and the second "this" receive a strong accent through
trochaic substitution; the third is in a technically unaccented position,
preceding the strongly accented word which ends the line. Thus one is
aware of the strain between the insistent pattern of accents on the re-

---

5. *Orator 65.*
6. *The Arte of English Poesie*, ed. Willcock and Walker, p. 198. Puttenham's first two
categories are "auricular figures" and "sensable figures."

peated word and the normal pattern of accents in the iambic line. In the third instance the strain becomes acute.

The frequent alliteration in Fletcher's verse (a figure which Puttenham naturally describes as making little appeal to the mind and hence "auricular" rather than "sensable") is one of the chief indications of the importance of sound patterns in the total effect. When the end-stopped line, the third of the most obvious characteristics of his verse, is added to the other two, it becomes clear that a formal arrangement of sounds is the basis upon which Fletcher builds. For the end stopping, especially when accompanied, as it so often is in Fletcher, by feminine endings, breaks the rhythmical flow of the verse into well-defined units. Thus, in spite of the irregularity of extra syllables, the regular beat of the iambic pentameter line is emphasized by incessant repetition:

Out thou impudence,

Thou ulcer of thy Sex; when I first saw thee,
I drew into mine eyes mine own destruction,
I pull'd into my heart that sudden poyson,
That now consumes my dear content to cinders:
I am not now *Demetrius,* thou hast chang'd me;
Thou, woman, with thy thousand wiles hast chang'd me;
Thou Serpent with thy angel-eyes hast slain me;
And where, before I touch'd on this fair ruine,
I was a man, and reason made, and mov'd me,
Now one great lump of grief, I grow and wander.

The Humorous Lieutenant, IV, viii; Cam., *2,* 358

The sound of such lines as these is their most formidable weapon for the assault upon the spectator's emotions. The patterns of repetition and alliteration are interwoven with the insistent pattern of the five-foot line, reinforced by frequent parallels of construction.

Neither Beaumont nor Massinger relies so heavily upon versification for the desired emotional effect. Specifically, neither of them uses so much repetition, so much alliteration, or so marked a rhythm. Fletcher's unfailing sense of rhythm, perhaps his greatest gift as a versifier, recalls Cicero's belief in the importance of rhythm to the orator.[7] Although no exact comparison can be made, since Cicero is solely concerned with prose rhythms, his comments reveal the recognition in rhetorical theory of the profound effect which rhythm may have upon an audience. Together with repetition and alliteration, Fletcher's rhythm makes of his verse a sort of incantation—a short cut to that "enchantment of the soul" at which the orator aims.

Quite contrary to the point of view which I have been maintaining is the opinion of certain critics of Fletcher's verse that it is extraordinarily

7. *Orator* 162–238.

unrhetorical, "natural," and "conversational."[8] It is true that Fletcher successfully imitates the vocabulary of conversation and its casual structure, and in scenes where the emotional tension is comparatively relaxed (such as those which primarily convey information or those which are devoted to light, satirical comedy) the characteristics I have been describing are much less in evidence. These are scenes for which a low style is appropriate. But whenever the tension increases, as it does in each important scene, the formal patterns of sound become prominent, and the effect is far from conversational. Even in some of the freest and most natural passages there is stricter adherence to the five accents of the line as a rhythmical unit than in the blank verse of many other poets. The following lines of Celia in *The Humorous Lieutenant,* lightly satirical in tone, are decidedly irregular and yet are more obviously patterned than the expository lines of Melantius in *The Maid's Tragedy* placed after them:

> If I stay longer
> I shall number as many Lovers as *Lais* did;
> How they flock after me! upon my Conscience,
> I have had a dozen Horses given me this morning,
> I'le ev'n set up a Troop, and turn She-souldier,   5
> A good discreet wench now, that were not hidebound
> Might raise a fine estate here, and suddenly:
> For these warm things will give their Souls—I can go
>   no where
> Without a world of offerings to my Excellence:
> I am a Queen, a Goddesse, I know not what—   10
> And no constellation in all Heaven, but I out-shine it;
> And they have found out now I have no eyes
> Of mortal lights, but certain influences,
> Strange vertuous lightnings, humane nature starts at,
> And I can kill my twenty in a morning,   15
> With as much ease now—
> Ha! what are these? new projects?
> Where are my honourable Ladies? are you out too?
> Nay then I must buy the stock, send me good Carding:
> I hope the Princes hands be not in this sport;   20
> I have not seen him yet, cannot hear from him,
> And that troubles me: all these were recreations
> Had I but his sweet company to laugh with me:
> What fellow's that? another Apparition?
> This is the lovingst Age: I should know that face,   25
> Sure I have seen't before, not long since neither.
>
>   IV, i; Cam., *2,* 333

8. See, for example, Oliphant, *Plays of Beaumont and Fletcher*, p. 36; Prior, *Language of Tragedy*, pp. 30, 100.

All joyes upon him, for he is my friend:
Wonder not that I call a man so young my friend,
His worth is great; valiant he is, and temperate,
And one that never thinks his life his own,
If his friend need it: when he was a boy,   5
As oft as I return'd (as without boast)
I brought home conquest, he would gaze upon me,
And view me round, to find in what one limb
The vertue lay to do those things he heard:
Then would he wish to see my Sword, and feel   10
The quickness of the edge, and in his hand
Weigh it; he oft would make me smile at this;
His youth did promise much, and his ripe years
Will see it all perform'd.

I; Cam., I, 2–3

The two long lines (8 and 11) in Celia's soliloquy are the major irregularities; the two short lines (16 and 17) are in reality the halves of one line, separated to emphasize the break in the train of thought. Most of the lines are end stopped, and of the three which are not (6, 8, and 12) the first two end with a slight hesitation produced by the final unaccented syllable. The accumulation of phrases whose grammatical connection is loose suggests the language of conversation but also aids in maintaining the line as a rhythmical unit, for the short phrase ("and suddenly," "I know not what") is paired with a longer one to fill out a line. Despite the extra syllables in almost every line, the feeling of pentameter is stronger here than in Melantius' speech, where the pauses are so distributed in the last seven lines that no sense of the line as a unit remains. This variety is a much closer approximation of normal conversational freedom than the irregularity of Fletcher, which is more apparent than real.

It is not only in conversational speeches that Fletcher uses the device of accumulating brief phrases to make up the line. In some of the more extravagant speeches, such as the following of Zenocia's in *The Custom of the Country*, this mannerism, accentuated by the device of repetition, is carried to exasperating lengths:

Do not do this

To save me, do not lose your self I charge you,
I charge you by your love, that love [you] bear me;
That love, that constant love you have twin'd to me,
By all your promises, take heed you keep 'em,
Now is your constant tryal.

IV, i; Cam., I, 359

The structure of the lines here is not essentially different from that in Celia's speech. In both a seemingly casual arrangement of words contributes to a regular pattern of rhythm that cannot be called either natural or conversational.

In some of Fletcher's noblest speeches brief phrases are similarly strung together and by their structure accentuate the cadence of the lines. Caesar's formal eulogy of the dead Pompey in *The False One* is an example of the sparing use of this device and of repetition and alliteration to produce a passage of impressive rhetoric:

> Oh thou Conquerour,
> Thou glory of the world once, now the pity:
> Thou awe of Nations, wherefore didst thou fall thus?
> What poor fate follow'd thee, and pluckt thee on
> To trust thy sacred life to an *Egyptian;*
> The life and light of *Rome,* to a blind stranger,
> That honorable war ne'r taught a nobleness,
> Nor worthy circumstance shew'd what a man was,
> That never heard thy name sung, but in banquets;
> And loose lascivious pleasures? to a Boy,
> That had no faith to comprehend thy greatness,
> No study of thy life to know thy goodness;
> And leave thy Nation, nay, thy noble friend,
> Leave him (distrusted) that in tears falls with thee?
> (In soft relenting tears) hear me (great *Pompey*)
> (If thy great spirit can hear) I must task thee:
> Thou hast most unnobly rob'd me of my victory,
> My love, and mercy.
>
> II, i; Cam., *3, 318–19*

Here the marked Fletcherian rhythm—the succession of five-foot units —is supported not only by the devices I have mentioned but by a more careful balancing of words and phrases than is usual in Fletcher: glory —pity, life and light—blind stranger, honorable war—nobleness, worthy circumstance—man, faith—greatness, study of life—goodness. The arrangement of these words is such that they define the length of the lines and sometimes pair two lines together in the manner of a couplet. The result is a rhythmical pattern whose somewhat hypnotic effect is well suited to aid in evoking the vague sense of decline and fall characteristic of Fletcherian tragedy.

It is only a short step from Caesar's nobility to that of Archas in *The Loyal Subject,* where the atmosphere of tragicomedy, as we have already seen, permits an even more luxuriant growth of heroic sentiments. In Archas' "farewell to the military profession" the hero's noble resig-

nation is supported by all the rhetorical devices which Fletcher favored;
their contribution to a marked rhythmical pattern is again apparent:

> I yet remember when the *Volga* curl'd,
> The aged *Volga,* when he heav'd his head up,
> And rais'd his waters high, to see the ruins;
> The ruines our Swords made, the bloudy ruins,
> Then flew this Bird of honour bravely, Gentlemen;
> But these must be forgotten: so must these too,
> And all that tend to Arms, by me for ever.
>
> I, iii; Cam., 3, 84

The same characteristics can be seen in the speech (quoted in the last
chapter) in which Archas defends himself against the attack of Borowski
and the "base ungrateful people." Fletcher's verse, with its strong element of incantation, adapts itself even more readily than the verse of
Beaumont or Massinger to the presentation of the extravagant attitudes
of tragicomedy. Perfectly fitted for declamation by the actor, it works
upon the listener to arouse a variety of ill-defined feelings.

The best illustration of the curious charm of Fletcherian rhetoric
may be Memnon's burlesque heroics in *The Mad Lover* as he contem-
plates cutting out his heart:

> 'Tis but to dye, Dogs do it, Ducks with dabling,
> Birds sing away their Souls, & Babies sleep 'em,
> Why do I talk of that is treble vantage?
> For in the other World she is bound to have me;
>
> .   .   .
>
> There love is everlasting, ever young,
> Free from Diseases, ages, jealousies,
> Bawds, Beldames, Painters, Purgers: dye? 'tis nothing,
> Men drown themselves for joy to draw in Juleps
> When they are hot with Wine: In dreams we do it.
>
> II, i; Cam., 3, 17

The pleasure which these lines give is partly due to the burlesque, but
even more to the sheer manipulation of words. The effect is essentially
similar to that of other passages we have considered, though the meaning here is comic rather than serious. It would be quite false to conclude that Fletcher's patterns of sound have an absolute value, divorced
from the meaning of the words, for in that case we should not be
aware of the differences between the speeches of Archas, Demetrius,
and Memnon. In all these speeches, however, the patterns of sound produce an excitement which greatly intensifies the emotions described by
the words. In Memnon's soliloquy even the burlesque of heroic feeling
becomes strangely moving. To look for the source of these emotional

effects in Fletcher's imagery is unrewarding, for there is comparatively little imagery in his language—almost none of the sort of metaphor by which Shakespeare, Chapman, or Tourneur achieves emotional intensity. In Fletcher the verbal texture—the sound of the words arranged in formal patterns—is what chiefly moves and pleases. This is Fletcher's version of Sophistic oratory.

The predominance of the oratorical effect in Fletcherian tragicomedy fits very well the taste of the times in which Beaumont and Fletcher wrote. The learned and licentious monarch from the north set the fashion for his court in more than one way and through the court influenced the upper strata of society in the city. The Jacobean court is known for its sensational intrigues and scandals, such as those which became public property during the trial of the murderers of Sir Thomas Overbury. Equally well known is the lavishness of the entertainment made possible when James I emancipated his court from the restrictions of Elizabethan thrift : it was the period of the elaborate masques of Jonson and Inigo Jones. As these masques clearly reveal, however, the king's pleasure-loving courtiers were accustomed to a liberal mixture of learning with their artistic distractions.

It is not surprising that an audience with such tastes should be capitivated by the extravagant eloquence of Sophistic rhetoric. There is a slight flavor of bookishness in the exploitation of a tradition so firmly rooted in the schools—an appeal to the educated spectator. Furthermore, the legalistic character of many of the forensic debates in Beaumont and Fletcher doubtless had a special appeal to the age which saw the wrangles of Chief Justice Coke with the sovereign. Sensational situations abound, each one fully developed as the basis of an intense emotional experience. Yet at the same time the pattern of Fletcherian tragicomedy tends, as we have seen, to nullify the total meanings which either comedy or tragedy may have and to substitute for them a more rarefied aesthetic satisfaction in purely formal relationships. Here is a direct appeal to tastes both cultivated and jaded. The emphasis falls upon a rhetoric which is itself formal in its reliance upon conspicuous patterns of sound and which is the chief means of projecting the emotion of the dramatic moments. Both the extravagance and the formality of this style were aptly designed to appeal to the Jacobean audience.

Technique becomes a matter of special interest for such an audience. Concerned with the separate dramatic effects of which the play is composed and familiar with the various literary precedents, the sophisticated spectator eagerly awaits not only the emotional experience but a revelation of how it is achieved. He is prone to admire sheer artistic dexterity. Thus the Jacobeans were apt to be pleased by the imitation of the masterpieces of declamation recorded by Seneca the Elder, for the enjoyment of such performances comes from a lively appreciation of rhetorical skill. The dramas of the younger Seneca, written in the declamatory tradition, had, as is well known, an immense appeal to the Elizabethans, and a large measure of the ranting verse of Kyd and others is doubtless attributable to this influence, but the rhetoric of the most Senecan plays did not long stay in fashion. It was far less durable than Seneca's bequest of sententiousness or of the Stoical concept of heroic personal integrity. By the time Beaumont and Fletcher began to write, the imitation of Seneca, though still popular, was no longer a fresh artistic enterprise, but the moment was propitious for exploiting the possibilities of the declamatory style. To turn from the tragedian to the rhetores was to expose a new facet of a familiar tradition and gratify the taste of an audience interested in technique and more eager for delight than instruction. Each age takes something different from the storehouse of the classics; Beaumont and Fletcher were clever enough to see what would suit the theatrical world of their time.

To push further the correspondences between Beaumont and Fletcher and the court of James I is to risk being unfaithful both to the plays and to the audience which admired them. Critics as widely separated by age and purpose as Coleridge and the contemporary historian Esmé Wingfield-Stratford have made much of the political absolutism of Beaumont and Fletcher, citing *The Maid's Tragedy* and *The Loyal Subject* as plays which pandered to the king's taste. But the playhouse audience was not composed entirely of people who agreed with James I, and one must grant the justice of G. C. Macaulay's comment: "Surely if these authors were such devoted royalists, and aimed so constantly at exhibiting their loyalty on the stage, it is strange and even unaccountable that so few sovereigns are represented in their plays as a sovereign would desire to be represented, and that so many are set up as objects of contempt and hatred."[9] If Archas is honored for being loyal, Virolet in *The Double Marriage* is honored for rebelling. Though Amintor's worship of sovereignty is presented as a virtue, the king who contrives his martyrdom is presented as a "libidinous tyrant," like the kings in *The Double Marriage* and *A Wife for a Month*. The literary ancestry of the tyrant as a stock type must also dissuade one from the simplicity of the argument that the Beaumont and Fletcher plays presented political views to please the court of their times. The attitudes toward tyrants in the plays would not have been pleasing to absolutists, if taken seriously, but were doubtless so familiar to readers of satire, romance, or the declamations that they were taken for granted as literary stereotypes. Finally, as I hope I have shown, there is no continuous specific meaning in plays like *The Maid's Tragedy* or *The Loyal Subject*. The

9. *Francis Beaumont* (London, 1883), p. 135. For a more thorough discussion of this point see Wallis, *Fletcher, Beaumont & Company*, pp. 133–42.

circumstances involving wicked monarchs and loyal subjects are used as are various other plot structures to create the situations in which honor eloquently defends itself against dishonor.

It is safest, then, to relate the great popularity of Beaumont and Fletcher not to the ideas expressed in their plays but to the artistic taste of the times.[1] The scandals and escapades of James I's courtiers must have made the sensational episodes in the plays more easily acceptable, and the successful imitation of the "conversation of gentlemen" would have had a similar effect, but this sort of timeliness was not what chiefly endeared Beaumont and Fletcher to their own generation. Shirley, whose flattering estimate was prefixed to the First Folio, praises them for the perfection of their art. He does not hesitate to say that the plays were a liberal education for the well-bred young men of the time, worth more than formal schooling and foreign travel combined. His reason for thinking so is an essentially aesthetic one, for his point (similar to Dryden's a few years later) is that Beaumont and Fletcher present in the most persuasive form every variety of human passion:

> You may here find passions raised to that excellent pitch and by such insinuating degrees that you shall not chuse but consent, & go along with them, finding your self at last grown insensibly the very same person you read, and then stand admiring the subtile Trackes of your engagement. Fall on a Scene of love and you will never believe the writers could have the least roome left in their soules for another passion, peruse a Scene of manly Rage, and you would sweare they cannot be exprest by the same hands, but both are so excellently wrought, you must confesse none, but the same hands, could worke them.
>
> "To The Reader," Cam., *I*, xii

This is an admirable description of the experience of a spectator who enjoys not only his emotional response but the "subtile Trackes" of his "engagement"—the strategy of the rhetorician.

To an age more apt to admire understatement than exaggeration, to an age shy of dramatic poetry, to an age brought up on the notion that it is more artful to express strong emotion on the stage by the smallest visible gesture or the briefest outburst, the exuberant rhetoric of Beaumont and Fletcher has very little appeal. The conventions of realistic tragedy and comedy have led the modern theater audience to expect something totally unlike Fletcherian tragicomedy. In our times the attitudes necessary for an enjoyment of this kind of artistic achieve-

---

1. Marco Mincoff discusses the baroque element in Beaumont and Fletcher in an interesting essay, with which I cannot wholly agree, "Baroque Literature in England," *Annuaire de L'Université de Sofia, Faculté Historico-Philologique*, 43 (1946–47), 1–71 (all articles in this volume are separately paginated).

ment have become attached exclusively to other arts—to music, for example, and to painting. There the most dramatic contrasts, the boldest designs, the purest abstractions, the most powerful emotional stimuli are frankly acknowledged and admired. Only in ballet, in opera, and in the more recent "musical drama" do such techniques enter the theater. One may speculate that if a modern audience approached Beaumont and Fletcher with the expectations it has on going to the opera, it would find much to enjoy, for it would accept the contrivance of the play more readily and would await the more declamatory passages as eagerly as the famous arias, duets, or quartets of grand opera.

Shakespeare has survived the changes of dramatic taste because his was never so narrowly a triumph of technique as was the triumph of Beaumont and Fletcher. We may, and do, misinterpret Shakespeare because of unfamiliarity with the dramatic conventions of his time, but the poetic integrity of his best work transcends these conventions. The genius of Beaumont and Fletcher is much more special. It is embodied in a particular rhetoric and in a dramatic genre which is, in effect, the projection of that rhetoric in the theater. Because the theatrical projection is fully and brilliantly achieved, Fletcherian tragicomedy may be enjoyed today, once it is recognized for what it is, as an extreme of dramatic formalism. Declamations were exercises in oratory which came to be valued in themselves as entertainment. In somewhat the same way these tragicomedies are superb examples of dramatic art —a series of hypothetical situations made compelling by sheer technical virtuosity. In the sharply delineated conflicts of Fletcherian tragicomedy is the basic design of all drama.

APPENDIX

Seneca the Elder and the Beaumont and Fletcher Plays

THE SENECAN DECLAMATIONS described in Chapter III, overlooked in previous source studies of the Beaumont and Fletcher plays, seem to have provided the chief complications for three of these plays and may have suggested a detail in one other. Since I have insisted upon the relationship of Fletcher and his collaborators to the Sophistic tradition of rhetoric, the evidence of these specific borrowings is important. Therefore, although I have given most of it elsewhere,[1] I include it here.

As I have explained in Chapter III, the Elizabethan schoolboy was very likely to encounter Seneca the Elder in the course of his schooling. However, one must also consider the possibility that translations of Seneca were used as sources of the plays. A complete French translation by Mathieu de Chaluet, *Les Controverses et suasoires de M. Annaeus Seneca rhéteur,* was published at Paris in 1605, and forty-five of the *Epitomes de cent histoires tragicques* (Paris, 1581) by Alexandre van den Busche (called Le Sylvain) are French translations of the Latin *Excerpta* made from the *Controversiae.* Since the *Epitomes* were in turn translated by Lazarus Pyott (or Piot) as *The Orator* (1596), these shortened versions of the *Controversiae* were also available to Fletcher and his collaborators in English. The following is a list of the *Epitomes* which are taken from Seneca:

Epitomes	*Controversiae*	*Epitomes*	*Controversiae*
35	vi. 3	46	vii. 6
36	ix. 1	47	v. 4
37	i. 1	48	i. 6
38	viii. 2	49	iv. 4
39	viii. 1	50	iv. 7
40	ii. 2	51	ii. 4
41	iii. 3	52	i. 3
42	iv. 6	53	i. 2
43	vi. 4	54	iv. 3
44	ix. 3	55	vi. 7
45	ix. 4	56	vii. 5

1. "John Fletcher and the Art of Declamation," *PMLA, 66* (1951), 226–34.

Epitomes	Controversiae	Epitomes	Controversiae
57	viii. 3	69	iii. 6
58	ix. 6	70	ix. 5
59	ix. 2	71	iii. 2
60	i. 4	72	vii. 7
61	i. 5	73	vi. 6
62	i. 8	75	vii. 3
63	ii. 3	76	viii. 4
64	ii. 5	82	viii. 6
65	ii. 7	83	vii. 4
66	iii. 1	84	v. 5
67	viii. 5	86	x. 4
68	vii. 8		

The plot of *The Double Marriage* (see chap. iv) is obviously a combination of the situations presented in *Controversiae* i. 6, "The Daughter of the Pirate Chief," and ii. 5, "The Woman Tortured by the Tyrant because of Her Husband" (see chap. iii). Virolet is both the son in the first controversia and the husband in the second. Pandulpho, like the father in Controversia 6 (bk. i), opposes Virolet's marriage to Martia, and Virolet's lawyer makes barrenness the legal basis for the divorce from Juliana, as in Controversia 5 (bk. ii). Since there are no close verbal parallels, it is impossible to say whether Fletcher and Massinger used the Latin, the complete French translation, the *Epitomes* (48 and 64), or *The Orator*. The story of Controversia 6 (bk. i) appears in the *Gesta Romanorum* (67 in the early English versions, E.E.T.S. edition,[2] pp. 306–07), but with the important modification that the daughter of the pirate chief becomes the daughter of an emperor. As the story of the tortured wife is not in this collection, the *Gesta* can be ruled out as the source of the play.

In the case of *The Queen of Corinth* the evidence points directly to the *Controversiae* in the original. There can be no possible doubt that the trial of Theanor for the dual rape of Merione and Beliza (see chap. iv) is based on the situation of Controversia 5 (bk. i), "The Man Who Raped Two Women" (see chap. iii). Once again the story occurs both in the *Epitomes* (61) and in the *Gesta* (19 in the Additional Stories of the early English versions, E.E.T.S. edition, p. 440). However, the major alteration of the story in the play—the ruse by which Merione is raped twice, while on the second occasion Theanor believes he is raping Beliza—recalls the insinuations of Cestius Pius and Pompeius Silon that the second woman was not really raped and was merely playing a role. These insinuations are not in either the *Epitomes* or

2. *The Early English Versions of the Gesta Romanorum*, ed. S. J. H. Herrtage, E.E.T.S., extra ser., 33 (London, Trübner, 1879).

the *Gesta*. Beliza's harangue is closely related to Seneca. Her question, "Shall one that is to suffer for a Rape / Be by a Rape defended?" (v, iv; Cam., 6, 73) is close to the Latin, "De stupro accusatur, stuprum defendit . . ." (*1*, 104.)[3] Chaluet's French is further from Seneca: "Estant accusé d'avoir forcé une fille, il est défendu par une autre qui a esté forcée." (P. 35.) Pyott's English translation of the *Epitomes* is an even greater departure: "Who did ever see anie man saved for one offence, by the meanes of another fault farre more hainous?" (*The Orator*, p. 255.) Beliza's strange suggestion, "May be I was ravish'd / For his lust only, thou for his defence" (Cam., 6, 74), appears in Seneca (*1*, 104) but not in the *Epitomes* nor in the *Gesta*. It does not even fit the situation in the play, where Beliza is thought to have been raped after Merione. Similarly, her implication that Merione might be an impostor (though of course Beliza knows that it is she who is pretending) echoes the insinuations of Cestius Pius and Pompeius Silon already referred to. A final example of the dependence upon the original controversia is the wording of the Queen's death verdict. She first points out why the law does not cover the present contingency:

> Ours, concerning Rapes,
> Provided that same latter [clause] of Marriage
> For him that had fall'n once, not then foreseeing
> Mankind could prove so monstrous, to tread twice
> A path so horrid.
>
> v, iv; Cam., 6, 75–6

There is nothing of this in the *Epitomes* or in the *Gesta*, but in the Latin we find: "Lex, inquit, quae dicit: 'rapta raptoris aut mortem optet aut nuptias,' de eis loquitur, qui singulas rapuerunt; non putavit quemquam futurum, qui una nocte raperet duas." (*1*, 112.) The Queen's conclusion is: "He cannot marry both, but for both dying, / Both have their full revenge . . ." (Cam., 6, 76.) Similarly Seneca: "Utrique raptae ultio debet contingere: utramque non potest ducere, utrique mori potest." (*1*, 112.) Again Chaluet's French is quite different: "il fault, que la vengeance soit pour toutes deux. Car tu ne les peux pas espouser toutes deux; & tu peux bien satisfaire à l'une & à l'autre." (P. 38.) The argument does not occur in the *Epitomes* or in the *Gesta*.

It is not necessary to adduce verbal parallels to show that the second controversia in the tenth book is the source of *The Laws of Candy;* the plot alone demonstrates the relationship and the controversia is not found in the *Epitomes* or the *Gesta*. It has usually been assumed that the source of the play is the ninth novel of the tenth decade of Cinthio's

---

3. As in chap. iii, specific references to the text of Seneca the Elder are to volume and page of Bornecque's edition.

Hecatommithi, in which the senate of Pisa announces that the man who does most for his city in war shall be given a golden hauberk and have a statue erected in his honor. A father and his son both claim the reward, but when the senate is unable to choose between them, the son offers to divide the honors. The father refuses this compromise, and after further discussion in which some of the soldiers energetically support the father, it is decided to settle the matter by lot, with the understanding that if the father wins he shall have both the hauberk and the statue but that if the son wins he shall have only the hauberk. The son wins and, as a gesture of filial piety, gives his father the hauberk as well. I give these details at length in order to show that the opening situation of *The Laws of Candy* is only rather vaguely similar. In Candy there are two laws: one that the man who fights most nobly may demand an unspecified reward; the other that ingratitude may be punished with death. Cassilanes and his son Antinous both demand the reward and are told to plead their cases before the senate. Antinous wins, supported by the soldiers, and asks as his reward that a statue be erected in honor of his father, who acknowledges the gesture by disinheriting him. The second law is invoked at the end of the play, where several characters accuse each other of ingratitude. In the second *controversia* of the tenth book it is stated that the best fighter may demand whatever reward he likes and that if two men claim the reward they shall plead their respective cases. When a father and son appear as rivals, the son is chosen and asks to have statues erected to his father, who promptly disinherits him. In several other *controversiae* (for instance in the one about the tortured wife) there are references to a law against ingratitude which does not figure in Cinthio. Clearly, *The Laws of Candy* owes more to the *Controversiae* than to the *Hecathommithi,* and it is not unlikely that Cinthio drew his inspiration also from Seneca, especially since the latter part of the novella in question bears some resemblance to *Controversia* 4 (bk. i). If further proof of the indebtedness of *The Laws of Candy* to Seneca is needed, it may be found in Cassilanes' bitter comment: "He would have my dishonour, and his Triumphs / Ingrav'd in Brass . . ." (1, ii; Cam., *3*, 249.) Just so the father in Seneca explains: "ne possem umquam victum me oblivisci, ignominiam meam in aes incidisti." (*2*, 366.)

It is plain, then, that neither the *Gesta* nor the *Epitomes* can have been the source of all three plays. And where verbal parallels exist, notably in *The Queen of Corinth,* the wording of the play is closer to the original Latin than to the English translation of the *Epitomes*[4] or to the French translation of Seneca. It is most reasonable to assume

4. I have not thought it necessary to complicate these comparisons further by including the French of the *Epitomes,* since Pyott translates rather closely and since the dramatists were more likely to have known Pyott than Busche.

that not only *The Queen of Corinth* and *The Laws of Candy* but also *The Double Marriage* were based on the Latin *Controversiae.*

Since Fletcher was certainly familiar with Seneca the Elder, it is quite possible that another controversia provided the basis of one scene in *The Loyal Subject,* though the relationship cannot be proved. In this scene (IV, v) Archas, returning from a victorious campaign, is accused of sacrilege for taking arms from the temple. It was suggested years ago[5] that Fletcher might have taken the idea from a story in the *Gesta* (4, E.E.T.S. edition, pp. 9–11) in which a knight takes arms from the body of a dead knight, saves a city from its enemies, and is then tried as a thief. He is acquitted by the judge but later murdered by some of the citizens. The story comes from the fourth controversia in the fourth book, where the situation is identical except that the hero is accused of violating a sepulcher; there is, of course, no verdict and no murder, since the case is left open for debate. The wording of Fletcher's scene never exactly parallels the wording of either the original or the *Gesta,* but in one respect the scene is closer to Seneca than to the *Gesta:* Archas, who did not steal arms from a body but merely took the arms which he himself had left in the temple with a vow never to wear them again, is accused of sacrilege rather than theft. When he says of his weapons,

> I wore 'em for my Countries health, that groan'd then:
> Took from the Temple, to preserve the Temple;
>
> IV, v; Cam., *3,* 151

his words are reminiscent of the Latin, "Pro re publica plerumque templa nudantur . . ." (*1,* 384.) It seems to me very likely that Seneca is again the source.

5. H. F. Schwarz, "John Fletcher and the *Gesta Romanorum,*" *MLN, 24* (1919), 146–9.

INDEX

Aphthonius, *Progymnasmata,* 95
Aristophanes, 51
Aristotle, 48, 118, 170, 172
Audiguier, Vital d', *Histoire trage-comique de nostre temps,* 132

Bacon, F., 38
Baldwin, C. S.: *Ancient Rhetoric and Poetic,* 88 n. 7, 170; *Medieval Rhetoric and Poetic,* 92
Baldwin, T. W., *William Shakspere's Small Latine & Lesse Greeke,* 95 n. 9
Bandello, M., 143, 144, 145, 146, 150
Beaumont, F., 30 n. 3, 107 n. 6; collaboration with Fletcher, 11 ff., 99, 100, 107, 111, 117; debt to Jonsonian comedy, 4; first plays not successful, 1, 3–5; *Masque,* x; part in *Philaster,* 19; style, 175, *176–81, 187–92,* 193, 197
Beaumont, F., and Fletcher, J.: fluctuation of reputation, 1–2; collaboration, 11, 19, 175; pattern of tragicomedy established in *A King and No King,* 28; characteristics of pattern, 36–41; meaning of term "tragicomedy" when they began to write, 43 ff.; influenced by satire of Jonson and Marston, 53, 65–6, 70, 80–5, by pastoral romance, 70, 77, 80–5, by Senecan declamation, 86, 97–8, 203–7; characteristics of pattern seen in all later plays, 99 ff.; language of plays studied, 170 ff.; appealed to taste of their times, 198–200; their success triumph of special technique, 201
Beaumont and Fletcher plays: anticipations of heroic drama in, 21, 127, of Etherege and Congreve in, 105; corpus of, 2; dating of, 3, 99 n. 1, 107 n. 5, 111 n. 8; editions referred to, First Folio, x, Second Folio, x, 99, *Works,* A. Glover and A. R. Waller, eds., ix, x, Variorum Edition, A. H. Bullen, ed., 29 n. 2, 143 n. 2; use of term, 2; *Barnavelt, Sir John Van Olden,* x, 117, 134; *Beggars' Bush,* 111, *114–17; The Bloody Brother, see Rollo, Duke of Normandy;*

Bonduca, 117, 134; *The Captain, 107–9,* 111; *The Chances,* 111; *The Coronation,* x; *The Coxcomb,* 3, *19–20,* 134; *Cupid's Revenge,* 3, *11–14,* 15, 16, 20, 21, 28, 29, 70, 102, 111, 124, 128, 129, 134, 152; *The Custom of the Country,* 135, 188–9, 195–6; *The Double Falsehood,* x; *The Double Marriage,* 15 n. 9, 16 n. 1, 97 n. 6, *132–4,* 135 n. 2, 163, 187–8, 199, 204, 207; *The Elder Brother,* 100; *The Fair Maid of the Inn,* 135; *The Faithful Friends,* x; *The Faithful Shepherdess,* 1, 3, *5–11,* 12, 13, 14, 15, 18, 19, 28, 31, 34, 41, 43, 46, 59, 62, 65 n. 8, 71, 97, 102, 111, 154, 163; *The False One,* 117, *124–9,* 134, 161, 183–5, 196; *Four Plays in One,* x, 135; *Henry VIII,* x, 99, 108, 117, *118–24,* 128; *The Honest Man's Fortune,* 135; *The Humorous Lieutenant,* 139, *151–4,* 159, 175, 176, 192, 193, *194–6; The Island Princess,* 139, *158–62,* 163; *A King and No King,* 3, *27–36,* 37, 38, 39, 41, 42, 70, 75, 80, 83, 84, 85, 97, 99, 106, 109, 111, 114, 117, 124, 129, 133, 157, 175, 176; *The Knight of the Burning Pestle,* 1, 3, 5, 11 n. 9, 19, 73, 80, 134, 135; *The Knight of Malta,* 135, *137–8,* 156, 157, 159; *The Laws of Candy,* 97 n. 6, 135, 136, *137,* 149, 205–7; *The Little French Lawyer,* 100; *Love's Cure,* 111; *Love's Pilgrimage,* 111; *The Lovers' Progress,* 132; *The Loyal Subject,* 66, 139, *143–51,* 156, 157, 161, 163, 196–7, 199, 207; *The Mad Lover, 139–43,* 151, 152, 197; *The Maid in the Mill,* 111, *112–14,* 117, 129; *The Maid's Tragedy,* 3, *20–6,* 28, 35, 38, 41, 59, 97, 128, 129, 134, 165, 178–9, 192, 194–5, 199; *Monsieur Thomas,* 107, *109–11,* 132; *The Nice Valor,* 107; *The Night-Walker,* 107; *The Noble Gentleman,* 100; *Philaster,* 1, 3, 11 n. 9, *15–19,* 20, 28, 29, 33, 38, 80, 111, 117, 129, 133, 163, 180–2; *The Pilgrim,* 111; *The Prophetess,* 118, 129, 134 n. 9; *The Queen of Corinth,* 97 n. 6, 135, *136–7,* 149, 169, 189–91, 204–